CliffsAP™
English Literature and Composition

2ND EDITION

by

Allan Casson

WILEY

Wiley Publishing, Inc.

About the Author

Allan Casson has been active in the reading and writing of the AP exams in English for more than 25 years. He was a member of the AP English Development Committee from 1985 to 1988 and Chairman from 1988 to 1992.

Publisher's Acknowledgments

Editorial

Project Editor: Stephanie Corby

Acquisitions Editor: Roxane Stanfield

Composition

Proofreader: Laura L. Bowman

Wiley Indianapolis Composition Services

CliffsAP™ English Literature and Composition, 2nd Edition

Published by:
Wiley Publishing, Inc.
111 River Street
Hoboken, NJ 07030
www.wiley.com

Copyright © 2001 Allan Casson, Inc.

Published by Wiley Publishing, Inc., Hoboken, NJ
Published simultaneously in Canada

Library of Congress Control Number: 00-109061

ISBN: 978-0-7645-8686-6

Printed in the United States of America

20 19 18 17 16 15 14

2B/TR/QT/QY/IN

Author's Acknowledgements

Charlotte Mew: "The Farmer's Bride" from *Collected Poems and Prose*, " Copyright 1981. Reprinted by permission of Carcanet Press Limited.

Wilfred Owen: "S.I.W." from *Collected Poems of Wilfred Owen*, " Copyright 1963 by Chatto and Windus, Ltd. Reprinted by permission of New Directions Publishing Corporation.

Claude McKay: "Flame Heart" from *Selected Poems of Claude McKay*, Harcourt, Brace, Jovanovich. Reprinted by permission of the Archives of Claude McKay.

George Orwell: "Some Thoughts on the Common Toad" from *Collected Essays, Journals and Letters of George Orwell, IV*, " Copyright 1968 by Sonia Brownell Orwell. Reprinted by permission of Harcourt, Brace, Jovanovich, Incorporated.

Dylan Thomas: "Credit Line" from *On The Air With Dylan Thomas*, edited by Ralph Maud, " Copyright 1953 by The Trustees for the Copyright of Dylan Thomas. Reprinted by permission of New Directions Publishing Corp.

Scott Momaday: "Introduction" from *The Way to Rainy Mountain*, " Copyright 1969 by University of New Mexico Press. Reprinted by permission of University of New Mexico Press.

Robert Hayden: "Magnolias in Snow" from *Collected Poems*, " Copyright 1948 by Robert Hayden. Published by Liveright Publishing Company.

Table of Contents

PART III: SIX FULL-LENGTH PRACTICE TESTS

PART I

INTRODUCTION

Format of the AP Literature and Composition Exam

The multiple-choice section accounts for 45 percent of the final grade and the essays 55 percent. Each of the three essay questions accounts for the same.

Format of the 1991 Test		
Section I	**Multiple-Choice**	**53 Questions**
60 minutes (one hour)	passage from a modern American novel (DiLillo)	15 questions
	soliloquy from an Elizabethan history play (Shakespeare)	14 questions
	modern American poem (Sarton)	9 questions
	passage of Victorian prose (Ruskin)	15 questions
Section II	**Essays**	**3 Questions**
(40 minutes suggested time)	analysis of a poem by Emily Dickinson	
(45 minutes suggested time)	analysis of a prose passage by James Boswell	
(35 minutes suggested time)	open question on two contrasting places in a novel or a play	

Format of the 1994 Test		
Section I	**Multiple-Choice**	**55 Questions**
60 minutes (one hour)	passage from a modern American novel (Baldwin)	14 questions
	seventeenth–century poem (Cowley)	14 questions
	passage from a Victorian novel (Thackeray)	12 questions
	modern American poem (Clampitt)	15 questions
Section II	**Essays**	**3 Questions**
(40 minutes suggested time)	analysis of two short poems (by Poe and H.D.)	
(40 minutes suggested time)	analysis of a prose passage from a Sarah Orne Jewett short story	
(40 minutes suggested time)	open essay on the use of a character who appears briefly or not at all in a play or novel	

Format of the 1999 Test		
Section I	**Multiple-Choice**	**55 Questions**
60 minutes (one hour)	passage from a nineteenth-century dialogue (Wilde)	13 questions
	nineteenth-century poem (Emily Dickinson)	12 questions
	passage from a seventeeth-century play (Ben Johnson)	9 questions
	passage from a modern poem (Yusef Komunyakaa)	9 questions
	passage from a nineteenth-century story (Mary Wilkins Freeman)	12 questions
Section II	**Essays**	**3 Questions**
(40 minutes suggested time)	analysis of a poem by Seamus Heaney	
(40 minutes suggested time)	analysis of a passage from a novel by Cormac McCarthy	
(40 minutes suggested time)	open question on effect of a character torn by equally powerful conflicting forces	

General Format and Grading of the AP Literature and Composition Exam

Contents of the Exam

The Advanced Placement literature exam has two parts, a multiple-choice section and an essay, or free-response, section. The one-hour multiple-choice part accounts for 45 percent, while the two-hour essay section determines 55 percent of the final grade.

The multiple-choice section of the exam is based on four selections from literature in English written from the sixteenth century to the present. (Once in a great while, instead of four, there will be five passages. Two of the selections will be shorter and have fewer questions.) Two passages are prose selections and two are poetry. They represent three or four different periods and include the work of a female or a minority writer. A characteristic selection would include a short poem by a metaphysical poet of the early seventeenth century (such as Herbert), a prose passage from an eighteenth-century writer (like Swift), a prose selection from a Victorian novelist (Charlotte Bronte, for example), and a poem by a twentieth-century American poet (like Gwendolyn Brooks). There are between 50 and 60 questions in the one-hour exam, normally 15 or 16 questions on each of two of the passages and 12 or 13 on the other two. An exam using five passages may have 7 or 8 questions on each of the two shorter selections, and from 12 to 16 questions on the other three.

The free-response section consists of three essay questions with two hours of writing. Though there is no absolute guarantee that the three essays will be alike every year, the form of the exam for the last 15 years has been one essay on a passage of poetry, one essay on a passage of prose (on rare occasions, a complete short story), and one essay on a topic allowing the student to choose an appropriate novel or play (and sometimes a poem or work of autobiography). Students usually spend 40 minutes on each of the essays.

How the Exam Is Written and Graded

The AP literature and language exams are written by a committee of eight English teachers — four men and four women — four teachers of Advanced Placement classes in public and private high schools and four teachers of English in colleges and universities. The committee is geographically and ethnically representative, and because most of the members serve for only three years, its membership is constantly changing. Working with testing professionals from Educational Testing Service, the committee selects the passages upon which the essay and multiple-choice questions are based and composes the questions for the free-response section of the exam. All of these questions are pretested in college literature or writing classes before they can be selected for use on an AP examination.

The examinations are read in a seven-day period in early June. In 1992, more than 450 readers from throughout the United States and Canada read more than 115,000 AP literature exams. In 2000, more than 500 readers from throughout the United States and Canada read just under 200,000 AP literature exams.

Slightly more than half of the readers are college teachers, and about 45 percent are high school and preparatory school AP teachers. Each grader reads essays for only one question throughout the reading week, so each exam has a minimum of three different readers. Because many essays are used as samples for grading standards and many more are read twice (by a reader and by one of 60 or so table leaders who check the readers' scoring), many essays have more than three readers.

Each student essay is scored on a scale from zero to nine. The standards for the grading are determined before the reading begins by a study of the essays students have written in May. The grading standards do not anticipate the students' performance, but are based on a wide sampling of actual tests. Sample papers that represent each digit on the scale are selected, and readers are trained to grade one of the three essays. After a test's three essays are scored, the individual scores (between zero and nine) are combined for a total score of between zero and 27. The result of the reading is three scores of zero to nine, or a total score of zero to 27.

The scores on the multiple-choice section and on the essay section are combined to make up a scale from zero to 150.

With current weighting of 55 percent for the essay section, the total score of zero to 27 is converted to a scale of zero to 82.5. The number of right answers on the multiple-choice section is converted to a scale of zero to 67.5, or 45 percent of the total scale. The chief reader then determines where the scale will be divided to determine the final scores of one, two, three, four, and five that are reported to the colleges and the students. The cutoff points are not predetermined nor are they chosen to guarantee a certain percentage of scores at any level. The results differ from year to year as do the percentage of scores in the one, two, three, four, and five categories.

Answers to Your Questions about the AP Literature and Composition Exam

Preparation for the Exam

Q. When should I study this book?

A. Browse through it early in the year before you take the AP exam, and read it carefully six weeks or so before the May exam. Don't spend too much time studying this book, especially time that could be spent reading or rereading poetry, fiction, or drama.

Q. What College Board publications do you recommend?

A. Students should have a copy of the AP Course Description in English (the Acorn book) and one or two of the earlier exams.

Teachers of an AP literature course will certainly want to have the most recent AP Course Description in English (the Acorn book), the Teacher's Guide to AP Courses in English Literature and Composition, and the latest AP English: Free Response Scoring Guide and Sample Student Answers. They will also probably want to own all or some of the complete exams that have been released.

The Student Guide to the AP English Courses and Examinations includes nothing that is not already available in the Course Description and Free Response Scoring Guide booklets, though it does cover the most recent exam each year. The English Literature CD-ROM is poorly written and overpriced. It contains nothing that is not already available in other College Board Publications and is a waste of money.

There are additional publications such as one on the language and composition examination. A list of publications and prices can be obtained from the Advanced Placement Program, P.O. Box 6670, Princeton, New Jersey, 08541-6670. Allow four to six weeks for delivery. For further information, you can consult the Web site at www.collegeboard.org/ap.

Q. As I prepare to take the literature exam, will it help me to consult the old language exams?

A. Perhaps. The multiple-choice section of the language exam has questions on four prose passages similar to the two prose passages on the literature exam. And the essay questions include a prose passage for analysis that is similar to the prose analysis question on the literature exam. The passages on the literature exam are more likely to come from fiction or criticism, but the language exam may use prose written by scientists, historians, or sociologists.

Q. If, shortly before the exam, I have time to review only one book, how do I decide which one?

A. Review the book you like best. If you're really short of time, review one or two plays instead of a long novel. The open question usually allows you to choose either a play or a novel, and because plays are so much shorter, it's easier to have command of the details of a play than a novel. Be sure to have more than one work ready, because you can't be sure your favorite will suit the question on the exam.

Q. What should I study the night before the exam?

A. Ask your AP teacher. He or she knows what you need better than I do. But don't stay up late. The exam is really testing all your years of English study, so there is no way you can make up for more than four years in one night. If you need to study the night before the exam, you're in trouble. You will probably perform better on the exam if you relax the night before. Watch television and, above all, get a good night's sleep. If you're so compulsive that you feel you must study, look over the definitions of some technical terms, and browse through the novels and plays you may use to refresh your memory of the names.

Multiple-Choice Questions

Q. How many passages and questions are on the multiple-choice part of the exam?

A. Usually there are four passages, two poetry and two prose. The exact number of questions may vary; as a rule, there are between 53 and 56 questions for four selections. Sometimes, as on the 1999 exam, for example, there will be five passages, two of which are shorter with fewer questions on each. The allowed time of one hour does not change.

Q. Where can I get old multiple-choice exams to practice with?

A. You can order the complete literature exams that have been released from the College Board at the address given earlier. The annually published AP Course Description in English (the Acorn book) has a few sample multiple-choice sets.

Q. Does it make sense that the multiple-choice exam, which takes only one hour, should account for 45 percent of the grade, while the essay exam, which takes two hours, accounts for only 55 percent?

A. No. But the grading of the multiple-choice section is more reliable, and it discriminates more widely than the essay section. There are now only three essay scores, and they do not spread out nearly as well as the multiple-choice scores. Statisticians argue that the 45 percent weighting of the multiple-choice scores makes the exam more reliable. That is, a student retaking the exam would be more likely to receive the same final score with a 45 percent weight for the multiple-choice than with 40 percent or 33 percent. If the essay answers were read by two readers, the reliance on the multiple-choice score could be decreased.

Q. When should I guess on the multiple-choice section?

A. Answer as many of the questions as you can. Avoid losing points by mismanaging your time and spending too long on one passage or one question. Don't be afraid to guess if you can eliminate at least two of the five choices. You get no credit for an unanswered question and lose a quarter of a point for each wrong answer. But if you reduce the options to three instead of five, your chances are one in three, which your loss, if you choose incorrectly, is one-fourth.

When a question seems hopeless, don't waste time on it. Leave it out and go on, taking care to skip the unanswered question's space on the answer sheet. If you are unsure of an answer, mark out the answers in the questions booklet you know are wrong:

A.

B. ?

C.

D. ?

E.

The question marks indicate possible answers. If you come back to the question later, you will not waste time considering wrong answers you have already eliminated.

Q. What if I don't finish all the multiple-choice questions?

A. Many students don't finish all the multiple-choice questions and still receive high scores on the whole exam. If you don't finish, don't worry about it. Go on and do a good job on the essays. You can afford to miss some points on the multiple-choice section if you write three good essays. If you find that you have no time left, don't fill in the answers for all the remaining questions on your answer sheet. Chances are four to one against your getting the right answer, and each wrong answer reduces your score by .25. Leaving the answer blank is zero.

Q. Are there any trick questions in the multiple-choice section?

A. No. If you read the passage carefully, you should be able to answer the question.

Q. Is it advisable to do the multiple-choice sets in the order they appear on the exam?

A. Do them in whatever order makes it easiest for you. If you find the passage that comes first very hard, go on and come back to it when you've finished the other parts. Remember, your score is determined by the number of correct answers, so you don't want to spend too much time on one section if it will prevent you from doing the other parts. Many students don't answer all of the multiple-choice questions, but you want to answer as many as possible in the hour allowed.

Q. What if a multiple-choice question seems too easy?

A. Be glad it's too easy rather than too hard. Don't assume that because a multiple-choice question seems obvious there must be some trick. In every set of multiple-choice questions, there are a few very easy questions and a few very hard ones. Don't throw away a chance to get easy points by trying to second-guess the exam. If the question asks for the name of the hero of *Hamlet* and the choices are Lear, Romeo, Othello, Macbeth, and Hamlet, take Hamlet. The first question of a multiple-choice set is often an easy one.

Q. What if I've had five consecutive answers of C in the multiple-choice section, and I'm pretty sure the sixth is C, but B is possible? Which do I choose?

A. Choose **C**. You've probably made a mistake in the five consecutive **C** choices. Don't play games with letter patterns in the multiple-choice section of the exam. Choose the answer that you think is right regardless of the pattern of the answers to the questions before it.

Q. Exactly what scores do I get for a wrong answer, a right answer, and no answer on the multiple-choice section?

A. A right answer is one point, an omitted answer is zero, and a wrong answer is minus .25. The total score is converted to equal 45 percent of 150, or 67.5 points, if you get all the multiple-choice questions right. If there were 55 questions and you got 45 minus 2, or 43 (or 52.7 out of a possible 67.5 — see the explanation of converting raw score to scaled score on page 18).

Q. How many multiple-choice questions do I have to get right to get a final grade of three on the exam?

A. It depends on your essay scores and on how well all the other students taking the exam perform.

Your final score is on a scale of 150, with a possible 82.65 points on the free-response (essay) section and a possible 67.5 points on the multiple-choice section. A student who gets nines on all three of the essays and answers all the multiple-choice questions correctly would score 150. But the number of points required for the final scores of one through five is determined anew each year.

The chart on page 19 will show you how your multiple-choice score determines your final grade.

Free-Response, or Essay, Questions

Q. Is the form of the three essay questions the same on all exams?

A. Essentially, but not exactly. You can count on a question on poetry, a question on prose, and a question that allows you to choose a literary work to write about. The poetry question may use a complete short poem, or part of a longer one, or two shorter poems for comparison. The prose question may use a selection from a work of fiction or non-fiction, or even a complete short story. The form of the open essay question may vary slightly. Usually it is followed by a list of authors or works that may be used in response, but every once in a while this list will be omitted.

Q. On the essay section of the exam, which question is the most important?

A. All three count one-third. Though you've probably spent much more time in your AP class preparing for the open question than for the others, the open question counts no more than the poetry or the prose analysis questions.

Because the multiple-choice section is all close reading of poems and prose, the exam has six passages for close reading but only one question about a novel or play of your choice. Because the multiple-choice section counts for 45 percent of your grade and the two passages in the essay section count for two-thirds of the other 55 percent, the open question determines only 18.3 percent of the final score.

9

Q. How should I begin my essay? Should I paraphrase or repeat the question?

A. Begin your essay in whatever way makes it easiest for you to write. If you simply cannot begin on your own without rephrasing the question, then do so. Your reader will not consciously hold it against you, but keep in mind that your reader is reading hundreds of essays that also begin with the same unnecessary restatement of a question he or she already knows by heart and that you've wasted a small amount of time. If you can, get to the point right away.

For example, assume a question on a prose passage asks you to "discuss Dickens's attitude to Pip and Joe and the stylistic devices he uses to convey his attitude." If you begin your essay — and thousands will — "Dickens in this passage conveys his attitude to Pip and Joe by using devices of style. This essay will discuss his attitude and also the devices of style he uses to convey it," all you have accomplished is to have bored the reader briefly. A better start is something like, "In this passage, Dickens regards Pip with a combination of sympathy and disapproval," or whatever the attitude is.

If you are one of those writers to whom writing a first sentence is like setting a first toe in the ocean on the coast of Maine, then use the question to get you started. Better still, begin by addressing the first task the exam calls on you to write about.

Q. Should I write an outline before I write my essay?

A. If you write better essays by writing an outline first, then do so. If not, then don't. The outline won't be graded or counted in any way. Do whatever makes it easier for you to write well-organized, specific, and relevant essays.

Q. Should I write a five-paragraph essay?

A. If, by a five-paragraph essay, you mean an essay in which the first paragraph is introductory and says what you're going to do in paragraphs two, three, and four, and the fifth recapitulates what you've done, write a three-paragraph essay and forget about the introduction and conclusion. Use the time you save to give more support to your argument or to develop other topics. Readers don't count paragraphs, and there is no advantage or disadvantage in writing five paragraphs as opposed to three or seven. You should write in well-developed paragraphs and let their number be determined by what you have to say in answer to the questions.

Q. How long should an essay be?

A. Long enough to answer all the parts of the question specifically and fully. There is no extra credit given to a very long essay, especially if it is repetitious or off the subject. A very short essay (one paragraph of only a few sentences) will fall into the scoring guide's "unacceptably brief" category and receive a very low score. If you've said all you have to say about a question, don't try to pad out your answer. Go on to the next question. A student with average-sized handwriting usually writes one and a half or two pages in the pink booklets, but many write more and many write less. Your reader will not count your words and will not thank you if you write an extra page repeating what you've already said.

Q. How important is spelling and punctuation?

A. Not very, unless yours is dreadful. The readers are not looking for spelling and punctuation errors, but if there are so many or if they are so flagrant that they interfere with a fluent reading, you will lose some points.

Q. How important is correct grammar?

A. The readers realize that you are writing rapidly, and they are tolerant of a lapse here and there. But if your writing suggests inadequate control over English prose, you may be penalized. On the literature exam, essays that are "poorly written" can score no higher than a three, but "poorly written" means much more than an occasional split infinitive, agreement error, or dangling participle.

Q. How important is handwriting or neatness?

A. I'd like to say not at all. Readers certainly try to avoid being influenced one way or the other by good or bad handwriting, but there may be an unconscious hostility to a paper that is very difficult to read. So make your writing as legible as you can.

Q. In the essay part of the exam, do I have to use a pen?

A. Your proctor will instruct you to write your essays with a pen, but every year some exams are written in pencil by students without pens or whose pens break down in midexam. A reader will certainly not penalize an exam written in pencil, but like bad handwriting, pencil is harder to read. Don't make it more difficult for your reader if you don't have to.

Q. What are the most important qualities of a good AP essay?

A. That it answers all the parts of the question fully and accurately.

That it is supported with specific evidence.

That it is well written.

Q. Should I use a title for my essay answers?

A. Suit yourself, but know that it almost certainly will not improve your grade. I don't recall ever reading one that I thought was good, but I do remember many inappropriate ones.

Q. Will the readers of my essays reward creativity?

A. The readers are looking for accurate and thorough answers to the questions on the exam. If you can combine "creativity" with answering the question well, then so much the better. But no amount of ingenuity will take the place of a response to the tasks set by the exam. If you write a brilliant poem that fails to answer the question, you will get a low score. If you write a straightforward essay that answers the question, you will get a high score. Remember that the direction on most questions is "write an essay" or "in a well-organized essay, discuss . . . ."

Q. Do the examiners want detail in the essays?

A. If, by detail, you mean specific evidence from the passages on the exam or from the novel or play of your choice, yes. But they don't want long passages quoted from memory or detailed plot summaries. Remember that your readers have a copy of the passage in front of them and that they have already read the novel or play you're writing about.

Q. Should I quote from the poem or the prose passages on the exam in my essay?

A. It depends. You must deal with the passages specifically, and quotation is the best way to do so. There is no point, however, in copying out five lines of poetry when you can say "in lines 1-5" and let your reader do the work. But if you're seeking to prove a point about the diction of a passage, for example, and there are single words throughout the passage that support your case, you should say something like "the optimistic tone is supported by words and phrases such as 'happy' (line 12), 'cheerful' (line 3), 'ecstatic' (line 7), and 'out of his gourd' (line 11)." Be specific, but don't waste time. Readers have copies of the passage in front of them and will look at a line if students direct them to it.

Q. What if I don't finish an essay in the free-response section?

A. Readers are told again and again to reward students for what they do well. If you have left out only a few sentences of conclusion but have answered the question, it will probably not affect your score at all. And if you have written three-fourths of an essay on the topic, you will certainly get credit for all you have done. A blank page earns no points at all, so if you find yourself with only a few moments, jot down as much as you can of what you were going to write, even if it's only in fragments. It may get one or two points, and any score is better than zero.

Divide your time evenly, or nearly evenly, among the three essays. They all count one-third, regardless of how much or how little you write on each.

Q. What suggestions about style would you make?

A. Avoid clichés. Nine out of ten AP exams written about the imagery of a passage will describe it as "vivid," regardless of how bland it may be. If the question suggests a proverb to you, resist the temptation to quote it because 50,000 other students will have thought of the same proverb and used it in their first paragraph.

Write naturally.

Q. In discussing the poem, should I write about the sound effects?

A. If the question calls for a discussion of the sound (prosody, metrics of the poem), you must answer the question. But if the question does not ask about this aspect, beware of overdoing it. Too many papers waste time finding "l's" that suggest sunsets or "s's" that denote deceit, death, and broccoli. Even more papers count alliterations and exultantly discover five "f's" in lines one and two of the poem without noticing that their own sentence has six.

Q. Should I write about the punctuation of a poem or a prose passage?

A. Only if it is very unusual or remarkably important and you can say something meaningful about it. Every passage on the exam will be punctuated, and the punctuation will almost never be worth discussing. Most students who waste time writing about the punctuation do so because they can't think of anything else to write about.

Q. Is it likely that the essay exam will not include a prose passage, a poem, and an open essay question?

A. No. Any change from this pattern would be a very slight variation, such as using a question on two poems or two prose passages or using a short story. If the form of the exam is going to change, the AP publications will say so in advance.

Q. What is a "rubric," or scoring guide?

A. The scoring guide ("rubric") is a one-page outline of essay characteristics and corresponding scores that readers of the free-response section of the exam use to score the papers. Each of the three essays is scored on a scale of zero to nine. The readers are trained using sample papers and a scoring guide that describes the characteristics of each of the scores. Like the questions, the scoring guides follow familiar patterns.

They begin with the general instructions to the reader that include judging the paper as a whole, rewarding students for what they do well, and scoring very poorly written essays no higher than a three.

Assume you wished to write a scoring guide for questions on a passage from Shakespeare on justice and mercy that call for an analysis of the author's attitudes and how the choice of details, imagery, and diction convey his attitudes. A scoring guide would probably look like this:

9–8 These responses are well written and discuss clearly and accurately the attitudes toward both justice and mercy. Using specific and appropriate references to the text, they analyze the choice of details, imagery, and diction of the passage. The student writing may not be errorless, but it will demonstrate a mature command of effective prose.

7–6 These essays also discuss the attitudes of the passage toward both justice and mercy, but they may do so less fully or less convincingly than the essays in the 9-8 range. They deal with the choice of details, imagery, or diction, but less well than the very best papers. These essays are written clearly and effectively, though they may be less mature than papers in the 9-8 range.

5 These essays attempt to deal with the author's attitudes toward justice and mercy and his use of detail, imagery, and diction, but they do so merely adequately. The attitudes they discuss will be simple or obvious ones, and the remarks on detail, imagery, and diction may be lacking in specificity or depth. These essays often summarize rather than analyze the passage. The writing is, as a rule, less clear and well organized than that of the upper-half essays, and the thinking is often simplistic.

4–3 These lower-half essays often fail to understand parts of the passage and/or fail to answer part or parts of the question. They may define Shakespeare's attitudes vaguely or inaccurately. Their handling of detail, imagery, and diction may be perfunctory or unclear. The writing may demonstrate weak compositional skills. These essays often contain errors in reading and writing and are rarely supported by evidence from the passage.

2–1 These essays are weaker than the papers in the 4–3 range. They have serious errors in the reading of the passage and often omit the second half of the question altogether. Some papers are unacceptably short. The writing is poor and lacks clarity, organization, or supporting evidence.

0 A blank paper or an essay that makes no attempt to deal with the question receives no credit. A table leader must reconfirm this score.

Open Questions

Q. **Will there always be a list of suggested works to choose from?**

A. No. Sometimes there will be only a list of authors, and, on rare occasions, no list at all.

Q. **On the open question, is it better to write about a book on the list of suggested works or to choose one that is not on the list?**

A. Every year some students pay no attention to the line in the instructions that says, "You may write your essay on one of the following novels or plays OR on another of comparable quality." You should choose the work that best fits the question and that you know best. Whether or not you choose a work on the list will not affect your grade. If the work you choose is not widely known, it will be read only by someone who knows the book. No reader has read all the works that are used on the open question, and a reader finding an essay on a work he or she does not know simply passes it on to another reader who is familiar with it. The important thing is to choose an appropriate work or an appropriate character within that work.

Q. **In answering the open essay question, can I write about works in translation?**

A. Yes. Many students use works by classical authors as well as those by more modern European, African, Asian, and South American authors. The list of suggested works on the exam frequently includes those of Achebe, Aeschylus, Camus, Cervantes, Chekhov, Dostoevski, Euripides, Homer, Ibsen, Sophocles, Tolstoi, and Voltaire, to name only some. Use the work that best fits the question.

Q. **On the open question, what if I don't know any of the books on the list of suggested works?**

A. Reread the question very carefully and think about the books you do know to see if one of them is appropriate. You don't have to use a book from the list, but the work you use must fit the question.

Q. **On the open question, is it better to use an older author or a modern one?**

A. Use the author that you know best that best fits the question. The time period doesn't matter.

Q. **In answering the open question, how can I tell whether or not the book I want to use is of "comparable quality" or "similar literary merit"?**

A. If you are in doubt about any of the works you may use on the exam, consult with your AP teacher before you take the exam. The works used on the exam should be ones that would be likely to be read in an introductory college literature class. The readers are not stuffy about the use of contemporary writers, but if you write about what is clearly light weight (Danielle Steel, the *Gone with the Wind* sequel) a popular mystery story (Agatha Christie), or an ephemeral mass-market bestseller, you will not get a good score.

Marginal works, for example, books written for younger readers, "novelizations" of popular films, and some works of science fiction, may slip by, but your reader cannot help noticing a doubtful choice. Unless you know no other works that suit the question, it is wiser to use a book that you studied in your AP class.

Q. If I write a really good essay using one of the books on the list but on a topic of my own rather than the question on the exam, what score will I get?

A. A really low one.

Q. On the open question, is it better to write on a long or difficult work (like *Moby Dick*) than a short or easy work (like *Ethan Frome*)?

A. The important thing is to answer the question. You don't get extra credit for using a hard book, and you lose no credit for choosing a short work. You can't use a short story if the question calls for a novel, but if you don't answer the question and write about *Ulysses* or *War and Peace*, you will get a much lower score than if you do answer the question and write about *The Secret Sharer* or *The Catcher in the Rye*.

Q. On the open question, may I write on two works when the question asks for one?

A. You may, but you shouldn't. The exam will be read and scored on the basis of one of the two works you write about, whichever is the better of the two. But you will probably have written only half as much as the other exams that followed directions and wrote on only one. You can, of course, refer to other works if doing so improves your essay, but focus on one work unless the question specifically calls for a comparison.

Q. Can I write on a novel or play that has been made into a film if I've read the book and seen the movie?

A. Yes, but be careful. Most of the classic (and many not-so-classic) novels have been made into films. Be sure what you say in your essay comes from your reading, not from the movie. The old Greer Garson movie of *Pride and Prejudice* changes the gorgon Lady Catherine into an ally who willingly brings Darcy and Elizabeth together, and the Hollywood *Wuthering Heights* ends at the halfway point in the novel. Olivier's and Mel Gibson's *Hamlet* leave out about one-third of the play. Be sure what you're remembering is what you've read, not what you've seen.

Q. What if I can't remember a character's name?

A. Do the best you can. You can sometimes use a phrase like "Hamlet's uncle" (if you forget Claudius), or you can explain that you've forgotten and substitute an X. If you make it clear, the reader will give you the benefit of the doubt. There have been quite good essays written about Hamlet in which he was (inadvertently) called Macbeth. The readers are aware that the essays must be written quickly and are tolerant of slips of the pen. I don't recommend inventing names. The effect can be unintentionally comic, as in "I can't re-member Othello's wife's name, so I'll call her Darlene."

Q. Do you have any further suggestions about answering the open essay question?

A. Be sure to understand whether or not the exam is asking about the author, the reader, or the characters in the work. There are, obviously, differences between our perception of Gatsby and Nick's, Daisy's, or Fitzgerald's. Ask yourself whether or not the question calls for a discussion of technique — that is, what the author does for specific purposes — or for a discussion of a character as if that character were alive. In *Lord of the Flies*, Piggy doesn't know that he is a symbol, but Golding and the reader do. And in *Hamlet*, Shakespeare and the reader use Horatio in ways that Hamlet doesn't know about. Don't confuse art and life.

Remember that a play or a novel is a play or a novel, and although Horatio is necessary to Fortinbras to tell him what has happened, or necessary to Shakespeare to say some things he wants to have said at the end of the play, we don't need him to tell us what has happened because we've just seen or read the whole play. Fortinbras, Horatio, and Hamlet, like Murphy Brown, are fictional characters, and educated people should recognize the difference between art's imitation of life and the real thing.

Q. **How many books should I prepare for the open question on the exam?**

A. There's no single answer, but the more, the better, as long as you know them well. Be sure to cover several periods and several genres. I'd recommend that you know one Shakespearean tragedy and at least two twentieth-century plays. And I'd recommend a minimum of at least one nineteenth-century and two twentieth-century novels. More would be better. Think about reviewing some of the works you read in tenth or eleventh grade. Choose works you like. Review the works carefully. A few years ago, a large number of students wrote on *Romeo and Juliet* on the open question on child-parent conflicts. But very few remembered the play well, probably because they had read it two or three years before and had not reviewed it.

Q. **Is the exam equally difficult each year or are there years when it is easier or harder?**

A. Although the Development committee that writes the exam tries to maintain the same level of difficulty, no two exams can be equally difficult or exactly alike. Each year one of the three essay questions turns out to be harder than the other two questions, but there is no pattern from year to year. The question on poetry was the most challenging when the poem was Sylvia Plath's "Sow," Emily Dickinson's "The last night that she lived," and Wilbur's "The Death of a Toad." But the prose question had lower scores when the passage was from Conrad's "Typhoon," from Joan Didion's "Self Respect," or from Hawthorne's "The House of the Seven Gables." The point to remember is that your exam will be graded by comparison with all the other exams written that year, so if a question seems harder to you than those on previous exams, it probably will seem harder to many of the other students against whom your score will be measured. That any exam is always hardest in the year I take it is a sad fact of human life. Fortunately, with the AP exam, the grading is not on an absolute standard, but by comparison of all the test takers.

One of the four sections of multiple-choice questions on each exam is repeated from an earlier examination, but this is the only exact measure of the performance of one year's AP students against that of another year, and the scores in a previous year have no effect on the final grades of this year's exams.

Q. **Are the passages on the exam taken from any set time period?**

A. The multiple-choice and the essay questions are based on passages of literature written in English from the sixteenth century to the present. Passages are in modern English, that is, the English written from 1575 to the present. The exam has never used Middle English (the language of Chaucer) or Old English (the language of Beowulf).

Q. **To do well on the exam, do I have to understand metrics?**

A. Chances are you can get by without knowing anything at all about metrics if you can read and write well. It has been a number of years since an essay question specifically asked for comments on the sound of a poem. In the multiple-choice section, you can expect two questions, at most, about metrics, but maybe only one. Obviously, the more technical knowledge you have about prose and poetry, the better off you are, if you use this learning knowledge with care. Essays on poetry are far more likely to say too much about metrics than too little. In fact, prosody (the art of versification) is not hard to master, and if you know the terms defined beginning on page 91, you should have no trouble with metrical questions in the multiple-choice section.

Other Questions

Q. **What is the difference between the AP literature and the AP language exams?**

A. The literature exam tests a student's ability to read and write about literature in English. It includes questions about poetry, drama, fiction, and nonfiction prose; the exam has one hour of multiple-choice questions and two hours of essay questions.

The language exam tests a student's ability to read and write about English prose and to write expository, analytical, and argumentative essays. Though a passage from a work of fiction can appear on the exam, the emphasis of the question or questions on the passage will be on language, style, and rhetoric. The exam has three 40-minute essays (two hours) and four sets of multiple-choice questions (one hour).

Q. **Can I take both the language and the literature exams in the same year?**

A. Yes. The exams are now given at different times, so students can take both exams in the same year if they wish to do so. Before this change in scheduling, many students took the language exam in their junior year and the literature exam in their senior year.

Q. **How can I tell what college credit I'll get for my AP scores?**

A. Look in the catalogs of the colleges you're interested in. Unfortunately, many college catalogs are vague about exactly what subject and unit credit each AP score will earn. With two English exams (literature and language) to add to the confusion, it's wise to get a statement from the admissions office. Write or call the admissions office and ask for an explicit statement of the policy on AP credit.

The Advanced Placement Course Description booklet names the colleges that give some credit for AP exams, but because the list gives no specific information and makes no distinction between the language and the literature exam, it is not very useful.

Q. **Will it affect my score if I check the box to refuse to allow my exam to be used as a sample for research?**

A. No. Nor will it affect your score if you check the "yes" box. The people who select samples consult these boxes to be sure no exams are used that have not been released by the students, but the readers of the exams never notice or care about what box you check.

Q. Can I find out my scores on the multiple-choice section and what I got on each essay?

A. No. The only score reported to you is the final grade of one to five, the score that is reported to the colleges.

Q. Will the college know my scores on the parts of the exam?

A. No. All the colleges receive is the single score. Colleges may request the essay exam, but they will not be told what scores each essay received.

Q. Can I take the exam without having taken an AP course?

A. Yes. Some schools have no designated AP English classes, and their students still do very well. And some students may do well without taking any course in an AP subject (speakers of a foreign language, for example, are likely not to need a course in their native tongue). Though the English language AP exam is designed for students who have taken an AP English language class, students who have had only an AP literature class will often do well on the test.

Q. How long does it take to receive the results of my AP exam?

A. The exams taken in May are read early in June, and the results are sent to the schools in July, usually just after the fourth, that is, about eight weeks after the exam is given.

Q. How do I convert my scores on a sample test to the one-through-five scores that are sent to the colleges?

A. The total score on the exam is 150. The essay and multiple-choice parts are weighted 55 percent to 45 percent respectively, (there are 82.5 points for the essays and 67.5 for the multiple-choice questions). Because the three essays are graded on a nine-point scale (plus zero), each point on your essay raw score is multiplied by 3.055. Three nines total 27, which, when multiplied by 3.055, total 82.5. There are 55 multiple-choice questions, and each point in the raw score is multiplied by 1.227, equaling 67.5. Remember that the raw score in the multiple-choice section is determined by the number of correct answers less one-quarter point for each wrong answer. A test with 30 right, 20 wrong, and 5 omitted answers would have a raw score of 30 minus 5, or 25. This raw score converts to a total of 30.675 (25 x 1.227).

The total number of points required for a final score of five, four, or three is different each year, but a very reasonable assumption is 100–150 for a score of five, 86–99 for a score of four, and 67–85 for a score of three. The following chart will give you an idea of the scores you need on the essay and the multiple-choice sections to receive final scores of three, four, or five. It assumes that there are 55 multiple-choice questions and three essay questions graded from zero to nine.

If a student received fives on all three essays, in order to receive a final score of three, he or she would need a raw score (the number correct less one-quarter times the number wrong) of at least 18 on the multiple-choice section; to receive a final score of four, the same student would need a raw score of at least 34 on the multiple-choice section; and to receive a five, that student would need a raw score of at least 46 on that section.

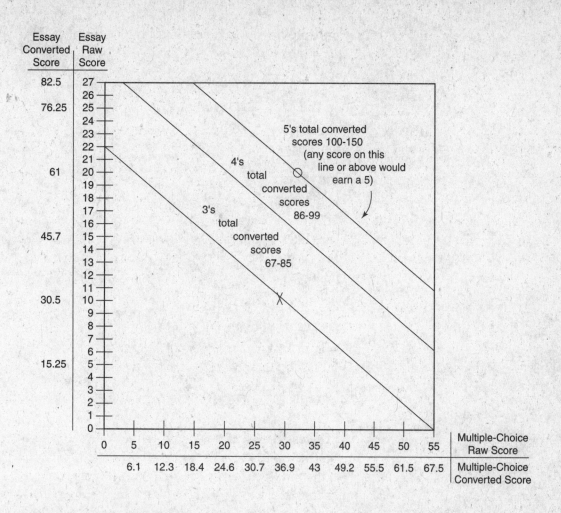

The angled lines on the graph tell you the minimum score you need on the multiple-choice and essay sections to earn a final score of 3, 4, or 5. For example: the point marked by a circle on the top line equals 61 converted points, the minimum score for a 5. The point marked by an x on the bottom line equals 30.5 converted points, the essay and 36.9 converted points on the multiple-choice section for a total of 67, the minimum score for a 3.

PART II

ANALYSIS OF
EXAM AREAS

The AP Literature Exam Section I: Multiple-Choice Questions

Introduction

The multiple-choice section of the exam normally contains between fifty and sixty questions on four different passages. One passage has at least fifteen questions and is reused on a future exam. Two of the passages are prose; two are poetry. Though the poems are usually complete works, the prose passages are likely to be taken from longer works such as novels or works of nonfiction.

The four passages represent different periods of British and American literature. It is likely that one is chosen from the sixteenth or the early seventeenth century and one from the restoration or eighteenth century, unless these periods are represented by passages on the essay section of the test. The two other sections are from nineteenth- and twentieth-century writers. The exam as a whole is likely to include several works by female and minority writers.

You may, by extraordinarily good luck, find a passage on the exam that you've studied in your English class, but the odds are heavily against it. The passages chosen for the exam are almost always those that have not found their way into textbooks and anthologies. Though your AP class should study shorter poems of poets like Shakespeare and Donne, and though a sonnet by one or the other may someday appear on the exam, it will not be one of the popular favorites like "My mistress' eyes are nothing like the sun" or "Death, be not proud." The passages are often by writers you are familiar with, but the text is not likely to be familiar to you. To be prepared for the multiple-choice section, you must be able to sight-read a reasonably complex poem or passage of prose written in English within the last five centuries. If your studies are limited to a narrow period — the twentieth century, say — you will be at a serious disadvantage on the multiple-choice section of the exam.

The passages chosen for the exam are not easy. They must be complex enough to generate fifteen or so multiple-choice questions that discriminate among the 200,000 students taking the exam. If the passages are too hard or too easy, they won't work.

To answer the multiple-choice questions, you don't need any special historical or philosophical knowledge. The passages are self-contained and self-explanatory. If a particularly difficult word occurs that is crucial to the understanding of the passage, it is explained in a footnote. But the exam expects you to be familiar with the common terms of literary analysis and to have some familiarity with classical mythology and the more popular parts of the Old and New Testaments. Because so much of British and American literature of the earlier periods is religious, it is quite possible that a religious poem by a writer like George Herbert or Edward Taylor or Anne Bradstreet may be on the exam. But the examiners are eager to make sure that no one is given any special advantage, and if a religious text is used, it should be just as accessible to a nonbeliever as to an evangelical and to a modern Moslem or a Jew as to a Christian. The questions will always be on literary, not doctrinal, issues.

Be glad if you have a teacher who insists on spending weeks on seventeenth- or eighteenth-century works when you would rather be talking about Vonnegut or Stoppard. Unless you're comfortable with the unfamiliar vocabulary, syntax, and conventions of the literature written before our time, you'll have trouble with the multiple-choice section of the exam and possibly with two-thirds of the essay section as well.

Though it will be helpful if you practice multiple-choice exams before you take the exam in May, your first task is to learn to analyze a poem and a prose passage. To practice your skills, you'll find the best exams are those published by the Advanced Placement Program of the College Board. The multiple-choice section of some past literature exams are available and can be ordered. Though several commercially published AP study guides contain sample multiple-choice exams, their questions and choice of texts are often not sufficiently like those on the real exams to make them very useful. (The exams in this book, it goes without saying, are an exception to this rule.)

There is no quick and easy way to master the analysis of literature. If there were, you wouldn't need to spend four years in high-school English classes, and English teachers would be selling real estate or practicing law or be out of a job. The Advanced Placement literature exam is testing all that you've learned about reading and writing English in junior and senior high school. But you can develop a method for approaching the literary texts you'll be asked to read on the AP exam.

Analyzing Poems

Some students have trouble with sight-reading poetry because they don't know where to start. They see the word "death" in the first line and "tomb" in the third and jump to the conclusion that this poem (which, in fact, is a sentimental lover's pitch to a woman who has turned him down) must be about mortality, and then spend the next ten minutes trying to make the poem fit these gloomy expectations.

To avoid premature conclusions, and to prepare yourself for the kind of questions the multiple-choice section asks, try going through each poem asking the following questions in something like this order.

1. **What is the dramatic situation?**

   That is, who is the speaker (or who are the speakers)? Is the speaker a male or female? Where is he or she? When does this poem take place? What are the circumstances?

   Sometimes you'll be able to answer all the questions: The speaker is a male psychopath living in a remote cottage, probably in Renaissance Italy, who has strangled his mistress and is sitting with her head propped upon his shoulder (Browning's "Porphyria's Lover"). Sometimes you'll be able to answer only a few, and sometimes only vaguely: The speaker is unnamed and unplaced and is speaking to an indeterminate audience. No matter. Already you've begun to understand the poem.

2. What is the structure of the poem?

That is, what are the parts of the poem and how are they related to each other? What gives the poem its coherence? What are the structural divisions of the poem?

In analyzing the structure, your best aid is the punctuation. Look first for the complete sentences indicated by periods, semicolons, question marks, or exclamation points. Then ask how the poem gets from the first sentence to the second and from the second to the third. Are there repetitions such as parallel syntax or the use of one simile in each sentence? Answer these questions in accordance with the sense of the poem, not by where a line ends or a rhyme falls. Don't assume that all sonnets will break into an 8–6 or a 4–4–4–2 pattern, but be able to recognize these patterns if they are used.

Think about the logic of the poem. Does it, say, ask questions, then answer them? Or develop an argument? Or use a series of analogies to prove a point? Understanding the structure isn't just a matter of mechanics. It will help you to understand the meaning of the poem as a whole and to perceive some of the art, the formal skills that the poet has used.

3. What is the theme of the poem?

You should now be able to see the point of the poem. Sometimes a poem simply says "I love you;" sometimes the theme or the meaning is much more complex. If possible, define what the poem says and why. A love poem usually praises the loved one in the hope that the speaker's love will be returned. But many poems have meanings too complex to be reduced to single sentences. When this is true, a good multiple-choice writer won't ask for a single theme or meaning.

4. Are the grammar and meaning clear?

Make sure you understand the meaning of all the words in the poem, especially words you thought you knew but which don't seem to fit in the context of the poem. Also make sure you understand the grammar of the poem. The word order of poetry is often skewed, and in a poem a direct object may come before the subject and the verb. ("His sounding lyre the poet struck" can mean a poet was hit by a musical instrument, but as a line of poetry, it probably means the poet played his harp.)

5. What are the important images and figures of speech?

What are the important literal sensory objects, the images, such as a field of poppies or a stench of corruption? What are the similes and metaphors of the poem? In each, exactly what is compared to what? Is there a pattern in the images, such as a series of comparisons all using men compared to wild animals? The most difficult challenge of reading poetry is discriminating between the figurative ("I love a rose" — that is, my love is like a rose, beautiful, sweet, fragile) and the literal ("I love a rose" — that is, roses are my favorite flower). Every exam tests a reader's understanding of figurative language many times in both the multiple-choice and essay sections.

6. What are the most important single words used in the poem?

This is another way of asking about diction. Some of the most significant words in a poem aren't figurative or images but still determine the effect of the poem. A good reader recognizes which words — usually nouns and verbs, adjectives and adverbs — are the keys to the poem.

7. **What is the tone of the poem?**

Tone is a slippery word, and almost everyone has trouble with it. It's sometimes used to mean the mood or atmosphere of a work, though purists are offended by this definition. Or it can mean a manner of speaking, a tone of voice, as in "The disappointed coach's tone was sardonic." But its most common use as a term of literary analysis is to denote the inferred attitude of an author. When the author's attitude is different from that of the speaker, as is usually the case in ironic works, the tone of voice of the speaker, which may be calm, businesslike, even gracious, may be very different from the satiric tone of the work, which reflects the author's disapproval of the speaker. Because it is often very hard to define tone in one or two words, questions on tone do not appear frequently on responsibly written multiple-choice exams. Tone is a topic you can't afford to ignore, however, because the essay topic may well ask for a discussion of the tone of a poem or a passage of prose.

8. **What literary devices does the poem employ?**

The list of rhetorical devices that a writer may use is enormous. The terms you should worry about are, above all, metaphor, simile, and personification.

9. **What is the prosody of the poem?**

You can, in fact, get away with knowing very little about the rhyme, meter, and sound effects of poetry, though versification is not difficult once you're used to the new vocabulary you need and can hear the difference between an accented and an unaccented syllable. The essay question has not asked about sound in a poem for several years now, and the last time a question asked about the "movement of the verse," the answers on that part of the question were so vague as to be of no use in the grading. But it is, of course, always possible that such a task may turn up as part of the essay question. Chances are that of the thirteen to fifteen multiple-choice questions asked on each of the two poems, only one question will ask about the meter or the use of rhyme or the sound effects of a line. So a total of just two of the fifty-five questions may be on metrics.

Answering Multiple-Choice Poetry Questions

Types of Questions

This process of analysis — or whatever your own method may be — should precede your answering of the multiple-choice questions. The question writer has already gone through the same process, and the questions that you find on the exam will be very much like the ones you've just asked yourself.

1. Questions on **dramatic situation:**

   Examples:

   Who is speaking?

   Where is she?

To whom is the poem addressed?

Who is the speaker in lines 5–8?

Where does the poem take place?

At what time of the year does the poem take place?

2. Questions on **structure:**

Examples:

How are stanzas 1 and 2 related to stanza 3?

What word in line 20 refers back to an idea used in lines 5, 10, and 15?

Which of the following divisions of the poem best represents its structure?

3. Questions on **theme:**

Examples:

Which of the following best sums up the meaning of stanza 2?

With which of the following is the poem centrally concerned?

The poet rejects the notion of an indifferent universe because . . .

4. Questions on **grammar and meaning of words:**

Examples:

Which of the following best defines the word "glass" as it is used in line 9?

To which of the following does the word "which" in line 7 refer?

The verb "had done" may best be paraphrased as . . .

When answering questions on grammar or meaning, you must look carefully at the context. In questions of meaning, more often than not, the obvious meaning of a word is not the one used in the poem. If it were, there would be no reason to ask you a question about it. The answers to a question about the meaning of the word "glass," for example, might include

(A) a transparent material used in windows

(B) a barometer

(C) a mirror

(D) a telescope

(E) a drinking vessel

Without a context, you would have to call all five answers right. On an exam, a poem with a line like "The glass has fallen since the dawn" might well ask the meaning of "glass" with these five options, and the logical answer would be **B**. The next line of the poem would make the correct choice even clearer.

Similarly, grammar questions may exploit double meanings. The verb form "had broken" looks like a past perfect tense: I had broken the glass before I realized it. But a poem might also say "I had broken my heart unless I had seen her once more" in which case "had broken" is not a past perfect indicative verb, but a subjunctive in a conditional sentence. And this sentence could be paraphrased as "If I had not seen her once more, it would have broken my heart."

5. Questions on **images** and **figurative language:**

You should expect a large number of these. Because the poems used on the exam must be complex enough to inspire ten to fifteen good multiple-choice questions, it is rare that a poem which does not rely on complex figurative language is chosen.

Examples:

To which of the following does the poet compare his love?

The images in lines 3 and 8 come from what area of science?

The figure of the rope used in line 7 is used later in the poem in line . . .

6. Questions on **diction:**

Examples:

Which of the following words is used to suggest the poet's dislike of winter?

The poet's use of the word "air" in line 8 is to indicate . . .

The poet's delight in the garden is suggested by all of the following words EXCEPT . . .

Notice that some questions use a negative: "all of the following . . . EXCEPT" is the most common phrasing. The exam always calls attention to a question of this sort by using capital letters.

7. Questions on **tone, literary devices,** and **metrics:**

Examples:

The tone of the poem (or stanza) can best be described as . . .

Which of the following literary techniques is illustrated by the phrase "murmurous hum and buzz of the hive"? (onomatopoeia)

The meter of the last line in each stanza is . . .

Examples of Poetry Selections, Questions, and Answers

Set 1

The following poem, a sonnet by Keats, is a good example of the level of difficulty of the poetry on the literature exam. The selected poems are usually longer than the sonnet, but shorter poems appear sometimes. Read this poem carefully. Then answer the twelve multiple-choice questions that follow. Choose the best answer of the five.

On the Sonnet

If by dull rhymes our English must be chained,
And, like Andromeda, the Sonnet sweet
Fettered, in spite of pained loveliness,
Let us find out, if we must be constrained,
(5) Sandals more interwoven and complete
To fit the naked foot of poesy;
Let us inspect the lyre, and weigh the stress
Of every chord, and see what may be gained
By ear industrious, and attention meet;
(10) Misers of sound and syllable, no less
Than Midas of his coinage, let us be
Jealous of dead leaves in the bay-wreath crown;
So, if we may not let the Muse be free,
She will be bound with garlands of her own.

1. The "we" ("us") of the poem refers to

A. literary critics

B. misers

C. readers of poetry

D. the Muses

E. English poets

2. Which of the following best describes the major structural divisions of the poem?

A. Lines 1–3; 4–6; 7–9; 10–14

B. Lines 1–8; 9–14

C. Lines 1–6; 7–9; 10–12; 13–14

D. Lines 1–4; 5–8; 9–12; 13–14

E. Lines 1–6; 7–14

3. The metaphor used in the first line of the poem compares English to

A. carefully guarded treasure

B. Andromeda

C. a bound creature

D. a necklace

E. a sonnet

4. In lines 2–3, the poem compares the sonnet to Andromeda because

I. both are beautiful

II. neither is free

III. both are inventions of classical Greece

A. III only

B. I and II only

C. I and III only

D. II and III only

E. I, II, and III

5. The main verb of the first grammatically complete sentence of the poem is

A. "must be" (line 1)

B. "be chained" (line 1)

C. "Fettered" (line 3)

D. "let . . . find" (line 4)

E. "must be" (line 4)

6. The phrase "naked foot of poesy" in line 6 is an example of which of the following technical devices?

    A. simile

    B. personification

    C. oxymoron

    D. allusion

    E. transferred epithet

7. In line 9, the word "meet" is best defined as

    A. suitable

    B. concentrated

    C. unified

    D. distributed

    E. introductory

8. The poet alludes to Midas in line 11 to encourage poets to be

    A. miserly

    B. generous

    C. mythical

    D. magical

    E. royal

9. In line 12, the phrase "dead leaves" probably refers to

    A. boring passages in poetry

    B. the pages of a book of poetry

    C. worn-out conventions of poetry

    D. surprising but inappropriate original metaphors

    E. the closely guarded secrets of style that make great poetry

10. All of the following words denote restraint EXCEPT

    A. "chained" (line 1)

    B. "Fettered" (line 3)

    C. "constrained" (line 4)

    D. "interwoven" (line 5)

    E. "bound" (line 14)

11. Which of the following best states the central idea of the poem?

    A. Poems must be carefully crafted and decorously adorned.

    B. Poets must jealously guard the traditional forms of the sonnet.

    C. Sonnets should be free of all restrictions.

    D. The constraint of the sonnet form will lead to discipline and creativity.

    E. Poems in restricted forms should be original and carefully crafted.

12. The poem is written in

    A. rhymed couplets

    B. blank verse

    C. rhymed iambic pentameter

    D. Shakespearean sonnet form

    E. rhymed triplets

Answers for Set 1

1. **E.** The first questions asks you to identify the speaker and his audience. This is one of the poems which tell us nothing about the time period or the location of the speaker. But we do know he is a poet, because the poem is called "On the Sonnet" and deals with his ideas about how the sonnet should be composed. Because he speaks of English as "chained" by the rhymes of poetry (and because he writes in English), we infer that the speaker and his audience are English poets. The correct choice is **E**. The next-best choice is **A**, but though the poem does include some literary criticism, **E** is the "best" answer. The very existence of this poem tells us the speaker is a poet, and his plural pronoun defines his audience as like himself.

2. **C.** The best choice here is **C**, dividing the poem at the semicolons (which may have been periods) at the end of lines 6, 9, and 12. Those of you familiar with other sonnets will recognize that this is an unusual poem. Most sonnets break naturally in units of eight and six lines (Italian sonnets especially) or into three four-line units and a closing couplet (the English, or Shakespearean, sonnet). But it is these restrictions Keats is complaining about. And so his poem falls into units of six, three, three, and two lines. And it pays no attention to the abba, abba, cdcdcd rhyme scheme of the Italian sonnet or to the abab, dcdc, efef, gg of the Shakespearean sonnet. Notice that you cannot stop at the comma in line 3. The first three lines are a dependent clause, and the sentence is not yet grammatically coherent.

3. **C.** The metaphor presents English chained without defining any more clearly whether the language is compared to a human or an animal. The comparison to Andromeda in line 2 is a simile.

4. **B.** This is an example of a question where part of your answer comes from reading the poem carefully and part from your general information. Both I and II are clear from the poem, because both Andromeda and the sonnet are said to be "sweet" and to have "loveliness" and both are "Fettered." Though Andromeda is the creation of Greek mythology — she was chained to a rock and rescued by Perseus — the sonnet is not an ancient Greek poetic form.

5. **D.** The main verb of the sentence is "let (us) find." The verbs "must be chained" and "Fettered" are part of the dependent clause.

6. **B.** There is no "like" or "as," so the figure is a metaphor, not a simile. It is also a personification, in this case, a metaphor in which poetry is represented as possessing human form, having a foot that can wear a sandal. Keats is probably punning here on another meaning of foot, the term to denote the metric unit of a line of verse.

7. **A.** As it is used here, "meet" is an adjective meaning "suitable" or "fitting" (compare Hamlet's line "meet it is I set it down" or the phrase "meet and just").

8. **A.** This question calls for a literal reading of the line, not an explanation of the figure. Surprisingly, because Midas is usually viewed as a fool or a villain, Keats urges poets to be miserly, like Midas, though not with money but with the sounds and syllables of their poems.

9. **C.** Here the question calls for an explanation of the metaphor "dead leaves." The adjective "Jealous" in this sentence does not mean "envious," as it usually does, but "watchful" or "very attentive to." The poet is urging other poets to scrupulously keep "dead leaves" from the bay-leaf crown that is traditionally associated with the poet. The metaphor, in keeping with the advice of the rest of the poem, is probably a reference to poetic practices that are no longer alive or natural like the green leaves of the laurel (bay) wreath. The word "leaves" here might be a play on "leaf" as "page," but the more important meaning is the metaphorical one, and **C** is the best of the five options.

10. **D.** The question combines diction and structure. The word "interwoven" in its context refers to the structure of the sandal. Arguably, because an interwoven sandal fits the foot, even this word suggests constraint, but the question calls for the best answer of the five, and constraint is much more clearly the denotation of the other four choices. The reference of the sandals metaphor is probably to the rhyme scheme into which the poem (the foot) must fit. The more interwoven rhyme scheme Keats has in mind is the one he uses here: not the abab, dcdc, efef, gg of the traditional English sonnet where new rhymes appear in each of the following quatrains, but the "interwoven" abc, abd, cabcdede.

11. **E.** This is the theme-of-the-poem question. Though Keats may agree with choice **A**, this poem doesn't make this point. In all multiple-choice sets, beware of the answer that in itself is true or morally uplifting or an idea that poems often express but which is not the issue in the poem you're dealing with. Good, wrong answers, test writers believe, must sound true even if they are irrelevant. Choice **B** is an idea some poets may hold, but this poem rejects the traditional forms if they have become "dead leaves." Choice **C** is not an issue here. Keats begins with the condition of English poetry chained by rhymes, and though this suggests some sympathy with the idea of even greater freedom, the poem never advocates giving up all restrictions. Choice **D** is another of those good-sounding wrong answers. It is an idea that many poets, perhaps including Keats, would endorse, but it is not the theme of this sonnet. Choice **E** is the best of the five.

12. **C.** This is an example of a question on the metrics of the poem. Choice **C** is right; **A**, **B**, **D**, and **E** are all untrue. Given the concern of this poem with the rhyme scheme of the sonnet, one should not be surprised to find a question about the rhyme scheme Keats uses here in a set of questions on the poem.

Set 2

The following poem, a sonnet by Wordsworth, was written twelve years before the Keats poem you just studied. Read this poem carefully, analyze it quickly, and then answer the multiple-choice questions that follow.

> Nuns fret not at their convent's narrow room;
> And hermits are contented with their cells;
> And students with their pensive citadels;
> Maids at the wheel, the weaver at his loom
> (5)   Sit blithe and happy; bees that soar for bloom,
> High as the highest Peak of Furness-fells,
> Will murmur by the hour in foxglove bells:

In truth the prison, unto which we doom
Ourselves, no prison is: and hence for me,
(10) In sundry moods, 'twas pastime to be bound
Within the Sonnet's scanty plot of ground;
Pleased if some souls (for such there needs must be)
Who have felt the weight of too much liberty,
Should find brief solace there, as I have found.

1. Which of the following best represents the structural divisions of the poem?

   A. Lines 1–4; 5–8; 9–12; 13–14
   B. Lines 1–7; 8–10; 11–13; 14
   C. Lines 1–7; 8–9½; 9½–14
   D. Lines 1–8; 9–11; 12–14
   E. Lines 1–9; 10–13; 14

2. Which of the following best describes the organization of the poem?

   A. A series of logically developing ideas with a concluding personal application
   B. A series of examples followed by a generalization and a personal application
   C. A generalization followed by examples
   D. A specific assertion followed by examples followed by a contradiction of the initial assertion
   E. An answer followed by a question that cannot be answered

3. In line 3, the phrase "pensive citadels" can be best paraphrased as

   A. towers in which students are imprisoned
   B. castles under siege

   C. dreary fortresses
   D. refuges for contemplation
   E. strongholds that inspire thought

4. The "we" of line 8 could refer to all of the following EXCEPT

   A. criminals
   B. poets
   C. nuns
   D. hermits
   E. students

5. In line 8, "prison" is parallel to all of the following EXCEPT

   A. "narrow room" (line 1)
   B. "pensive citadels" (line 3)
   C. "Peak of Furness-fells" (line 6)
   D. "foxglove bells" (line 7)
   E. "scanty plot of ground" (line 11)

6. Lines 8–9 ("In truth the prison, unto which we doom/Ourselves, no prison is") is an example of

   A. hyperbole
   B. personification
   C. alliteration
   D. simile
   E. paradox

7. In line 10, the assertion "'twas pastime" is parallel to all of the following phrases EXCEPT

    A. "fret not" (line 1)

    B. "are contented" (line 2)

    C. "Sit blithe" (line 5)

    D. "Will murmur" (line 7)

    E. "we doom" (line 8)

8. The figure of speech in line 11 ("Within the Sonnet's scanty plot of ground") is

    A. a simile comparing the writing of poetry to a field

    B. a simile comparing the poet and a farmer

    C. a metaphor comparing the sonnet and a small piece of land

    D. a metaphor comparing the pleasures of writing poetry and the pleasures of gardening

    E. an apostrophe

9. In line 14, "there" refers to

    A. the sonnet (line 11)

    B. the soul (line 12)

    C. pleasure (line 12)

    D. weight (line 13)

    E. liberty (line 13)

10. Which of the following phrases from the poem best sums up its central idea?

    A. "hermits are contented with their cells" (line 2)

    B. "Maids at the wheel . . . / Sit blithe and happy" (lines 4–5)

    C. "the prison, unto which we doom / Ourselves, no prison is" (lines 8–9)

    D. "such there needs must be" (line 12)

    E. "Who have felt the weight of too much liberty" (line 13)

11. From the poem, the reader may infer all of the following about the speaker EXCEPT that he

    A. feels deep compassion for the nuns

    B. sometimes finds liberty onerous

    C. respects literary conventions

    D. finds conventional verse forms congenial to his talent

    E. has written a number of sonnets

12. The rhyme scheme of this poem is especially appropriate because

    I.   lines 1–8 employ the traditional abba, abba, of the Italian sonnet

    II. it is restricted to only four rhymes in the 14 lines

    III. it makes judicious use of slant rhymes

    A. III only

    B. I and II only

    C. I and III only

    D. II and III only

    E. I, II, and III

Answers for Set 2

1. **C.** Line 8 and half of line 9 state the thesis of the poem: that a self-chosen restriction is not a restriction at all. The first seven lines of the poem give six different examples of self-chosen restrictions: the nuns in their convent, the hermits in their cells, the students withdrawn to contemplation, the maids at their spinning wheels, the weaver at the loom, and finally the bee which seeks nectar in the narrow confines of the foxglove blossom. Lines 9, 10, and 11 apply the idea of self-elected restrictions to the poet's choosing to write in the difficult and limiting sonnet form. Lines 12–14 express the poet's satisfaction in others' finding the same pleasure in his sonnets. The structure then is that described in **C**.

2. **B.** The organization is explained by **B**. Notice that one of the divisions of the poem falls in the middle rather than at the end of a line. Though the rhyme scheme of abba, abba suggests an eight-line unit to begin the poem, the real unit is seven lines.

3. **D.** A citadel is a tower, a fortress, a refuge. The adjective "pensive" means thoughtful, meditative. Because a citadel cannot think, the phrase is surprising. The device the poet uses here is a transferred epithet, the shift of a word or phrase from the noun it would logically modify to another. Shakespeare writes of a sailor high on the "giddy mast" of a ship in a storm. It is, of course, the sailor, not the mast, who is "giddy." It is the students here who are "pensive," but the adjective is transferred to modify the place where they meditate.

4. **A.** The exception is the criminals. A criminal in prison has not chosen prison voluntarily, while, according to the poem, the nun, poet, hermit, and students have chosen the restrictions of the convent, the sonnet, the cell, or the citadel.

5. **C.** The prison is parallel to other self-chosen forms of restriction such as the narrow room, citadels, bells (or flowers) of the foxglove, and the scanty plot of the sonnet. In line 6, the reference to bees flying as high as the mountain peak is to demonstrate the freedom the bees might enjoy contrasted with the narrow space inside the foxglove flower, which they choose instead. Choice **C** is the opposite of prison, not a parallel.

6. **E.** This is a paradox, an apparently self-contradictory statement. To say a prison is not a prison is paradoxical. Another term for this figure is oxymoron.

7. **E.** The phrase is the expression of the speaker's pleasure in restriction. The phrases parallel to this are "fret not," "are contented," "Sit blithe," and "Will murmur," all of which are used to express satisfaction with elected restraints. The exception, and right answer, is "we doom."

8. **C.** This is a metaphor (a simile would use "like" or "as") comparing the sonnet and a small plot of land. Apostrophe is direct address to a person or thing.

9. **A.** The "there" refers to the sonnet, where the poet has found and, he hopes the reader will find, some pleasure.

10. **C.** This option, using the prison metaphor, explicitly states the theme of the sonnet.

11. **A.** There is no reason to feel compassion for the nuns, whose confinement is self-chosen. That he has "felt the weight of too much liberty" supports **B**. That he finds pleasure in the restrictions of the sonnet suggests his respect for tradition and for conventional restrictive forms.

12. **B.** Among a number of possible rhyme schemes for the sonnet, the poet has chosen one of the most restrictive, in keeping with the thesis of the poem that a chosen restraint is not restraining. The first eight lines have only two rhymes (as in the Italian sonnet), and only two more rhymes are used in lines 9–14. A slant rhyme is an off-rhyme, a rhyme that is incomplete. If "bells" were rhymed with "calls" or "ills," both rhymes would be slant rhymes. This poem, predictably, does not take advantage of this license.

Analyzing Prose

Though the analysis of a prose passage is like the analysis of a poem in many ways, there are important differences quite apart from the absence of meter. The prose selections are normally longer than the poems, running from 450 to 850 words. Like the poetry, they represent writing in English in the sixteenth, seventeenth, eighteenth, nineteenth, and twentieth centuries. Some of the prose is more difficult because of differences between style in the earlier periods and that of our time. Some passages are on unfamiliar subjects. Excerpts come from a variety of both fictional and nonfictional sources: novels, short stories, history, philosophical writing, sermons, journals, letters, essays, biographies, autobiographies, or literary criticism, and the list could go on.

One approach to sight-reading prose is to deal first with the issues of genre (the kind of work, such as novel or essay) and content, then, of structure, and finally, of style.

1. **genre**

   From what kind of a work is the selection taken? Is it fiction or nonfiction?

   If you're dealing with a work of fiction, chances are you'll have to think about the character or characters in the passage, while a work of nonfiction probably focuses on an issue, on an idea, or on the narrator, him or herself.

2. **narrator**

   Whether the passage is from a work of fiction or of nonfiction, you must be aware of who is speaking and what his or her attitudes are toward the characters or the subject of the passage. If you can, identify who is speaking, where and when, why, and to whom. You will often be unable to answer all of these questions, but answer as many of them as you can.

3. **subject**

   Ascertain what the purpose of the passage is. Is it to present an argument or to introduce a character? To cajole, or entertain, or stir to action? If you can define an author's purpose clearly, most of the questions on the interpretation of meaning will fall neatly into place.

4. **structure**

   The normal unit of prose is the paragraph, and the passages on the AP exam run from a single long paragraph (the prose writers of the seventeenth century sometimes wrote paragraphs that seem as long as chapters to modern readers) to ten shorter paragraphs. As with a poem, try to see how each part advances the progress of the whole. How are the paragraphs related to each other and to the passage as a whole?

5. **style**

The style of prose is determined by diction, imagery, figurative language, and syntax — all matters you deal with in the analysis of poetry. In addition, the analysis of prose is certain to raise questions about the rhetoric of a passage, that is, its use of words to persuade or influence a reader. There is, of course, a rhetoric in poetry, but the questions about rhetoric are more likely to be asked about prose passages.

Answering Multiple-Choice Prose Questions

Types of Questions

Most of the multiple-choice questions on the prose passage take the following forms:

1. Questions on **situation and content:** on the passage as a whole; on a single paragraph; on a single sentence.

   Examples:

   The main subject of the passage is . . .

   The primary distinction made in the first paragraph is between . . .

   According to lines 3–7, which of the following is the chief . . .

   In the third paragraph, the author is chiefly concerned with . . .

2. Questions on **meaning of words or phrases:**

   Examples:

   As it is used in line 2, the word x can be best understood to mean . . .

   In line 7, the word x employs all of the following meanings EXCEPT . . .

   The phrase xyz is best understood to mean . . .

3. Questions on **grammar:**

   Examples:

   In the opening clause, the word "which" refers to . . .

   In line 12, the antecedent of "it" is . . .

   The subject of the long sentence that makes up the third paragraph is . . .

4. Questions on **diction:**

   Examples:

   The speaker's choice of verbs in the paragraph is to stress the . . .

   The speaker's anger is suggested by all of the following EXCEPT . . .

5. Questions on **figurative language:**

Examples:

The comparison in lines 1-3 compares . . .

The analogy of the second paragraph compares . . .

The phrase xyz is best read as a metaphor relating to . . .

The purpose of the astronomy metaphor in line 9 is to . . .

6. Questions on **structure:**

Examples:

The transitions from the first to the second and the second to the third paragraph are dependent upon . . .

The last paragraph of the passage is related to the first chiefly by . . .

7. Questions on **literary techniques:**

Examples:

In the third paragraph, the description of the cat on roller skates is an example of . . .

All of the following phrases are paradoxes EXCEPT . . .

The phrase "silent scream" is an example of . . .

8. Questions on **rhetoric:**

Examples:

The rhetorical purpose of lines 1–6 is to . . .

The argument of the passage can best be described as progressing from . . .

Which of the following best describes the function of the last sentence?

The effect of shifting from the past to the present tense in the third paragraph is . . .

The happiness of the speaker is conveyed primarily by the use of . . .

9. Questions on **tone:**

Examples:

The tone of the passage may be described as . . .

In discussing x in the second paragraph, the speaker adopts a tone of . . .

Examples of Prose Selections, Questions, and Answers

Set 1

The following passage is taken from George Eliot's novel *Adam Bede* (1859). Though the passage comes from a work of fiction, it could just as well have appeared as a short essay. To read it, you do not need to know anything about the rest of the novel. The passage was used in the essay section of an AP exam. Read it very carefully. It is not so easy or straightforward as it may at first appear to be. Then answer the multiple-choice questions that follow.

Leisure is gone — gone where the spinning-wheels are gone, and the pack horses, and the slow waggons, and the pedlars, who brought bargains to the
(5) door on sunny afternoons. Ingenious philosophers tell you, perhaps, that the great work of the steam-engine is to create leisure for mankind. Do not believe them: it only creates a vacuum for eager
(10) thought to rush in. Even idleness is eager now — eager for amusement: prone to excursion-trains, art-museums, periodical literature, and exciting novels: prone even to scientific theorising, and
(15) cursory peeps through microscopes. Old Leisure was quite a different personage: he only read one newspaper, innocent of leaders, and was free from that periodicity of sensations which we call
(20) post-time. He was a contemplative, rather stout gentleman, of excellent digestion — of quiet perceptions, undiseased by hypothesis: happy in his inability to know the causes of things,
(25) preferring the things themselves. He lived chiefly in the country, among pleasant seats and homesteads, and was fond of sauntering by the fruit-tree wall, and scenting the apricots when they
(30) were warmed by the morning sunshine, or of sheltering himself under the orchard boughs at noon, when the summer pears were falling. He knew nothing of weekday services, and thought none the
(35) worse of the Sunday sermon if it allowed him to sleep from the text to the blessing — liking the afternoon service best, because the prayers were the shortest, and not ashamed to say so; for he
(40) had an easy, jolly conscience, broadbacked like himself, and able to carry a great deal of beer or port-wine, — not being made squeamish by doubts and qualms and lofty aspirations. Life was
(45) not a task to him, but a sinecure: he fingered the guineas in his pocket, and ate his dinners, and slept the sleep of the irresponsible; for had he not kept up his charter by going to church on the
(50) Sunday afternoons?

Fine old Leisure! Do not be severe upon him, and judge him by our modern standard: he never went to Exeter Hall, or heard a popular preacher, or read
(55) *Tracts for the Times* or *Sartor Resartus*.*

*Exeter Hall was a London building used for lectures and meetings, especially of a religious nature. Tracts for the Times and Sartor Resartus are important Victorian religious and philosophical books.

1. The phrases "Even idleness is eager now — eager for amusement" (lines 10–11) exemplify which of the following devices?

    I.   metaphor
    II. personification
    III. paradox

    A. III only
    B. I and II only
    C. I and III only
    D. II and III only
    E. I, II, and III

2. According to the passage, all of the following are the activities of the present EXCEPT

    A. restoring antiques
    B. railway excursions
    C. reading fiction
    D. amateur biology
    E. attending lectures

3. The phrase "innocent of leaders" (line 17–18) can be best said to mean

    A. guiltless of ambition

    B. free of editorials

    C. ignorant of competition

    D. pure as a commander

    E. blameless of power

4. Old Leisure had not been "made squeamish by doubts and qualms and lofty aspirations" (lines 43–44) because

    A. he has no reason to feel guilty

    B. his honesty protects him against doubt

    C. he never thinks about doubt or aspiration

    D. he has fulfilled his charter by attending church

    E. they are inventions of the modern age

5. The word "sinecure" in line 45 can be best defined as

    A. a well-rewarded but undemanding position

    B. a paid vacation

    C. a hard-won and deserved triumph

    D. an irresponsible indulgence in pleasure

    E. an assuming of responsibility for the well-being of others

6. The point of view in the question "had he not kept up his charter by going to church on the Sunday afternoons?" (lines 48–50) is that of

    I.   old Leisure

    II. new or modern leisure

    III. the narrator of the passage

    A. I only

    B. II only

    C. III only

    D. I and III only

    E. II and III only

7. In lines 39–41, the phrase "he had an easy, jolly conscience, broad-backed like himself" employs

    A. only one simile

    B. only one metaphor

    C. one metaphor and one simile

    D. two metaphors and one simile

    E. two similes

8. The social position of old Leisure is suggested by all of the following words EXCEPT

    A. "gentleman" (line 21)

    B. "pleasant seats" (line 27)

    C. "port-wine" (line 42)

    D. "guineas" (line 46)

    E. "charter" (line 49)

9. Old Leisure's observance of his religious obligations may be best described as

   A. hypocritical

   B. ardent

   C. grudging

   D. perfunctory

   E. skeptical

10. Of the following phrases, all of them work to make a similar point about old Leisure EXCEPT

   A. "rather stout" (line 21)

   B. "of excellent digestion" (lines 21–22)

   C. "undiseased by hypothesis" (lines 22–23)

   D. "able to carry a great deal of beer" (lines 41–42)

   E. "ate his dinners" (lines 46–49)

11. Of the following techniques, which is the most important in the presentation of old Leisure?

   A. hyperbole

   B. simile

   C. personification

   D. paradox

   E. apostrophe

12. Compared to the leisure of modern times, old Leisure is characterized as more

   A. religious

   B. cynical

   C. unthinking

   D. eager

   E. carnal

13. The passage implies all of the following contrasts between the leisure of the past and of the present EXCEPT

   A. rural vs. urban

   B. science vs. art

   C. mind vs. body

   D. complacency vs. aspiration

   E. belief vs. doubt

14. From the whole passage, the reader can infer that the narrator feels

   I. some nostalgia for the leisure of the past

   II. an awareness of the complacency of the present

   III. a concern for the anti-intellectual self-interest of the past

   A. I only

   B. II only

   C. I and II only

   D. I and III only

   E. I, II, and III

15. The tone of the passage is best described as

   A. gently satirical

   B. harshly sarcastic

   C. mawkishly sentimental

   D. coolly objective

   E. cheerfully optimistic

Answers for Set 1

The instructions tell you that the passage is from a novel but that it may have come from an essay. What is striking about the passage is the characterization of the idea of old Leisure. George Eliot personifies the leisure of the past and devotes most of the passage to describing this fictitious character. In the course of the passage, the speaker or narrator reveals her views about the leisure of her own era and about old Leisure, and she cautions her contemporaries not to be too quick to pronounce the up-to-date to be superior.

1. **E.** The first question asks you to identify the technical devices in "even idleness is eager." All three terms apply. "Idleness" is personified (and personification is a form of metaphor in which an abstract quality is compared to a person), and an eager idleness is a paradox, an apparent contradiction, because eager and idle seem to be opposites.

2. **A.** The passage lists all of the activities except restoring antiques as leisure activities of the mid-Victorian world.

3. **B.** This question is an example of a vocabulary word where the obvious modern meaning is not relevant. A "leader" is a newspaper editorial. The word is still used by journalists, but it is more common now in England than in the United States. The context of the phrase, introduced by "newspaper," as well as what we are told of old Leisure's lack of interest in almost anything requiring some thought, could suggest the right answer even if you had never heard of a "leader" as a "newspaper editorial."

4. **C.** Doubts, qualms, and lofty aspirations do not bother old Leisure because he never thinks about such serious or disturbing things. He is, we have been told, glad to be ignorant of causes and unconcerned with theories. This phrase is one of several which suggest that the narrator is not wholly on old Leisure's side. Can we really endorse an approach to life that avoids doubts and aspirations?

5. **A.** A "sinecure" is a position that is well paid but that requires very little work. Unlike the Victorians, celebrated for their earnest approach to life, old Leisure is in the happy position to regard life as a free ride.

6. **A.** Old Leisure, thoughtless as he is, would see no irony in the question and assume the answer is yes. But the narrator is not quite so sure. Though she tweaks old Leisure gently by putting this question in his mouth, it's hard for a modern reader to believe that the author thinks a snooze in church is an adequate fulfillment of religious duties.

7. **D.** The figurative language here is complex. To begin with, we have the basic metaphor of the passage in which the abstraction, old Leisure, is compared to a person (metaphor one) with the phrase "he had an easy, jolly conscience." But this conscience is also personified as "jolly" and "broad-backed" (metaphor two) and in being stout is said to be "like himself" (a simile). So the phrase has a simile and two metaphors, both personifications.

8. **E.** One of the subtle touches in George Eliot's portrait of old Leisure is her clearly placing him in the moneyed class. He is not a farmer who plants crops or gets up early, though he no doubt owns agricultural lands that others work for his profit. He is a "gentleman" (often in British parlance a man of good birth and social position whose wealth is inherited — Mr. Bennet in *Pride and Prejudice,* as Elizabeth proudly tells Darcy, is a "gentleman"). He drinks port, lives among pleasant seats, and fingers his guineas. His guineas, notice, not his pennies or shillings. A guinea was a gold coin equal to a year's wages of a serving girl in

nineteenth-century England. Only the word "charter" here does not suggest old Leisure's social position.

9. **D.** A case could be made for "grudging," but given the fact that he does go to church on Sunday, sleeps comfortably, and is satisfied with his performance, "perfunctory" is a better choice.

10. **C.** Another of the pleasures of the passage is the suggestion that old Leisure eats a lot and is, perhaps, a bit overweight — certainly "stout" and "broad-backed." Though his digestion may be relevant to old Leisure's girth, the phrase "undiseased by hypothesis" is only a metaphor revealing his anti-intellectuality.

11. **C.** The chief technique is personification.

12. **C.** Old Leisure is presented as more unthinking. Modern leisure may think too much; old Leisure avoids thought at all costs.

13. **B.** The passage does not use the art-science contrast. In fact, modern leisure is said to be interested in both art museums and microscopes, while old Leisure would be indifferent to both.

14. **E.** All three of these ideas are implied. The author sees the charm as well as the limitations of old Leisure and warns against complacency in the paragraph.

15. **A.** The best choice here is **A**, though it is not the whole story. Sometimes you have to select an imperfect answer because the other four are inferior or outrightly wrong. Here, **B**, **C**, **D**, and **E** are all clearly worse than **A**.

Set 2

The following passage, from Joseph Conrad's short novel *Typhoon*, was used on the essay section of the 1989 literature exam, but it could have been used for multiple-choice questions. Read the passage carefully and choose the best answer of the five options in the multiple-choice questions following the passage.

Captain MacWhirr, of the steamer Nan-Shan, had a physiognomy that, in the order of material appearances, was the exact counterpart of his mind: it pre-
(5) sented no marked characteristics of firmness or stupidity; it had no pronounced characteristics whatever; it was simply ordinary, irresponsive, and unruffled...

Having just enough imagination to
(10) carry him through each successive day, and no more, he was tranquilly sure of himself; and from the very same cause he was not in the least conceited. It is your imaginative superior who is touchy,
(15) overbearing, and difficult to please; but every ship Captain MacWhirr commanded was the floating abode of harmony and peace. It was, in truth, as impossible for him to take a flight of
(20) fancy as it would be for a watchmaker to put together a chronometer with nothing except a two-pound hammer and a whipsaw in the way of tools. Yet the uninteresting lives of men so entirely given to
(25) the actuality of the bare existence have their mysterious side. It was impossible in Captain MacWhirr's case, for instance, to understand what under heaven

(30) could have induced that perfectly satis-factory son of a petty grocer in Belfast to run away to sea. And yet he had done that very thing at the age of fifteen. It was enough, when you thought it over, to give you the idea of an immense, potent,
(35) and invisible hand thrust into the ant-heap of the earth, laying hold of shoul-ders, knocking heads together, and setting the unconscious faces of the mul-titude towards inconceivable goals and in
(40) undreamt-of directions.

His father never really forgave him for this undutiful stupidity. "We could have got on without him," he used to say later on, "but there's the business. And
(45) he an only son, too!" His mother wept very much after his disappearance. As it had never occurred to him to leave word behind, he was mourned over for dead till, after eight months, his first letter ar-
(50) rived from Talcahuano. It was short, and contained the statement: "We had very fine weather on our passage out." But evidently, in the writer's mind, the only important intelligence was to the effect
(55) that his captain had, on the very day of writing, entered him regularly on the ship's articles as Ordinary Seaman. "Because I can do the work," he explained. The mother again wept

(60) copiously, while the remark, "Tom's an ass," expressed the emotions of the fa-ther. He was a corpulent man, with a gift for sly chaffing, which to the end of his life he exercised in his intercourse with
(65) his son, a little pityingly, as if upon a half-witted person.

MacWhirr's visits to his home were necessarily rare, and in the course of years he dispatched other letters to his
(70) parents, informing them of his succes-sive promotions and of his movements upon the vast earth. In these missives could be found sentences like this: "The heat here is very great." Or: "On
(75) Christmas day at 4 p.m. we fell in with some icebergs." The old people ulti-mately became acquainted with a good many names of ships, and with the names of the skippers who commanded
(80) them — with the names of Scots and English shipowners — with the names of seas, oceans, straits, promontories — with outlandish names of lumberports, of rice-ports, of cotton-ports—with the
(85) names of islands — with the name of their son's young woman. She was called Lucy. It did not suggest itself to him to mention whether he thought the name pretty. And then they died.

1. The word "physiognomy" in line 2 can be best defined as

   A. temperament
   B. personality
   C. face
   D. manner of behaving
   E. pragmatism

2. The point of the simile in lines 18–23 ("It was, in truth . . . way of tools") is to illustrate

   A. a difficulty
   B. an impossibility
   C. a subtlety
   D. a technicality
   E. an unlikeness

3. The passage represents the young MacWhirr's decision to go to sea as

    A. youthful rebelliousness

    B. a search for adventure

    C. personal ambition

    D. romantic escapism

    E. an unexplainable action

4. In line 42, the word "undutiful" may be best defined as

    A. unusual

    B. extreme

    C. unexpected

    D. disobedient

    E. uncharged

5. The phrase "undutiful stupidity" in line 42 reflects the point of view of which of the following?

    I. the narrator of the passage

    II. MacWhirr's father

    III. MacWhirr's mother

    A. I only

    B. II only

    C. I and II only

    D. II and III only

    E. I, II, and III

6. Of the following phrases, which has the effect of reducing our feelings of sympathy for MacWhirr's parents?

    I. "but there's the business. And he an only son, too!" (lines 44–45)

    II. "His mother wept very much after his disappearance." (lines 45–46)

    III. "Tom's an ass," (lines 60–61)

    A. II only

    B. I and II only

    C. I and III only

    D. I, II, and III

    E. III

7. MacWhirr does not comment on the prettiness of the name Lucy in his letters to his parents because

    A. he wants them to know only the external events of his life

    B. he does not think they care enough about him to be interested

    C. he has not thought about it himself

    D. such a comment would be effeminate

    E. such a comment would suggest that her face was not pretty

8. The word "names" is repeated six times in the last paragraph to

    A. contrast with the single repetition of the singular "name"

    B. suggest the slow passage of time at sea

    C. expose the unnatural absence of feeling in Captain MacWhirr

    D. emphasize Captain MacWhirr's commitment to actuality

    E. enhance the poetic quality of the prose

9. In the last sentence of the passage, the antecedent of "they" is probably

   A. the old people
   B. skippers
   C. Scots ship owners
   D. English ship owners
   E. Captain MacWhirr and Lucy

10. MacWhirr's prose style is best characterized as

   A. episodic
   B. baroque
   C. metaphorical
   D. ironic
   E. factual

11. The narrator's prose style differs from that of captain MacWhirr in its use of

   I. figurative language
   II. irony
   III. generalization

   A. III only
   B. I and II only
   C. I and III only
   D. II and III only
   E. I, II, and III

12. To which of the following does the passage attribute MacWhirr's success as a commanding officer?

   I. his attention to detail
   II. his lack of imagination
   III. his ability to do the work

   A. II only
   B. III only
   C. I and III only
   D. II and III only
   E. I, II, and III

13. All of the following words accurately describe Captain MacWhirr EXCEPT

   A. fanciful
   B. ordinary
   C. cool
   D. serious
   E. confident

Answers for Set 2

The Conrad passage is centrally concerned with the character of Captain MacWhirr, and it also includes brief comments on and dialogue of his parents. The passage establishes what is to be the key to Captain MacWhirr and to the action of the story. MacWhirr is so completely lacking in imaginative ability that he cannot imagine the power and the peril of a typhoon. And so when others are paralyzed by fear, MacWhirr keeps his head and steers his ship through the storm.

1. **C.** "Physiognomy" is a long word for face. Notice that this paragraph does not call MacWhirr firm or stupid or their opposites. It says his face, like his mind, had "no pronounced characteristics."

2. **B.** The point of the simile is to show impossibility: "as impossible for him . . . as". Don't be surprised if you find some multiple-choice questions that strike you as very easy, and don't assume that because a question seems easy there must be a trick and the right answer must be the unexpected choice. Each set of questions contains a few very hard questions and a few very easy questions. No set is all of one or the other.

3. **E.** The narrator admits that MacWhirr's decision is unexplainable: "impossible . . . to understand" and wholly "mysterious."

4. **D.** The word "undutiful" means lacking in a sense of duty, disobedient, disrespectful.

5. **B.** Remember that, in the first paragraph, the narrator doesn't charge MacWhirr with stupidity. MacWhirr's mother doesn't say enough for us to know her opinion, but the idea is certainly one the father would endorse.

6. **C.** The first of the father's remarks is not that of a dutiful parent, as it suggests that the business is more important than the loss of the company of the child. The third remark is even clearer. The mother's tears — at least on the first occasion — don't reduce our sympathy. And why did MacWhirr go off without telling his parents he was leaving? Why didn't he spare them all their needless worry? The answer, we infer, is that it never occurred to young Tom MacWhirr that his parents would worry. Such an idea requires some ability to imagine what others will feel, and MacWhirr, as we know, has no imagination at all.

7. **C.** Again the key to MacWhirr's actions is his inability to imagine, to think in terms other than the starkly factual. It would not occur to him to comment on the prettiness of a name because he would never think about whether a name was pretty or not.

8. **D.** To MacWhirr, a name is a name and no more, and the repeated use of the word in the last paragraph drives home the notion of MacWhirr's life "entirely given to the actuality of the bare existence." The purpose of a name, to MacWhirr, is to denote a reality.

9. **A.** It is grammatically possible to refer the pronoun to "Lucy" and to "he," which are, in fact, closer to the "they." But the logic of the passage as a whole, the focus from the beginning on MacWhirr, should suggest that there is more to follow and that MacWhirr will be more fully described.

10. **E.** MacWhirr's style is, of course, factual: "The heat here is very great."

11. **E.** Fortunately, the narrator writes a more sophisticated prose than does MacWhirr, employing all three of these devices, which MacWhirr would not understand.

12. **A.** According to the second paragraph, MacWhirr's lack of imagination makes for harmony on the ship. MacWhirr may possess the other qualities, but the passage attributes his success to II.

13. **A.** Again, it is MacWhirr's lack of imagination, his inability to be fanciful, that answers the question.

The AP Literature Exam Section II: Essay Questions

The Prose Passage

Answering All Parts of the Question

This section would say the most important thing it has to say if it simply repeated the following sentence for five pages:

Answer all the parts of the question on the exam.

And, unfortunately, there would still be students who paid no attention.

If the question asks you to discuss the narrator's attitude toward cars, toys, and pigs and the literary devices he uses to convey this attitude, the directions on the scoring guide for the top scores will read like this: "These essays accurately discuss the narrator's attitude toward cars, toys, and pigs. They deal fully and specifically with the literary devices (such as diction, figurative language, and irony) used in the passage." And if the question should ask you to write an essay without ever using the letter "z" (it won't), the first line of the scoring guide describing the best papers would begin, "These well-written essays completely avoid the letter z." Which is to say, answer all the parts of the question. Don't write your own question, regardless of how much more interesting it may be than the dull one on the exam. If a question calls for a play or a novel, write about a play or a novel — one play or one novel, not two plays or one play and one novel. Not one short story or one essay. If the question calls for tone, diction, and syntax (and it will), write about tone, diction, and syntax.

In preparing for the exam, you should practice reading AP questions as if your life depended on it. Your life doesn't, but your grade does. Go over in class with your teacher and fellow test takers as many of the old AP exam questions as you can stand. You don't have to write essays on all the old questions, but you should use them to train yourself to answer all the parts of the question.

Don't be in a hurry to begin writing. A well-thought-out, well-organized, and specific essay of three paragraphs will score higher than a disorganized and repetitive essay two or three times as long. You must answer all the question, and because the essay questions usually have three or four tasks, a very short answer — say, a single paragraph — is not likely to be adequate. But papers earning the highest scores are often distinguished by their economy as well as by their insights. Remember that your readers are spending all day reading essays on a single topic. They don't need to be told what the question asks, and frankly, they don't care if Shakespeare is your favorite writer or that your reading of *A Tale of Two Cities* has transfigured your life.

What they do want to see is whether or not you understand the question, understand the passage, and can write an essay demonstrating this mastery. You don't need to write an introductory paragraph outlining what you will do in your next three paragraphs. And you shouldn't write a final paragraph repeating what you've just said. Assume you have a reader smart enough to understand it the first time. If you answer the question the exam has put before you, you don't need a cute title, a dramatic opening, or a snazzy close.

Questions often ask you to identify an "attitude," a "state of mind," or a "tone." A common mistake is the assumption that the answer requires only one word, that there is only one attitude, one state of mind, or one tone. More often than not, the best answer is the one that sees complexity or a change. The good student sees that, though an author endorses a character or a position, he or she may do so with reservations. And though a character may feel relief or elation at the beginning of a passage, the second or third paragraph may present a change, a new feeling of disillusion or disappointment, for example. Don't assume that the singular or plural ("attitude" may really mean "attitudes," and "state of mind" might more clearly be called "states of mind") makes it perfectly clear. Chances are, if the answer is too simple, you're missing something. On the essay exams, if an answer is obvious, everyone will get it right, and the readers will be unable to discriminate among the papers. Don't let this warning lead you to be too inventive, to see too much, or to see what isn't there. But read carefully, and understand that a poem or a passage which simply says "Mothers are good" or "Murder is not nice" is an unlikely prompt for 200,000 essays.

Determining the Task on Essay Questions

Practice reading AP questions before you begin to practice writing answers. None of the following questions has appeared on the AP exam, but they closely mimic the real ones. Practice for the exam by studying them and determining exactly what it is the question asks you to do. Formulate your answers to each of the questions before reading the commentary that follows. There are three mock-prose questions.

1. The following passage is the opening of a novel. Read it carefully. Then write an essay in which you analyze how the speaker conveys her attitude to the marriage of Mr. and Mrs. Smith, paying special attention to the diction, figurative language, and tone.

This looks like a straightforward question, but notice that it asks "how" not "what." Your first job is to figure out what the speaker's attitude to the marriage is. Then, you must think about how she conveys this attitude. The question, then, is chiefly about means — more about style than content. Those stylistic techniques that you must talk about are the three listed in the question: diction, figurative language (metaphor and simile, especially), and tone. All of them probably relate to characterizations of Mr. and Mrs. Smith or to specific assertions about the nature of their marriage.

2. The author of the following letter questions the traditional distinctions between comedy and tragedy. Read the passage carefully. Then write a cohesive essay in which you discuss his agreement and disagreement with the definitions of other writers and the literary devices he employs to justify his definitions of the two dramatic forms.

Without the passage, it's impossible to say how many other writers are mentioned, but you do know that the question expects you to talk about more than one. And you must talk about the writer's agreement and disagreement with at least two of the other writers' definitions. And you must also talk about at least two devices he uses (diction is usually one, and imagery or figurative language is often the easiest second choice), being sure to refer to his definitions of both comedy and tragedy.

This question is probably asking more than the real test would ask, but the point here is to be sure you understand all the things the question requires you to do. Mercifully, you don't have to write real essays on these three questions.

3. The passage that follows presents the conversation of a man and woman looking back on forty years of their marriage. Write an essay in which you discuss the differences between the husband's and the wife's attitude toward marriage and the family. Explain how the author uses the resources of language to make a reader more sympathetic to the wife's point of view than to the husband's.

You should have highlighted or underlined "husband's," "wife's," "attitude to marriage," and "family." You have four tasks already. A fifth task would be an analysis of the "resources of language" (another test phrase for "style," "devices," or "techniques") that work to favor the wife and/or to disfavor the husband. Here, too, you have a choice among topics like diction, images, syntax, contrast, irony, and others.

Almost every prose passage question begins with the injunction "Read the following passage carefully." Obey this order. All your care in understanding what the question asks you to do is useless if you don't read the passage well enough to give convincing answers.

Examples of Prose Passages and Student Essays

Prose Passage 1

The following George Eliot passage, which you've already read in the multiple-choice section, originally appeared as the subject for an essay on the AP exam of 1987.

Leisure is gone — gone where the spinning-wheels are gone, and the pack horses, and the slow waggons, and the pedlars, who brought bargains to the
(5) door on sunny afternoons. Ingenious philosophers tell you, perhaps, that the great work of the steam-engine is to create leisure for mankind. Do not believe them: it only creates a vacuum for eager
(10) thought to rush in. Even idleness is eager now — eager for amusement: prone to excursion-trains, art-museums, periodical literature, and exciting novels: prone even to scientific theorising, and cursory
(15) peeps through microscopes. Old Leisure was quite a different personage: he only read one newspaper, innocent of leaders, and was free from that periodicity of sensations which we call post-time. He was
(20) a contemplative, rather stout gentleman, of excellent digestion — of quiet perceptions, undiseased by hypothesis: happy in his inability to know the causes of things, preferring the things themselves.
(25) He lived chiefly in the country, among pleasant seats and homesteads, and was fond of sauntering by the fruit-tree wall,

and scenting the apricots when they were warmed by the morning sunshine, or of
(30) sheltering himself under the orchard boughs at noon, when the summer pears were falling. He knew nothing of week-day services, and thought none the worse of the Sunday sermon if it allowed him
(35) to sleep from the text to the blessing — liking the afternoon service best, because the prayers were the shortest, and not ashamed to say so; for he had an easy, jolly conscience, broad-backed like him-
(40) self, and able to carry a great deal of beer or port-wine, — not being made squeamish by doubts and qualms and lofty aspirations. Life was not a task to him, but a sinecure: he fingered the guineas in his
(45) pocket, and ate his dinners, and slept the sleep of the irresponsible; for had he not kept up his charter by going to church on the Sunday afternoons?

Fine old Leisure! Do not be severe
(50) upon him, and judge him by our modern standard: he never went to Exeter Hall, or heard a popular preacher, or read *Tracts for the Times* or *Sartor Resartus*.

Comments on Prose Passage 1

Students were asked to discuss the attitudes of the speaker to both the leisure of the present and the leisure of the past. They were also required to discuss the style used to present both the past and the present. There are, then, four tasks: defining the attitudes to the past and to the present and discussing the style the passage uses to present "old Leisure" and contemporary leisure.

If you take the time to enumerate the required tasks of the question with care, you usually find that the question offers you an organizing scheme for your essay. This scheme may be mechanical, but it's foolproof; it's safe. If you can invent a more interesting and original way to organize your paper without losing sight of all the required tasks, do so. If not, take the secure road. Here, you can begin with a well-developed and specific paragraph on what George Eliot thinks about the leisure of her day; your second paragraph can discuss (at even greater length, because the passage is chiefly about "old Leisure") the leisure of the past. The third paragraph can deal with the stylistic devices used to describe modern leisure — for example, diction (words like "eager," repeated three times, or "rush," or the "cursory peeps" which undercut any claim to genuine intellectuality) — and the contrast of these words suggesting haste with the diction of old Leisure, suggesting a more quiet and more slowly paced time ("slow waggons" vs. "trains," "sauntering," "sheltering"). The fourth paragraph can go on to the other devices of style used to describe old Leisure. You will probably want to talk about personification, by which George Eliot transforms the abstract idea of leisure into a pudgy country gentleman, bored by sermons, theories, science, or debates, but appreciative of summer pears, beer, and port. If you are especially perceptive, you will talk about the irony of the passage, the reservations George Eliot suggests about both leisures despite her apparent preference for the old over the new. As you know now from answering the multiple-choice questions on the passage, the stylistic devices can also include other figures of speech, other personifications. You can allude to the use of allusion (the proverbial "slept the sleep of the irresponsible"). All these aren't necessary. Papers that understand George Eliot's approval of and reservations about both leisures and discuss only her use of contrast and personification would get top scores.

The four papers that follow were written by high school seniors near the end of their AP course. The essays were part of a full-length practice exam, and the students spent thirty-five minutes on this question.

Student Essay 1

George Eliot presents "old leisure" in a more relaxed way than on leisure in society of her own time through the uses of tone, syntax, and imagery.

Eliot's views on old leisure are way more relaxed than on leisure in the society of her own time and this is clearly shown in the tone. Eliot writes about old leisure in a lazy tone where all the time is leisure to the people who "slept the sleep of the irresponsible." The tone on the leisure of her times is much more serious trying to imply that there was no leisure. Her opposing views of leisure are directly shown in her tone.

The syntax used tells us a lot about her attitude toward leisure. The syntax on old leisure is long and redundant showing us that old leisure had too much leisure time. Her attitude is saying that it was much easier then than in her time. She has a negative attitude toward old leisure and it clearly shows in the writing she spends three fourths of the passage on old leisure putting it down.

Imagery is used by personification of the ideas. She exaggerated how much leisure time there was in old leisure. Trying to prove a point but she has stepped over the line, gone too far.

Eliot's devices used to help her convey the message were tone, syntax, and imagery but she mainly just stated that old leisure was too relaxed and that people of that time just sat on their butts. Her views are clearly shown and overly exaggerated.

Student Essay 2

In this selection, George Eliot reminisces about "Old Leisure" — "Old Leisure" that was killed with the introduction of the Industrial and Scientific Revolution (represented by the steam engine), "Old Leisure" that incorporated spinning wheels, pack horses, and slow wagons. She describes her longing for this Old Leisure through personification, contrast, diction, and gentle sarcasm.

George Eliot describes leisure as being a man — a chubby, rather laid back man. In doing this, she is representing all the people and their habits of that era into this one man. By contrasting this gentleman to the impersonal feeling of the "new leisure," George Eliot inclines the reader toward the "Old Leisure." Whereas the New Leisure is very rushed and mechanical ("prone to excursion-trains, art museums . . . scientific theorising . . ."), "Mr. Old Leisure" was relaxed, reading only one newspaper. George Eliot describes old leisure as innocent and free of leaders; had no sensational periodicals to read and fill his mind with, no corrupted politicians to listen to. He was contemplative on his own, uncontaminated by other people's ideas and theories, as new Leisure is. He was simple, not bothering to discover the mechanism of everything around him, but content with simply enjoying his surroundings. He loved nature rather than being caught up in the man made things. Here, Eliot describes nature with temperature, scent, and view, drawing the reader into the aura of the surroundings. Old Leisure smelled the apricots, sat in the shade of orchard boughs, watched the summer pears fall. Old Leisure was carefree; he did not have to worry about goals, about being judged, or of "making the best use of his time." Instead, he could relax at home, and sleep irresponsibly. By glamourizing Old Leisure, Eliot put the New Leisure into a bad light, deeming the rush for learning and developing unnecessary and secondary to complete relaxation and enjoyment. By personifying Old Leisure as a stout gentleman, Eliot conjures an image of a jolly old man, one who is perfectly content and happy. Finally, Eliot ends the comparison by gently mocking new Leisure, requesting forgiveness for old leisure for not going to Exeter Hall, hearing a popular preacher, or reading Tracts for the Times. In doing this, she takes one final poke at the ridiculousness of the activities New Leisure found so fulfilling.

Response to Student Essays 1 and 2

These two essays are examples of a weak answer (the first) and a good response to the question. With a below-average performance on the multiple-choice questions, a student who wrote three essays of the quality of the first paper would probably get a reported exam score of two. Assuming a good performance on the multiple-choice section, a student who wrote three essays of the quality of the second would get a final score of five, and this essay would probably get a seven on the nine-point scale used for evaluating the three essays.

Though essay 1 is a poor essay, it is, surprisingly, one of the very few that saw that the passage expresses reservations about "old Leisure." It overstates the case and fails to see that new leisure is also criticized. Its real deficiency is in the handling of the stylistic devices. Though the first paragraph promises an account of tone, syntax, and imagery, the three paragraphs on these topics are all inadequate. The student's writing problems compound the problems in the paragraph on tone. Though the student approaches a real and important difference between the old ("lazy") and the new ("more serious"), the essay is not really sure what tone is, and it misses the nostalgic, tolerant, affectionate, and sensuous tone that is used to describe the leisure of the past.

The bad writing interferes with the paragraph on syntax. The student probably meant to say that the sentences on old leisure are long, not the syntax. The rest of the paragraph talks about attitude rather than syntax, and what it says is inaccurate.

The fourth paragraph uses the word "personification" but doesn't make clear whether or not the student understands exactly how the device is used. The whole essay fails to use enough specific evidence from the passage.

The final paragraph says nothing new. The slang phrase "just sat on their butts," incidentally, has nothing to do with the low scoring of the essay, and slang is a device that good writers may use. The trouble here is that the student is not a good writer and has not answered the question on the exam clearly or coherently.

You should notice that it wouldn't take much to turn this paper into a first-rate essay. Of course, the quality of the writing would have to be improved, and the evaluation of George Eliot's attitudes would have to be expanded. This done, a paragraph on tone that contrasted the lazy quiet of the old with the frantic activity of the new, followed by a paragraph on syntax that saw how short sentences like "Do not believe them" and "Even idleness is eager now" contrast with the more langorous and much longer sentences associated with old Leisure, followed by an accurate account of how the passage uses personification, would make a fine response to the question.

Essay 2 is, as far as it goes, excellent. Its reading of the passage, though incomplete, is sensible, and its specific and well-supported discussions of diction, contrast, and personification are very good. There can be no doubt that this student knows just what these terms mean and how these techniques are used in George Eliot's prose. The essay does not deal with the implied criticism of old Leisure, but many papers on this topic scored well without seeing the most subtle aspect of the passage. Readers reward student essays for what they do well. They don't expect perfection on an essay that a student must plan and write in only forty minutes.

Student Essay 3

In this passage, Eliot presents a conception of leisure in which he begins by comparing the absence of leisure to the absence of the Old West. The author has a very pessimistic view towards today's leisure, or what people consider to be leisurable. The present form of leisure is only discussed in the first eleven lines of this passage, and the good, old leisure is discussed in the rest.

In describing "Old Leisure," the author of this passage describes the typical man who enjoys this leisure. The author obviously believes that "ignorance is bliss" by the way that he optimistically describes the man's actions and blinded knowledge.

In describing the leisure of the present time, at the beginning of the passage, the language is very straightforward and it is very obvious that the author does not believe that it is true leisure. The old leisure is not described as straightforward, but it is more indepth and descriptive.

In the last sentence of the passage, the author defends old leisure from those who believe that somehow a steam-engine is leisurable.

Student Essay 4

George Eliot longs for a time long gone. She laments the replacement of "old Leisure" by the leisure of her own society. Eliot feels that it has lost feeling, lost personality. She feels that leisure has become a representation of the masses rather than the individualistic whims of the few.

Eliot refers to "Old Leisure" as being "innocent" and "free . . . of sensations." She presents him as "contemplative" and perceptive, yet simple. He is a man "undiseased by hypothesis, happy in his inability to know . . . things." She admires this view of "Old Leisure" and sees it as a symbol of individual freedom. She sees him "living . . . in the country." He is a man who saunters rather than walks, who scents the apricots rather than smells them. "Old Leisure" has "an easy, jolly conscience," characteristic of the free and independent.

Eliot despises the new leisure. It is a symbol of rush, hustle and bustle, and impersonality. She immediately relates it to "the steam engine" which serves "mankind," not individual men. She sees the leisure of her time as a tool of idleness and primitive amusement, referring to "excursion-trains," "exciting novels" and "cursory peeps through microscopes."

Eliot conveys her views by personifying "Old Leisure." She presents him as the respectful, humble gentleman that every girl wants to bring home to the parents. She uses exalting phrases, giving her gentleman a special grandeur and reverence. She states that he is "rather stout" and "of excellent digestion." She has created the perfect man: one who is free of problems from "doubts and qualms and lofty aspirations."

Eliot also makes a statement by her omission of new leisure as a person. She feels that new leisure is impersonal and unfeeling, therefore undeserving of a personality. She describes it very briefly, condensing her phrases in the exact same way that new leisure has condensed the individual wants of mankind.

Eliot leaves the reader with no doubt about her feelings for old and new Leisure. Her love for the former and hatred of the latter are convincingly presented. The contrast between her perfect gentleman and the non-person plainly reveals her heart.

Response to Student Essays 3 and 4

This pair of essays also illustrates the lower and the upper half of the grading scale. The surprising reference in the first sentence of essay 3 to the Old West arises, I suppose, from the student's association of spinning wheels and slow wagons (covered, I suspect) with the American past. Be sure to look carefully at the context and the details of the passage. The old Leisure here must have been some time before the 1830's. Another lesson is to beware of thinking that everything is about the United States. The details of this passage such as "guineas" or "Exeter Hall" place it in England.

The essay does suggest an awareness of a preference for the old Leisure but does not explain clearly or with support from the passage George Eliot's attitude. It is even weaker on technique. A phrase like "the language is very straightforward" or "in-depth" and an adjective like "descriptive" are useless. In fact, the language is not at all straightforward, and any adjective can be called "descriptive." You must be ready to talk about specific stylistic devices, even when the question does not enumerate specific ones.

Essay 4 does a decent job on the question without reaching the level of essay 2. The second paragraph illustrates the use of diction, and the fourth handles personification, but the case for old Leisure ("the perfect man") and the case against the new leisure ("despises") are both over-stated. The essay would probably get a score of six on the nine-point scale, an upper half paper but not an upper third.

Prose Passage 2

Let's look at one more example of a question on a prose passage. This passage on the escaped slave Frederick Douglass's response to his arrival in the North appeared on the English language AP exam, but it could just as easily have been used on the literature exam.

The wretchedness of slavery, and the blessedness of freedom, were perpetually before me. It was life and death with me. But I remained firm, and according (5) to my solution, on the third day of September, 1838, I left my chains, and succeeded in reaching New York without the slightest interruption of any kind. How I did so — what means I (10) adopted, — what direction I travelled, and by what mode of conveyance, — I must leave unexplained, for the reasons before mentioned.

I have been frequently asked how I (15) felt when I found myself in a free State. I have never been able to answer the question with any satisfaction to myself. It was a moment of the highest excitement I ever experienced. I suppose I felt (20) as one may imagine the unarmed mariner to feel when he is rescued by a friendly man-of-war from pursuit of a pirate. In writing to a dear friend, immediately after my arrival at New York, I (25) said I felt like one who had escaped a den of hungry lions. This state of mind, however, very soon subsided; and I was again seized with a feeling of great insecurity and loneliness. I was yet liable to (30) be taken back, and subjected to all the tortures of slavery. This in itself was enough to damp the ardor of my enthusiasm. But the loneliness overcame me. There I was in the midst of thousands,

(35) and yet a perfect stranger; without home and without friends, in the midst of thousands of my own brethren — children of a common Father, and yet I dared not to unfold to any one of them (40) my sad condition. I was afraid to speak to any one for fear of speaking to the wrong one, and thereby falling into the hands of money-loving kidnappers, whose business it was to lie in wait for (45) the panting fugitive, as the ferocious beasts of the forest lie in wait for their prey. The motto which I adopted when I started from slavery was this — "Trust no man!" I saw in every white man an (50) enemy and in almost every colored man cause for distrust. It was a most painful situation; and, to understand it, one must needs experience it, or imagine himself in similar circumstances. Let him be a (55) fugitive slave in a strange land — a land given up to be the hunting-ground for slave-holders — whose inhabitants are legalized kidnappers — where he is every moment subjected to the terrible (60) liability of being seized upon by his fellow-men, as the hideous crocodile seizes upon his prey! — I say, let him place himself in my situation — without home or friends — without money or credit — (65) wanting shelter, and no one to give it — wanting bread, and no money to buy it, — and at the same time let him feel that he is pursued by merciless men-hunters,

(70) and in total darkness as to what to do, where to go, or where to stay, — perfectly helpless both as to the means of defense and means of escape, — in the midst of plenty, yet suffering the terrible gnawings of (75) hunger, — in the midst of houses, yet having no home, — among fellow-men, yet feeling as if in the midst of wild beasts, whose greediness to swallow up the trembling and half-famished fugitive (80) is only equalled by that with which the monsters of the deep swallow up the helpless fish upon which they subsist, — I say, let him be placed in this most trying situation, — the situation in which I (85) was placed, — then and not till then, will he fully appreciate the hardships of, and know how to sympathize with, the toil-worn and whip-scarred slave.

— Frederick Douglass

Comments on Prose Passage 2

Students were asked to discuss Douglass's response to finding himself in a free state. They were also required to write about the language, especially the figurative language and the syntax, of the passage that reveals Douglass's feelings.

An essay that defines Douglass's states of mind (excitement, relief, joy at first but followed by fear, insecurity, loneliness, suspicion) and discusses only the figures of speech and the syntax would fulfill the requirements of the question. Though the techniques for discussion are specified here (figures of speech and syntax), the literature exam has shown no preference for the specific or the nonspecific requirement. Often, an exam with a prose and poetry question that call for a discussion of style specifies the devices on one question and allows students to choose their own on the other.

The figures of speech in the passage are easy to identify, because most of them are similes rather than metaphors. They include the following:

1. Douglass feels like the unarmed sailor rescued from pirates.
2. Douglass feels like a man who has escaped a lion's den.
3. Kidnappers are like ferocious beasts waiting to capture their prey (the fugitive slave).
4. The fugitive slave may be seized like the prey of a crocodile.
5. Douglass feels as if wild beasts surrounded him.
6. The enemies are as greedy as monsters of the deep devouring helpless fish (the fugitive slaves).

The principle of organization here is clear at once; five of the six similes liken the slaveholders or their allies to savage beasts and the fugitive slave to the sought-after victim of their powerful jaws.

Many students, expecting a slave's prose style to be simple and direct, were taken by surprise by Douglass' ornate syntax. Regardless of the evidence on the page, a number of students praised Douglass' prose as "simple and sincere." It may be sincere, but simple it isn't. It has far more in common with the writing of Dr. Johnson, or Winston Churchill, or Martin Luther King, Jr., than the naïve colloquialism of Sojourner Truth.

In discussing the syntax of the passage, the essays could deal with the interplay of long and short sentences or the array of specific contrasts ("wretchedness of slavery," "blessedness of freedom;" "life and death;" "plenty . . . hunger;" "houses . . . no home") or the series of parallel phrases and clauses ("in the midst of" repeated five times in the second paragraph or "let him" repeated four times). Let anyone who imagines this prose to be artless read aloud the blockbuster last sentence, 225 words long.

Student Essay 1

In the old days of slavery, there were many slaves who rebelled and obtained their freedom. Once free, the ex-slaves were thrust into a terrifying, new environment. Such was the case with Fredrick Douglass.

In his essay, Fredrick Douglass uses a large vocabulary to create a concise essay. This is unusual for a black in the 1800's. Douglass' education despite his difficult background shows his determination to become free. Douglass uses many metaphors and figures of speech to show the reader his strong feeling toward the people in his new "free" environment. Phrases such as "Den of hungry lion," "ferocious beasts . . . lie in wait for their prey," and "legalized kidnappers" show his hatred and distrust of whites. Douglass came out of the evil of slavery into a world of poverty and hardship. The fact that he survived with no home, no money, no food, and no friends shows the reader his adaptability and courage.

"Trust no man!" This was the phrase that Douglass lived by for many years. He could not trust the whites. If he were to tell his sorrowful story to a slave-hunter, he would be subject to a "legalized" kidnapping, and all his pains and sacrifices would have been for nothing. This mistrust and hatred of whites lead to a mistrust of blacks, who could have been in league with the whites in exchange for money. Douglas lived a life filled with paranoia, always fearing that he would be sent back to be a slave once again. Douglas was not relieved of this terrifying way of life until the outbreak of the civil war, and the passing of the 16th Amendment to the Constitution, which forever abolished slavery.

Fredrick Douglass set a great example for generations of blacks, but he himself led a painful, tortured life.

Student Essay 2

What is more freedom? To be enslaved on a Master's land as property toiling in the sun or to be enslaved in the horrid reality of loneliness and inexperience in a cruel world? Frederick Douglass represents all runaway slaves, the unfortunate souls who struggled all their lives to escape slavery only to find later that freedom was just as bad. Douglass effectively conveys his disturbed state of mind after escaping slavery in this passage by using good syntax and diction and several figures of speech.

Syntax is effectively used throughout the passage. Douglass arranges the sentences in such a way as to impact the reader fully. In many instances, long sentences are followed by terse sentences to achieve a dramatic essence. "This in itself . . . of my enthusiasm" is suddenly followed by "But the loneliness overcame me." Parallelisms in sentence structure are also shown in the passage. "let him be a fugitive slave . . . upon his prey!" The parallelisms show the importance of each point Douglass makes because each point adds to his uneasiness and anger. As he continues explaining why freedom was so wretched, he again uses parallelisms to describe point by point the pain and struggling he dealt with. " — without home or friends — without money or credit — wanting shelter. . . . ."

The irony Douglass portrays in this passage is obvious. He describes escaping slavery as "escaping a den of hungry lions" and that "it was a moment of the highest excitement." Immediately following these statements, Douglass realizes being free meant living in fear of "money-loving kidnappers," no home, food, or money. He describes this condition as "ferocious beasts of the forest lie in wait for their prey." This figure of speech is much more vivid than his analogy of escaping slavery. Taking this into consideration, we realize that these dire conditions are not exactly ironic because it is so common to any "whip-scarred fugitive slave."

Douglass succeeds in convincing the reader how loneliness surpasses almost all hardships. The diction is well-chosen. The adjectives he chooses causes the reader to sympathize deeply with his pain. ". . . in the midst of plenty, yet suffering the terrible gnawings of hunger." "The motto . . . 'TRUST NO MAN' I saw in every white man an enemy." The hatred in his tone and the frustration is immediately relevant in Douglass's voice.

Douglass uses a final figure of speech ". . . half-famished fugitive is only equalled by that with which the monsters of the deep swallow up the helpless fish upon which they subsist . . ." It is here that Douglass manifests a deep truth to all fugitives . . . the hopelessness of inevitably being devoured by inexperience and prejudice.

As Douglass states in his first paragraph, "I left my chains" when referring to his escape from slavery, he only escaped to new territory still bounded by the wretchedness of reality.

Response to Student Essays 1 and 2

Essay 1 as a generalized response to the Douglass passage is not bad, but as a response to the question it exemplifies a very common and mortal mistake. It simply paraphrases the passage without addressing the tasks the question sets. It sees one of Douglass's states of mind, and it alludes to two similes of the passage, but it is too intent on summarizing the content of the passage to answer the question. On a nine-point scale, this essay would score no higher than a three.

On the other hand, essay 2 is excellent. It isn't without minor flaws, but the nines on a nine-point scale aren't flawless. They are simply the best answers to the question compared to the other essays written in that year. The second paragraph handles several aspects of the syntax with accuracy and precision. The third paragraph defines clearly Douglass's two states of mind, while the third and fifth paragraphs discuss the figures of speech. In addition, the student deals with the irony and the diction of the passage. The student's writing throughout is controlled and effective.

The Poetry Question

The AP poetry essay and the essay on prose are similar. There's no reason for any student to think he or she can do one but not the other. If you can read the prose passage well, you can read the poem well too. And vice versa.

Of course, there are some differences. The poem has fewer words. It is probably more dense. It probably uses more figurative language. Its rhythm and other effects of sound are probably more important. It's likely to be more private, more interior, and more personal than the prose passage.

Determining the Task on Poetry Questions

There is one kind of question about a poem that appears occasionally that is unlikely to be used with a prose passage. The student is asked to discuss how one part of a poem is related to another part. For example, the question may require an explanation of how the first four stanzas of a poem prepare, or do not prepare, the reader for the attitudes expressed in the fifth stanza. Or a student may have to contrast the first half and last half of a poem or relate the images of one section to the images of another section.

But most of the poetry questions resemble the prose questions. There is, in fact, an archetype, a paradigm, a mother of all AP prose and poetry questions. This is it:

Read the following (prose passage or poem) carefully. Then write an essay in which you discuss the *author's* (or the speaker's, or x's, or x's and y's) *attitude(s)* toward *a* (or a and b) and the *devices* the author uses to convey this (these) view(s).

The question has two parts. The first calls for a reading of meaning, an interpretation of what the passage conveys. The question may ask for the *attitude*, or *views*, or *response*, or *feelings* of the *author*, or the *speaker*, or a *character*, or *two characters* who appear in the poem or the passage.

The second part of the question is about style. It calls for a discussion of *devices, or literary devices*, or *techniques*, or *language* or *resources of language*, or *stylistic devices*, or *style*. Half of the time the devices will be unspecified; half of the time the question will contain a list of two or more. The most commonly specified techniques are diction, imagery, figurative language, choice of details, tone, and syntax. Less often, the list may include the following: organization, devices of sound, allusion, and point of view.

Look for a form of this question. Remember, it may ask for one or more attitudes or states of mind. Be sure to deal with more than one technique. If the question reads, "such as diction, imagery, tone, and syntax," you could safely skip one of the four, but if the question says, "discuss diction, imagery, tone, and syntax," deal with all four.

Before beginning to write your essay on the poem, you should go through the same analytical processes that you used on the poetry in the multiple-choice section of the exam. And you must be sure you've defined clearly all the parts that must be included in your essay.

Practice defining the tasks by using the three following poetry questions:

1. Both of the following short poems are sonnets spoken by a man to the woman he loves. Write a well-organized essay about their similarities and differences. Deal with both theme and style.

If you highlight, you should hit the words "similarities," "differences," "theme," and "style." What you have is four tasks: similarities of theme, similarities of style, differences of theme, and differences of style. The question allows you to choose what devices of style you want to discuss. Good essays talk about several, such as diction, figurative language, and if relevant, another. With questions like this, you can skip the areas where you feel insecure (syntax or metrics, perhaps?), but if you're a whiz with metrics, you could show your knowledge in your section on style.

2. Read the following poem carefully, and write an essay in which you discuss how the author's diction and syntax reveal his attitudes toward the city and the country in time of war.

Notice that "attitudes" here is plural, though even if it were singular, the question may still require more than one (his attitude to the city and his attitude to the country). And remember, this attitude may be complex (for example, he likes the friendliness of the country but objects to its excessive curiosity). Here you have no choice in stylistic devices; you must write on diction, and you must write on syntax. There are four main tasks: diction and city, syntax and city, diction and country, and syntax and country. This question is an example of the archetypal AP question.

3. Read the following poem carefully. Write a well-organized essay in which you discuss how the imagery of the last three stanzas is related to and different from the imagery of the first three stanzas. Explain how this difference determines the tone and meaning of the poem as a whole.

To explain how the images of the first three stanzas are like and unlike those of the last three, you must first understand what the images are (the literal sensory objects as well as the figures of speech such as simile or metaphor that evoke sensations). Then you must determine how the images of the beginning of the poem are (1) like and (2) unlike those of the end. Having done this (with specific examples, of course), you can go on to explain how the differences in imagery determine the (3) tone (which you must define, probably in several words, not just one). Finally, you must define (4) a meaning or several meanings of the poem as a whole (that life is transient, that the imagination consoles us for the loss of loved ones, or some such notions) and relate what you've said about the differences in imagery to this meaning. Fortunately, a question with as many demands as this one wouldn't be used on the exam. A real exam would be more likely to ask only how the imagery of the last three stanzas is related to and different from that of the first three. Or it might ask only how the difference in the images at the beginning and end of the poem determine its tone and meaning.

Examples of Poetry Selections and Student Essays

Poetry Selection 1

Most of the poetry questions on the exam have used complete poems, usually lyrics of 14 to 50 lines. But a few questions have been based on selections from longer poems such as Pope's "Moral Essays" or Wordsworth's "The Prelude." The poem used in 1990 was an excerpt from Shakespeare's "Henry IV, Part II." This play was chosen because it's almost never taught in the high schools. The examiners are at pains to select poetry that is like the poetry taught in AP classes but that is not likely to have been used in the classroom.

> How many thousand of my poorest subjects
> Are at this hour asleep! O sleep! O gentle sleep!
> Nature's soft nurse, how have I frighted thee,
> That thou no more wilt weigh my eyelids down,
> (5) And steep my senses in forgetfulness?
> Why rather, sleep, liest thou in smoky cribs,
> Upon uneasy pallets stretching thee,
> And hush'd with buzzing night-flies to thy slumber,
> Than in the perfum'd chambers of the great,
> (10) Under the canopies of costly state,
> And lull'd with sound of sweetest melody?
> O thou dull god, why liest thou with the vile
> In loathsome beds, and leav'st the kingly couch
> A watch-case or a common 'larum-bell?
> (15) Wilt thou upon the high and giddy mast
> Seal up the ship-boy's eyes, and rock his brains
> In cradle of the rude imperious surge,
> And in the visitation of the winds,
> Who take the ruffian billows by the top,
> (20) Curling their monstrous heads and hanging them
> With deaf'ning clamour in the slippery clouds,
> That with the hurly death itself awakes?
> Canst thou, O partial sleep, give thy repose
> To the wet sea-boy in an hour so rude,
> (25) And in the calmest and most stillest night,
> With all appliances and means to boot,
> Deny it to a King? Then, happy low, lie down!
> Uneasy lies the head that wears a crown.

Comments on Poetry Selection 1

Students were asked to paraphrase the passage and to discuss how the feelings of the king are reflected in his word choice, his images, and his syntax.

Before you look at some exam answers, you can begin to analyze this passage. The speaker is King Henry and the piece is a soliloquy, that is, a speech in which a character voices his or her thoughts while alone (solus = alone, and loqui = to speak). The first lines of the passage seem to be self-addressed, but in line 2 ("O sleep!"), he speaks directly to a personified sleep and continues to do so for most of the passage. The second half of the next-to-last line (line 27) is addressed to the "happy low," and the final line may also be spoken to these poorest subjects, or like the first line of the speech, it may be self-addressed.

The 28 lines of the speech are composed of opening and closing assertions of one and a half lines and 25 lines made up of a series of questions to the sleep that eludes the king. The basic organizing method of the passage is the contrast of the low born, who are able to sleep despite their noisy and uncomfortable surroundings, with the king, sleepless amid trappings that would seem to be the most conducive to sleep. The thesis of the speech is the commonplace that high position brings with it responsibilities and disadvantages (such as sleeplessness) that the humble need not endure.

Much of the notable diction in the passage supports the contrast of the "happy low" and the restless king. The "poorest" subjects must suffer "smoky cribs," "uneasy pallets," "buzzing night-flies," and "loathsome beds," while the king lies in a "perfum'd" chamber, under "canopies of costly state," "lull'd" with sweet melodies. The choice of words to describe sleep is also important, as it reflects the changes of strategy of the king. At first, sleep is "gentle" and "soft," but when flattery doesn't work, the king insults the god as "dull," punning on its meanings of slow or lacking spirit and its meaning of stupid.

A wise student, baffled by the difficult comparison of the kingly couch to a "watch-case" would simply leave it out and deal with the other images in the passage. The critics have not satisfactorily explained the figure (they suggest that the watch-case is a sentry box or that, if the bed is the watch-case, the king would be the workings of a watch, which are constantly in motion). In the reading of this essay, any reasonable interpretation of this phrase was treated tolerantly. The most important comparison is the extended image of the sea-boy in what may well be called an epic metaphor, because the figure moves from the sea-boy able to sleep high on the mast in a tempest at sea to the storm itself with the personifications of the surge, winds, and waves whose hair the winds curl, hurling the waves to the clouds with a tumult to awaken the dead.

As usual, syntax was the major problem for the students answering the question. Because grading is determined by comparing one paper with the others, students who could deal with syntax in even the most perfunctory way got some credit. Good students saw the balance in the use of exclamations, then questions, then exclamations, or the breathless piling up of clauses in the sea-boy lines, or the careful balance of opposites in lines 6–8 ("smoky cribs," "uneasy pallets," "buzzing night-flies") versus lines 9–11 ("perfum'd chambers," "canopies of costly state," "sweetest melody").

An unusual aspect of this question is its calling first for a brief summary of the king's thoughts. This task was assigned to help rather than trip up the exam-takers. Aware of the fact that a poetry question based upon a text written before the nineteenth century had not appeared on the exam for many years, the examiners wanted to make sure that the students had worked through the passage carefully and understood its argument before they began to deal with the more challenging topics of its diction, imagery, and syntax. A careful summary of the content of the passage, it was hoped, would lead the students to an understanding of the king's state of mind.

Predictably, on this point, some students were eager to find a single answer, and they failed to see how the tone of the passage shifts from the quiet, cajoling beginning to the annoyance of the middle section to the excitement of the sea-boy figure to the rueful acceptance of the last lines. The techniques that must be discussed were specified in this question, but many papers failed to deal adequately with syntax. So long as students continue to omit or deal weakly with questions about syntax, questions about syntax will continue to appear on the exam.

Here are some examples of high school seniors' responses to this question.

Student Essay 1

In King Henry's lamenting soliloquy, he pleadingly chastises "partial sleep" for failing to "weigh" his "eyelids down." His desperate desire for sleep is conveyed in Shakespeare's choice of words, imagery and rhythmic construction.

In the passage's diction, the beauty and comforts of sleep are exemplified. It is made so appealing that we can understand the King's sorrow for lack of it. Shakespeare chooses soft, soothing words, like "smoky," "sweetest," "dull," and "rock." They reflect the quiet rest that the King desires.

The images that Shakespeare uses also reflect the desirable tranquility of sleep. He describes the "buzzing night flies" in line 8 and the rocking of the stormy sea in line 16. These are relaxing sounds and sensations that might induce slumber. The King, however, is deprived of such slumber, and his personification of sleep, as he questions it, is conveyed in such images as "seal up the ship-boy's eyes" and "nature's soft nurse." He makes sleep seem like a living thing, and therefore justifies his anger at its evasiveness.

Along with diction and imagery, structure plays an important part in conveying the King's desperation. The passage's rhythmic feel contributes to the lulling effect of sleep. It soothes and relaxes, and once more allows us to see its desirability for King Henry. Such a smooth and rhythmic flow could probably not be accomplished, were the passage not in verse form.

Thus Shakespeare's methods of diction, imagery, and structure all work together to create the soothing effects of sleep, and help us share in the King's anger at its unwillingness to find him.

Student Essay 2

Sleep, like other forces of nature, does not scurry obediently to satisfy the whims of man; it knows no law but that of its own, and the hand that holds the golden spectre is as equal in its eyes as the hand of one who holds a ragged fishing net — unfortunately for men such as King Henry, some have not yet learned the impartiality of sleep's judgement, and Henry's elevated status above his subjects does little to prevent his begrudging of that force of nature.

In the first portion of his soliloquy, the King seems to be imploring (something, I would venture to say, he is not used to in the least — nor does he like it) to the indifferent deity for her favor. The diction here is as close to humble as the proud King can stand — "O sleep" O gentle sleep!" . . . but even in his extremities of homage, Henry still manages to toss in a little reminder of his arrogance: He asked sleep, ". . . how have I frighted thee?" Oh, this is indeed noble of him — so gentle, so considerate, so . . . condescending of him to say such a thing! In asking sleep, "nature's soft nurse," whether he, a king and of royal blood but a mortal man nonetheless, had frightened her away, Henry reveals the pomposity and pride that is, doubtless, unavoidable when one ascends the throne and becomes absolute monarch — another added bonus to the crown is the foolishness that stems from being so powerful (among men!).

He talks of sleep in a way that invokes an image of a mother bending to kiss her child on the cheek; and this flighty and desirable kiss "weigh(s) (the) eyelids down, and steep(s) . . . senses in forgetfulness." The imagery Henry has drawn makes the state of sleep all the more seductive and wonderful . . . and it is this same imagery that makes his inability to sleep all the more tortuous and excruciating.

Following this subtly hidden invocation of sleep, Henry then proceeds to berate sleep for avoiding him and visiting, in his stead, his lowly subjects in their miserable hovels and parasite-infested dwellings. "Why rather sleep, liest thou in smoky cribs . . . than in perfumed chambers of the great . . . and lull'd with sound of sweetest melody." ("What is the reason for your visitation upon the wretched peasantry and their stinking "uneasy pallets" when you could be frolicking in my house — perfumed, immaculate, richly adorned and beautiful?") Here then is the most blatant of the King's show of arrogance and annoyance — he's very put off by the fact that sleep chooses to habit the houses of his subjects and skip over his own dwelling: inconceivable!

After more embellishing on the subject (Henry complains about the ship-boy — even the ship-boy can sleep!) the King finally heaves a colossal sigh and bows his head in resignation; he has finally come to the realization that he is, in some ways better off than his subjects, but he also has responsibilities that weigh him down further than others. He sadly says, "Then, happy low, lie down! Uneasy lies the head that wears the crown." In spite of all his arrogance and presumptuousness we should pity Henry. But he should be glad: throughout the passage, we notice three major tones — first, his imploring but vastly disguised pride, then his unveiled arrogance in full glory, then finally, resignation and sadness. Maybe King Henry has been enlightened by the whole wretched affair — after all, he's learned that even kings can be insomniacs.

Response to Student Essays 1 and 2

Essay 1 is not a good essay, but it is useful to illustrate a common mistake. The second paragraph discusses the diction of the passage and quite rightly specifically cites words from the speech ("smoky," "sweetest," "dull," and "rock") that "reflect the quiet rest" that Henry longs for. The reference to specific words is estimable, but you must see the words in their context in the passage, not in isolation. Why "smoky" should be "soothing" is hard to understand; the "smoky cribs" here are huts with no ventilation for their fires and not at all something "quiet" or "soothing." As it is used in line 12, "dull" means stupid, while the verb "rock" refers not to a baby's cradle but to the motion of the sea-boy, high on the "giddy mast" in a storm. Three of the four words are wholly inappropriate choices. Similarly the "buzzing night-flies" and "rocking" of the ship in the storm are not images of "desirable tranquility" or relaxing sounds that might induce slumber, as anyone who has been kept awake by a pesky mosquito can attest.

It's fine to talk about the rhythm of a poem, but you must do so much more specifically and accurately than the fourth paragraph here. Like Henry's mood, the rhythm of the passage changes. Lines 19–22 describing the sea in a storm cannot be called "lulling." They do not "soothe and relax." This essay does not say nearly enough about the King's state of mind. What it says about diction and imagery is largely untrue, and it never mentions syntax at all.

Essay 2, on the other hand, though it fails to deal with syntax, does a good job on the King's changes of mood. It handles diction well but is thin on the imagery of the passage. It shows that a competent essay can be written without mentioning the terms the question had called for. But this student, who clearly understands the speech, would probably have scored better if he or she had referred to diction, citing the examples used here, and to imagery, citing some other examples, and to syntax. The essay should remind you that you can't deal too exclusively with only one part of the question.

Student Essay 3

Henry is a king. He is a king who cannot sleep. He believes it is his divine right yet sleep will not visit him and he resents it. The protagonist of Shakespeare's Henry IV, Part II, the restless king cannot understand this denial.

King Henry pleads for sleep to come. He coaxes it, gently nudges it, then begs it. He tries to reason with sleep, asking "how have I frighted thee, that thou no more wilt . . . steep my senses in forgetfulness?" The entire speech is a plea to a personified sleep. The King knows that thousands of his subjects have been visited, yet he has not.

Henry feels that royalty is special. He believes that it deserves special privileges. He asked why sleep will not come to "the perfumed chambers of the great"? This haughty old man chastises sleep for granting "the wet sea-boy" repose yet denying "it to a King." He feels outraged by this blatant irreverence.

To convey Henry's feeling of bitterness and jealousy, Shakespeare uses a consistent imagery. The reader is bombarded with pictures of the lowly and destitute in simple fulfillment. These are contrasted to a lonely and restless king unaccustomed to such discomforts.

Henry refers to "smoky cribs," "uneasy pallets," and "buzzing night-flies." He compares these to his "canopies of costly state . . . lull'd with sound of sweetest melody." He derides "the vile in loathsome beds" while praising "the kingly couch."

Shakespeare gives an effective personification to sleep. He creates a spirited nymph who delights in toying with the great King. The King tries to persuade her to help, gently calling out to "Nature's soft nurse." When he is refused, his anger flares and he slanders "thou dull god, why liest thou with the vile."

Shakespeare also uses a consistent diction in this passage. When Henry describes his subjects his spite and jealousy are evident. He uses hateful and hurtful phrases. He refers to "poorest subjects," "smoky cribs," "uneasy pallets," "buzzing flies" and even the ship's "ruffian billows." When the King refers to his trappings he uses positive and exalting phrases. He praises his "perfumed chambers," "canopies of costly state," and "sweetest melody." He mentions, "the kingly couch" and "the calmest and most stillest night" which exists in his abode.

King Henry is a man who feels high rights have been stolen from him. His bitterness and resentment are convincingly portrayed through the language of his speech.

Response to Student Essay 3

Essay 3 is better than essay 2, though it also has no discussion of syntax. But its answers to the questions about Henry's state of mind, about the diction, and about the imagery are accurate and detailed. In the sixth paragraph, the essay refers to a personification of sleep as "nymph," though this figure does not appear in the passage. It goes on to quote "Nature's soft nurse" and "thou dull god." The unnecessary remarks on the nymph would not affect the scoring of this paper. The rest of the paragraph makes it clear that the student does see the personifications accurately, and the readers of the exams are trained to overlook trivial errors and to reward students for what they do well. The flaw in this essay is its failure to discuss the syntax of the speech, and this omission would probably cost the writer two points on the nine-point grading scale.

Poetry Selection 2

Let's look at another poem, a lyric this time, written by Emily Dickinson. This poem was used on the exam many years ago but is still relevant today. An essay question on this poem today would read:

Read the following poem by Emily Dickinson carefully. Then write a well-organized essay in which you briefly summarize its content and discuss how the diction and imagery reveal the speaker's attitude toward religious belief.

> I never lost as much but twice,
> And that was in the sod;
> Twice have I stood a beggar
> Before the door of God!
>
> (5) Angels twice descending
> Reimbursed my store.
> Burglar, banker, father!
> I am poor once more!

Comments on Poetry Selection 2

The summary task is appropriate here, because the second line of the first stanza is crucial, but it is not easy to say just what it means. And because the poem is so short, the task doesn't take too much time. The first stanza tells of a loss, equaled only by two such losses in the past. Line 2 is problematic because it is so hard to determine the antecedent of "that." The line probably refers to death and burial as the two earlier losses, and you can infer that the occasion of this poem is the death of a third loved one. The second stanza is a cry for comfort, for reconcilement to the loss as the speaker, through divine aid, had been able to come to terms with the two previous deaths.

The diction and images of the first six lines of the poem present the speaker, who in these lines appears to be speaking to herself (let us assume a female speaker) or to an unspecified audience as a "beggar" at the door of God. The petitions of the beggar have been answered on both of the earlier occasions. The figures here and the diction are financial: "lost" (line 1), "beggar" (line 3), "Reimbursed" (line 6; the literal meaning of the verb is to pay back, and its root is the word for "purse"), and "store" (line 6; a supply, reserve, or stock). The attitude toward religious belief, to this point, is that of the grateful suppliant whose prayers have been answered and whom the angels have comforted. Had the poem ended at line 6, it would be a conventional assertion of the restoring powers of prayers using, as often in the Bible, the language of monetary profit and loss.

The extraordinary line of the poem, a line that it is impossible to imagine written by anyone but Emily Dickinson, is line 7: "Burglar, banker, father!" By calling God a burglar, the speaker reveals her blame of Him for her losses. The Lord giveth, and the Lord taketh away. But if God is a thief, He is also a banker able to lend as well as to call in loans. And finally, in a simple, moving statement of her dependence, the speaker calls Him "father." Only this banker father can restore the pauper of the last line to solvency.

The Open Question

If there can be such a thing as a favorite among exam questions, the third question in the essay section, the open question that allows students to select what work they write about, is certainly the choice among AP students and teachers. Many nationally administered tests on literature depend upon a specifically assigned list of works from which the examination questions will be selected. This is the method most used in Europe, and some of the AP exams in foreign languages also use the "set texts" system. Almost every year someone suggests that the AP literature exam adopt this method and assign four or five works upon which one or more exam questions can be based. The development committee has always resisted this proposal. One of the strengths of the AP literature course is its variety. Many of the best teachers agree to teach AP because it gives them the freedom to choose the works the class will study and allows them to teach works that would not be part of the standard high school curriculum. A list of set texts, the committee fears, would take away this freedom and may lead to too great an emphasis on the exam itself rather than on the skills of reading and writing that the exam in its present form tests.

When the examiners choose an open question for the exam, they are looking for one that will allow the student to select from the widest possible choice of works and at the same time discriminate among the well trained and the unprepared. Some questions work much better than others. The 1990 question, for example, on the conflict of a child and parents, allowed students to write about an extremely wide range of works from Antigone to the present day. On the other hand, the 1985 question calling for a discussion of a work that produced both "pleasure and disquietude" in the reader resulted in essays that were almost all about twentieth-century works, especially works by the novelists and playwrights of the period after World War II. Similarly, the 1989 question on the "distortion" produced interesting essays, but almost all of them were on works by modern authors.

69

The last thing the examiners want to happen is a student's turning to the open question and realizing that he or she doesn't know any work that suits this question. If this happens, both the student and the exam have failed. You must prepare several works, of several genres, of several periods. But if you've done that, there's no reason in the world for you to worry about finding an exam question that you can't answer. If you're still worried about not knowing appropriate books, read over the list in the section on previous exam questions. If you don't know any of these, your worst fears are justified, but chances are you know half a dozen of them or more. If you're still nervous, read over the summary of previous open questions and think about what work and, when relevant, what character in that work you could use to answer. If after reading these questions and this list of works you still find yourself unable to find a work you know or one that could be used on these questions, your AP class is a very unusual one, and you should speak to your AP teacher about the problem.

One reason that students and teachers universally prefer the open question is that it's about a work the student has studied and often about a work the student enjoys and admires. The prose passage and the poem are always going to be something of a surprise, and you can never quite get rid of the fear of misreading. Another reason for the preference of the open question is, I think, the nature of the questions. The questions on passages of prose and poetry are almost always one-half to two-thirds questions about style ("literary devices," "techniques," and so on). But the open essay is much more often solely about content. Students can't be expected to write well about style without an example in front of them, and the open question can't possibly give examples from all the plays and novels that may be chosen. So the questions focus upon characterizations, theme, relations of a part to the whole, and the function of characters, events, or settings. When questions do call for literary techniques, they are likely to ask about the handling of point of view or the angle from which the story is told.

Students writing on the open question are not expected to remember every detail of plot or even every character's name. Still the difference between a merely competent and an outstanding essay is often specificity. The student who can point to a relevant specific scene or even a specific line of dialogue has an advantage over a student who can't. There's no reason to prepare for the exam by memorizing page after page of plays or novels. Readers will often come upon, say, ten lines of Hamlet's "To be or not to be" quoted in the middle of an essay on the role of the supernatural, and the student will not have improved his or her grade. But there may be a question (the question on pleasure and disquietude, for example) where a specific and informed discussion of a speech would be very impressive.

You must have more than one string to your bow, but be careful not to overload yourself. The student who has spent weeks preparing *Othello* to the exclusion of all other works may be confronted with a question on the novel, on a work written after 1900, or on a comedy. On the other hand, it's much better, I think, to know five works very well than ten works vaguely. The more you know well, the better. Then you can choose among more than one suitable work, the one that fits the question ideally.

Your choice of work, character, or scene within a work is crucial. A brilliant essay on a wholly inappropriate work will not score as high as a pedestrian essay on a work that fits the question. And just because the work you write about is on the recommended list on the exam doesn't end your responsibility. You must then select the best character (Ahab or Starbuck? Heathcliff or

Hindley?) or best scene, place, or whatever the question calls for you to write about. A bad choice of work or subject on the open question places an essay at an almost insurmountable disadvantage.

Determining the Task on Open Questions

Even before you select the work you'll write on, you must understand exactly what the question asks you to do. The questions below haven't appeared on the exams, but they will accustom you to the format and demands of the questions that do. Read them carefully and determine what the exact tasks are. Most of the open questions deal with meaning rather than style. Most of the time, you can choose to write on either a novel or a play but not always. The first thing to be sure about is the kind of work called for. It may be just a play, just a novel, or just a tragedy. Or the question may simply say "work" and leave you free to choose an epic poem or a short story. So far, films and television plays have been forbidden, and there are no signs of this rule being changed.

1. In many novels, a child plays an all-important part. Choose a novel of recognized literary merit in which a child is significant and write an essay that explains how the author presents the child's point of view and how the child's values are related to the central themes of the work as a whole. Do not merely summarize the plot.

Right away you should notice that you must choose a novel — *Great Expectations* or *Oliver Twist,* but not Joyce's "Araby" or *The Children's Hour.* Task one, how the author presents the child's point of view, may be a technical question that requires comment on subjects like who tells the story (it may be told by the child in the first person or by an adult remembering his or her childhood, as in *Great Expectations* or *Jane Eyre*) or how other characters interact with or comment on the child. It may also mean the author's attitude toward the child's position.

The second half of the sentence calls for a definition of the child's values and a definition of some of the central themes of the book before you can begin to relate the former to the latter. With most books, especially novels of the nineteenth century, the moral values of the uncorrupted child are those of the novel. *A High Wind in Jamaica* by Richard Hughes would provide a unique and refreshing response to this question.

2. The conflict between an idealistic and a pragmatic, or realistic, response to life is a recurrent theme in literature. Choose a work in which such a conflict is central. Write an essay in which you analyze the reasons for the conflict and its effect upon one idealistic character and one representative of the realistic attitude.

Here, only a "work" is specified, so you can use a novel, a play, or even a short story or a poem. The important point is that the realist-idealist conflict must be central to the work. The tasks are analyzing the reasons (note the plural) for the conflict and describing its effect on each of the two characters (both Antigone and Creon if you choose *Antigone*).

3. Plays and novels frequently argue the issue of the freedom of the individual will as opposed to the controlling pressures of the environment or public world. Choose a play or novel in which this theme is prominent. Write an essay in which you discuss a character who represents this issue, analyzing the nature of the conflict, its effect upon the character, and the meaning of its resolution at the end of the work.

71

On this question, a play or a novel can be used as long as the freedom of the will versus environmental control is a prominent theme (as, for example, in Hardy). The question requires that you choose a character to represent the issue, explain the conflict and its effect upon the character, and interpret the significance of the conflict at the conclusion of the work.

You may have noticed that a number of the open questions ask you to discuss "the meaning," "a meaning," or "the meanings" of a novel or a play. Because this task is so often a part of the open questions, you should carefully prepare for it in your last-minute studies. To define "the meaning" is a task that will reduce or demean some works. What is the meaning of *Hamlet* or *King Lear*? It almost seems that the greater the work of art, the more impossible it becomes to reduce its meaning to a sentence or a paragraph. And conversely, the more simple and sometimes simple-minded works are easy to encapsulate in a single morally uplifting aphorism. Because the question still appears on the exam, you should prepare for it. When you've decided on the novels and plays that you might use on the open question, go over each with a mind to define just what the "meanings" you would write about are. Depending on the nature of the question, you may find that several but not all of the meanings in your list will be relevant in your essay.

Examples of an Open Question and Student Essays

Open Question

One of the open questions from a previous test in the early 1980s asked for the discussion of a villain in a novel or a play. Students were asked to describe the villainy of the selected character and to relate this evil to meaning in the work. Suggested authors included Melville, Faulkner, Hawthorne, Fitzgerald, Dickens, Austen, Brontë, and Conrad among novelists and such playwrights as Shakespeare, Ibsen, Jonson, and Miller.

Student Essay 1

In the novel "Pride and Prejudice" the author creates Wickham to give us a villain. Wickham provides some action and conflict for an otherwise dull novel about a prim and proper life.

In the book, Wickham is portrayed as the villain simply because he steals away one of the Bennet's daughters for primarily sexual purposes. Whereas the daughter would have otherwise gotten married to a wealthy man in town somewhere, Wickham elopes with her despite his lack of money. Their romps throughout many a motel room reach epic proportions.

Wickham throws on a little spice into an otherwise actionless and rather boring novel. Wickham also serves to shake up the small town community that the Bennets live in.

Wickham is perhaps not a villain in the true sense of the word in that he does not have harmful intentions towards the daughter it just ends up being that way because of the society they live in.

Wickham spices up the plot and makes the novel less dull as a villain.

Student Essay 2

Mr. Wickham came to town a stranger. Arriving with his best friend Mr. Bingley, he was perceived as a nice, respectable young man. Mr. Wickham was a deceptive villain in Pride and Prejudice by Jane Austen. He was vital in three important aspects: to the character development of Elizabeth, to show the blindness of other characters, and to teach the lesson of looking past the outside to the real person inside.

Elizabeth was immediately taken in by Mr. Wickham. He was very charming and he used that to toy with her emotions. Carrying her along on a string, he managed to make her blind to her real feelings toward Mr. Darcy. His interference is vital in her learning. He hurts and betrays her by eloping with her younger sister. This throws her into the open arms of Darcy who she had detested. She begins to see past his seemingly rude behavior to the real loyal Darcy who had loved her all along. It took that hurtful, but necessary blow from Wickham for her to see what was important to see in people. She learned that what may seem like a person outside may not be very good inside and that's what mattered. She learned how to swallow her prejudice and hold up her pride.

Wickham's character also showed how deceptive people could be. After everything that happened, Mr. Bennett said that Wickham would always be his favorite son-in-law. He managed to fool almost everyone with his charming and cool exterior. Wickham serves as a warning that not everyone is as they seem.

This brings us to Wickham's third function. He was not what he seemed and operated strictly for his own benefit and showed by contrast how someone perceived as the villain could turn out to be good like Mr. Darcy. People need to learn about the real inner person they're dealing with before they should completely trust them.

It is because of Wickham that Elizabeth may truly be happy. In a way, their flirtations and her being taken in by him could've been a blessing. His deceptions made her see how wrong she had been about people. Now that she saw past the outside mask of Darcy they have a possibility of a happy future together with a more open and honest relationship. Wickham taught her what to stay away from and served as a warning.

Response to Student Essays 1 and 2

Both of these essays choose Mr. Wickham in Jane Austen's *Pride and Prejudice* as their villain. The exam question gives no definition of the word but assumes that students know that the word refers to a wicked person, a scoundrel, one who opposes the hero or heroine, or would offer their own definitions. As with all the open questions, choosing a work and a character in the work that fits the question is the crucial first step, and the choice of Wickham is appropriate. He is, after all, a liar, a fortune-hunter, a seducer, perhaps even a blackmailer, though a charming and good-looking scoundrel.

The wise choice of Wickham is about the only point in the first essay's favor. Anyone who has read Jane Austen will be enchanted by the notion of two characters in her novels on epic "romps throughout many a motel room" a century before the automobile, let alone the motel, has been invented. The analysis of the nature of Wickham's villainy is incompetent, inaccurate, and self-contradictory, because the essay suggests that Wickham is not, after all, a villain. And though some readers may agree with the contention that Wickham's role is to liven up an otherwise dull novel, this is not the kind of answer to the question that will impress readers of the exam. Don't use your essays as a platform from which to express your views on life or literature. To denounce Jane Austen to an audience of English teachers is self-destructive behavior, but the student who imagines that praising Jane Austen's art will earn points is also mistaken. Answer the question on the exam.

Essay 2 does answer the question. It begins with an error, confusing Mr. Wickham with Mr. Darcy, who does arrive with his friend Mr. Bingley. But this is the sort of error that readers are trained to overlook. It's a minor slip of the pen like misspelling Austen or forgetting a name or a place, but it doesn't mar the essay in any important way. The rest of the paper makes clear that the student knows exactly who Wickham is and why he can be called a villain.

The essay refers to more than one meaning in the novel that is revealed through Wickham. The essay does answer both parts of the question, but it also has mechanical weaknesses and a misguided third paragraph. The student takes Mr. Bennett, the ironist of the novel, seriously when he calls the villainous Wickham his favorite son-in-law. This is a different kind of error from the confusion of Wickham and Darcy in the first paragraph of the essay, because it reveals a misunderstanding of a character, not just a lapse of memory. The good points of this essay outnumber its weaknesses, however, and it would receive a score in the upper half of the scale.

Student Essay 3

In Pride and Prejudice by Jane Austen, the villain in the novel is the mother of the five girls. The mother is a villain because she sees love as money, and money as love. This unloving, villainous attitude comes from the fact that she married an unwealthy man and her relationship with her husband is not very loving. She sees the absence of wealth as the reason for the absence of love. She wants her daughters to have a better life than she has had and she sees that the only way they can achieve this is by marrying wealthy men — not to mention that she also believes that she will receive some of the happiness and money too. This enhances the meaning of the work because the mother wants the wealth more than the daughters do so it would be easy for them to just go along with the mother's beliefs and marry whichever rich guy that their mother sets them up with. Luckily, Elizabeth is a strong-willed individual and she knows that her mother is unfeeling and villainous because she is taking advantage of other people's money. Elizabeth is interested in real love and the only wealth she is after is wealth of their heart and mind.

The mother's villainous beliefs start to break down at the end when one of her daughters marries a man with no wealth and also when she begins to realize that although two of her other daughters are marrying wealthy men. They are marrying them for their love not for their money because they are smart, and caring enough to know that love and money are two separate things.

Student Essay 4

I think that most people would say that Heathcliff is the villain of "Wuthering Heights." But he is the hero, and the reader feels a sympathy with him as he grinds the "puny" Lintons because we think that they are puny. Edgar and Isabella are uninteresting people, but they aren't villains. Hindley Earnshaw is the best choice for villain in Emily Brontë's "Wuthering Heights."

His first action is to refuse to give the orphan Heathcliff a place in his bedroom and then to tease and torture him until his father's death. He then makes him a stableboy and tries to prevent his associating with Cathy. Hindley's villainy can be explained as jealousy at Heathcliff taking his place in his father's affection, but it continues after Mr. Earnshaw's death. Hindley never stops hating Heathcliff and doing all he can to injure him.

Hindley's drinking is motivated by the death of his wife. A good sign of his villainy is his indifference and cruelty to his own son, Hareton. When Heathcliff returns, Hindley is a pitiful drunk and gambler, and Heathcliff easily outwits him. In his drunkenness, Hindley almost kills his son, and he is guilty of the attempted murder of Heathcliff, which he bungles. He dies in debt and drunk at 27, leaving his son in the hands of his enemy, Heathcliff. It is hard to find anything to say in defense of Hindley's actions. He is the best example of a villain in the novel, but the novel is not really about villains versus heroes or evil versus good.

The meaning of "Wuthering Heights" is not moral like it is in a Dickens novel. Catherine Earnshaw's marriage to Edgar while she loves Heathcliff is the turning point, and Heathcliff explains this meaning in their scene before Catherine's death. Hindley, like Catherine, has been guilty of social ambition, and his contempt for Heathcliff is based on his belief that Heathcliff is a "gypsy," a lower order. Catherine has avoided this mistake with Heathcliff but cannot resist the attraction of the Grange, and so she makes the fatal mistake of marrying Edgar. The novel is not about a class war. It is about following one's true nature. Whatever good was in Hindley was destroyed by the arrival of Heathcliff and by the early death of his wife. Hindley's villainy throws the actions of Heathcliff into relief, for however terrible Heathcliff's actions become, they are caused by a frustrated love and desire to right what he sees as the wrongs of his childhood. Hindley doesn't have this excuse.

Response to Student Essays 3 and 4

Essay 3 selects Mrs. Bennet as the villain of *Pride and Prejudice* and gives her preference of money to love as the cause of her villainy. Mrs. Bennet is a foolish woman, a materialist, a hypochondriac, but is she a villain? She unwittingly injures her daughters' chances for a happy marriage, and she can't tell a good man from a bad (she really does like Wickham). But if a villain is wicked, evil, or unprincipled, Mrs. Bennet doesn't qualify. One is tempted to say she is too stupid to be a villain, too dim to scheme or hatch a plot. So from the start, this essay is in trouble.

A reader of this essay would begin by deploring the choice of Mrs. Bennet but then look for redeeming features. Does the essay analyze the nature of the villainy and relate it to the meaning in the work? It is true that the novel condemns marriage solely for material motives (though Charlotte Lucas's marriage is, in its way, a success), and Mrs. Bennet is all in favor of marrying money. But the essay gets little else quite right: Mrs. Bennet doesn't marry an "unwealthy man," want a "better life" for her daughters, or expect to cash in on their wealth. The attitudes of the novel toward wealth are far more hard-headed than this essay suggests. It would probably be scored a three.

Essay 4, on the other hand, would score very high. Almost all of the essays on *Wuthering Heights* used Heathcliff as villain, and while a good case can be made for his villainy, it's not an easy essay to write. This student may have thought first about using Heathcliff, seen the difficulties, and realized that as good a case can be made for Hindley Earnshaw as the villain without the problem of his being, like Heathcliff, the hero of the novel as well. The first paragraph explains this decision, and it is an original and convincing opening.

The second and third paragraphs accurately record the evidence of Hindley's villainy. That he is an ineffectual villain does not disqualify him for the title.

The fourth paragraph rightly refuses to pin "a meaning" on *Wuthering Heights* but refers to the issue of social prestige and class distinctions and to the central idea of keeping faith with one's nature and shows how Hindley's revenge differs from Heathcliff's. Notice how this student has allowed the question to organize the essay. The first paragraph is introductory. The second and third paragraphs do the first assignment ("the nature of villainy"); the final paragraph does the second task. There is no padding, no repetition. The student never loses sight of what the question has asked.

Questions on Two Texts and Other Questions

Questions on Two Texts

Every so often, the exam includes a prose or a poetry question using two texts. The prose question used passages from Ralph Ellison and Henry James in 1980 and two versions of a paragraph from Hemingway's *A Farewell to Arms* in 1985.

The poetry section has included comparisons of poems on spring by Louise Gluck and William Carlos Williams. Poems by Wordsworth and Frost on nature, poems by Keats and Frost on a star, and poems by Poe and H.D. on Helen. Some of these questions have been more general than the questions on a single poem, calling simply for a discussion of the similarities and differences of the two poems.

A question using two prose passages still regularly appears on the AP language exam, but in the last ten years, there has been only one, a comparison of two drafts of a passage from Hemingway's *A Farewell to Arms*, on the literature test. This question was used in 1985 at a time when the prose analysis question was the same on both the language and the literature exams. There has been no question calling for a comparison of two prose passages on the literature exam since the common question was dropped in 1986, and though it remains a possibility, the comparison of two prose passages is much more likely to appear on the language test.

Questions using two poetry texts, however, are likely to continue to appear on the literature exam, and you should think about a method to use in answering them. The poems used are short ones, because a student is expected to read and write about two poems in the same 35 or 40 minutes that are usually allowed for an essay on one. The two works must have something in common (a response to nature, a star), but as the Frost-Keats question demonstrates, the connection may be superficial. A good comparison essay can be written using the two poems about the sonnet by Wordsworth and Keats discussed in the section on multiple-choice questions. The two poems are short, and the subject is the same in both. The question would read like this:

The following poems by Wordsworth and Keats are about the sonnet. Read them carefully. Then write a well-organized essay in which you discuss their similarities and differences in style and meaning.

On the Sonnet

If by dull rhymes our English must be chained,
And, like Andromeda, the Sonnet sweet
Fettered, in spite of pained loveliness;
Let us find out, if we must be constrained,
(5)   Sandals more interwoven and complete
To fit the naked foot of poesy;
Let us inspect the lyre, and weigh the stress
Of every chord, and see what may be gained
By ear industrious, and attention meet;
(10) Misers of sound and syllable, no less
Than Midas of his coinage, let us be
Jealous of dead leaves in the bay-wreath crown;
So, if we may not let the Muse be free.
She will be bound with garlands of her own.

— Keats

Nuns fret not at their convent's narrow room;
And hermits are contented with their cells;
And students with their pensive citadels;
Maids at the wheel, the weaver at his loom,
(5)   Sit blithe and happy; bees that soar for bloom,
High as the highest Peak of Furness-fells,
Will murmur by the hour in foxglove bells:
In truth the prison, unto which we doom
Ourselves, no prison is: and hence for me,
(10) In sundry moods, 'twas pastime to be bound
Within the Sonnet's scanty plot of ground;
Pleased if some souls (for such their needs must be)
Who have felt the weight of too much liberty,
Should find brief solace there, as I have found.

— Wordsworth

Before you begin to write an answer to a comparison question like this, you should quickly list as many similarities and differences of both theme and style as you can. Your essay can then be based upon a selection of the most important ones. Your notes on the poems may look something like this:

	Wordsworth	Keats
Speaker	Poet — first person singular ("I")	Poet — first person plural ("we")
Audience	Unspecified general audience, readers of sonnets	Other poets, writers of sonnets
Structural divisions	Lines 1–7, 8–9, 9–14	Lines 1–6, 7–9, 10–12, 13–14
Rhyme scheme	abba, abba, cddccd	abc, abd, cabcedede
Subject	The sonnet	The Sonnet
	The restrictions that are self-chosen are liberating	The restrictions of the sonnet should be made freer, more organic
Images	Sonnet = small plot of earth	Poetry = woman in chains
	Restriction = prison	Rhyme = interwoven sandals
	Nuns, hermits, students as restricted by choice	Poetry personified
	Bees in flowers = also chosen restraint	Stale verse conventions = dead leaves
		Rhyme = garlands
Allusions	Furness-fells (a peak in the Lake District of England)	Classical references including Andromeda, Midas, the Muse
Diction	Contented, happy, blithe, pastime, solace	Chained, fettered, pained, constrained

Using this information, your essay would probably discuss the likenesses and important differences in the poets' views of the restrictions of the sonnet rhyme scheme. Both use the sonnet to talk about the sonnet, but Wordsworth's point is that the restrictions we choose are not really restrictions but can become a pleasure, a relief from the oppression of too much freedom. Keats, on the other hand, is impatient with unnatural restrictions or dead conventions and urges a natural and organic poetry. The structural divisions and the rhyme schemes are different; both reflect the ideas about freedom and restriction the two poems express.

The images of the two poems are very different. Keats relies heavily on classical allusion, not only to persons, but also to classical symbols for poetry such as the lyre, garlands, or the bay-wreath crown. Wordsworth uses five human examples of self-chosen enclosure as well as one from nature (the bee) and, unlike Keats, uses paradox. The contrast in diction reflects the difference in the two poets' attitudes toward restraints. Keats suggests its harsh side ("pained"), Wordsworth its pleasures ("blithe").

Let's look at another pair of short poems, two Renaissance lyrics by Edmund Spenser and Thomas Carew (pronounced Carey).

Write a well-organized essay in which you discuss the similarities and differences in the two following poems about spring.

Fresh spring, the herald of love's might king,
In whose cote-armor[1] richly are displayed
All sorts of flowers the which on earth do spring
In goodly colors gloriously arrayed,
(5) Go to my love, where she is careless laid,
Yet in her winter's bower not well-awake:
Tell her the joyous time will not be stayed
Unless she do him by the forelock take.
Bid her therefore herself soon ready make
(10) To wait on Love amongst his lovely crew:
Where every one that misseth then her make[2]
Shall be by him amerced[3] with penance due.
Make haste therefore, sweet love, whilst it is prime,
For none can call again the passed time.

— Edmund Spenser

[1]garment [2]mate [3]punished

The Spring

Now that the winter's gone, the earth hath lost
Her snow-white robes; and now no more the frost
Candies the grass, or casts an icy cream
Upon the silver lake or crystal stream:
(5) But the warm sun thaws the benumbed earth,
And makes it tender; gives a second birth
To the dead swallow; wakes in hollow tree
The drowsy cuckoo and the bumble-bee.
Now do a choir of chirping minstrels sing,
(10) In triumph to the world, the youthful Spring:
The valleys, hills, and woods in rich array
Welcome the coming of the long'd-for May.
Now all things smile; only my love doth lower;
Nor hath the scalding noon-day sun the power
(15) To melt that marble ice, which still doth hold
Her heart congeal'd, and makes her pity cold.
The ox which lately did for shelter fly
Into the stall, doth now securely lie
In open field; and love no more is made

(5)   By the fire-side, but in the cooler shade.
       Amyntas now doth by his Cloris sleep
       Under a sycamore, and all things keep
       Time with the season: only she doth carry
       June in her eyes, in her heart January.

— Thomas Carew

The notes on these poems would be something like this:

	Spenser	Carew
Speaker	The male lover	The male lover
Audience	Lines 1–12, spring; Lines 13–14 the female beloved	No specific audience (the real, unnamed audience is the beloved)
Situation	Springtime	Springtime
Structural divisions	Lines 1–8, 9–12, 13–14	Lines 1–4, winter (A); Lines 5–12, spring (B); Lines 12–16, the lady (C); Lines 17–23, spring (B); Lines 23–24, the lady (C) as both winter (A) and spring (B)
Rhyme	abab, bcbc, cdcd, ee	12 pentameter couplets
Subject	Make use of youth, spring, because time passed cannot be recalled	Everyone and everything in the spring is happy and in love except the cold and beautiful lady
Images	Spring = herald Spring's clothes = flowers Lady as if in hibernation Time personified Love as god, Love	Snow = earth's clothing Frost = sugar Ice = cream Birds = choir Ice = her heart Rich array = spring flowers Spring, nature personified
Diction	Focus on time: time, not stayed, take by the forelock, soon, ready, haste, prime, passed time	Focus on hot versus cold contrast: winter, frost, icy, benumbed, dead, ice, congeal'd, cold, January versus spring, warm sun, tender, birth, smile, scalding noonday sun, June.

Both poets make use of spring to argue for a warmer response from the women they love. Spenser uses the *carpe diem* line; Carew simply points out the stark contrast between the warmth of the natural and human world of lovers and the icy disdain of the lady (who incidentally is as beautiful as June). Predictably, the diction and images of Spenser support his argument and stress the rapid and inevitable passage of time, while Carew exploits the contrast of winter and spring, of hot and cold. With this sort of detailed evidence in front of you, your essay should be easy to write.

Other Questions

The wheels of the AP exam move slowly, and the chances of your finding a new kind of question on your exam are very small. In the early 1970s when the multiple-choice section had only fifteen to twenty questions, the exam had four essays, and occasionally one of the four was not a critical analysis of literature question. The 1971 exam asked for a creative essay, fable, or letter criticizing some facet of contemporary life, and the 1973 exam asked for a dialogue with two incompatible points of view. Since the multiple-choice exam increased to fifty to sixty questions in 1975, this sort of assignment has vanished.

The 1977 exam used a different kind of comparison-of-two-texts question by giving an earlier and a later draft of D. H. Lawrence's poem "Piano." Since then, the exam has stayed close to the one poem for analysis, one prose passage for analysis, and one open essay question format. There have been four uses of a complete short story as the question on prose. Joyce's "Eveline" was used in 1972, Par Lagerkvist's "Father and I," a banal existential parable in 1975, John Cheever's seriocomic "Reunion" in 1988, and Sandra Cisneros' "Eleven" in 1995. There is always the possibility that another complete short story will appear on the exam. Though the stories are longer than the usual excerpt, there has not been a problem with student's finishing the exam, though the student essays are often shorter than usual. The questions on short stories may well take the familiar form of asking for the definition of an attitude and the discussion of the techniques used to convey that view — in other words, the old paradigmatic AP exam assignment.

Definitions of Terms Used in AP Literature Exams

Terms Used in Essay Instructions

The following are the most important terms used in the instructions for essay questions. All of them have been used at least once and often more frequently. You should be familiar with the meaning of these terms.

allusion: A reference in a work of literature to something outside the work, especially to a well-known historical or literary event, person, or work. Lorraine Hansberry's title *A Raisin in the Sun* is an allusion to a phrase in a poem by Langston Hughes. When T. S. Eliot writes, "To have squeezed the universe into a ball" in "The Love Song of J. Alfred Prufrock," he is alluding to the lines "Let us roll all our strength and all / Our sweetness up into one ball" in Marvell's "To His Coy Mistress." In *Hamlet,* when Horatio says, "ere the mightiest Julius fell," the allusion is to the death of Julius Caesar.

attitude: A speaker's, author's, or character's disposition toward or opinion of a subject. For example, Hamlet's attitude toward Gertrude is a mixture of affection and revulsion, changing from one to the other within a single scene. Jane Austen's attitude toward Mr. Bennet in *Pride and Prejudice* combines respect for his wit and intelligence with disapproval of his failure to take sufficient responsibility for the rearing of all of his daughters.

details (also **choice of details**): Details are items or parts that make up a larger picture or story. Chaucer's "Prologue" to *The Canterbury Tales* is celebrated for its use of a few details to bring the characters to life. The miller, for example, is described as being brawny and big-boned, able to win wrestling contests or to break a door with his head, and having a wart on his nose on which grew a "tuft of hairs red as the bristles of a sow's ears."

devices of sound: The techniques of deploying the sound of words, especially in poetry. Among devices of sound are rhyme, alliteration, assonance, consonance, and onomatopoeia. These are defined later under metrical terms. The devices are used for many reasons, including creating a general effect of pleasant or of discordant sound, imitating another sound, or reflecting a meaning.

diction: Word choice. Nearly all essay questions on a passage of prose or a poem will ask you to talk about diction or about "techniques" that include diction. Any word that is important to the meaning and the effect of a passage can be used in your essay. Often several words with a similar effect are worth discussion, such as George Eliot's use in *Adam Bede* of "sunny afternoons," "slow waggons," and "bargains" to make the leisure of bygone days appealing. These words are also details.

figurative language: Writing that uses figures of speech (as opposed to literal language or that which is actual or specifically denoted) such as metaphor, simile, and irony.

Figurative language uses words to mean something other than their literal meaning. "The black bat night has flown" is figurative, with the metaphor comparing night and a bat. "Night is over" says the same thing without figurative language. No real bat is or has been on the scene, but night is like a bat because it is dark.

imagery: The images of a literary work; the sensory details of a work; the figurative language of a work. Imagery has several definitions, but the two that are paramount are the visual, auditory, or tactile images evoked by the words of a literary work or the images that figurative language evokes. When an AP question asks you to discuss the images or imagery of a work, you should look especially carefully at the sensory details and the metaphors and similes of a passage. Some diction (word choice) is also imagery, but not all diction evokes sensory responses.

irony: A figure of speech in which intent and actual meaning differ, characteristically praise for blame or blame for praise; a pattern of words that turns away from direct statement of its own obvious meaning. The term irony implies a discrepancy. In verbal irony (saying the opposite of what one means), the discrepancy is between statement and meaning. Sometimes, irony may simply understate, as in "Men have died from time to time . . ." when Mr. Bennet, who loathes Wickham, says he is perhaps his "favorite" son-in-law, he is using irony.

metaphor: A figurative use of language in which a comparison is expressed without the use of a comparative term like "as," "like," or "than." A simile would say, "Night is like a black bat;" a metaphor would say, "the black bat night." When Romeo says, "It is the east, and Juliet is the sun," his metaphors compare her window to the east and Juliet to the sun.

narrative techniques: The methods involved in telling a story; the procedures used by a writer of stories or accounts. Narrative technique is a general term (like "devices," or "resources of language") that asks you to discuss the procedures used in the telling of a story. Examples of the techniques you might use are point of view, manipulation of time, dialogue, or interior monologue.

omniscient point of view: The vantage point of a story in which the narrator can know, see, and report whatever he or she chooses. The narrator is free to describe the thoughts of any of the characters, to skip about in time or place, or to speak directly to the reader. Most of the novels of Austen, Dickens, or Hardy employ the omniscient point of view.

point of view: Any of several possible vantage points from which a story is told. The point of view may be omniscient, limited to that of a single character, or limited to that of several characters. And there are other possibilities. The teller may use the first person (as in *Great Expectations* or *Wuthering Heights*) or the third person (as in *The Mayor of Casterbridge* or *A Tale of Two Cities*). Faulkner's *As I Lay Dying* uses the point of view of all the members of the Bundren family and others as well in the first person, while in *Wuthering Heights*, Mr. Lockwood tells us the story that Nelly Dean tells him, a first-person narration reported by a second first-person narrator.

resources of language: A general phrase for the linguistic devices or techniques that a writer can use. A question calling for the "resources of language" invites a student to discuss the style and rhetoric of a passage. Such topics as diction, syntax, figurative language, and imagery are all examples of resources of language.

rhetorical techniques: The devices used in effective or persuasive language. The number of rhetorical techniques, like that of the resources of language, is long and runs from apostrophe to zeugma. The more common examples include devices like contrast, repetitions, paradox, understatement, sarcasm, and rhetorical question.

satire: Writing that seeks to arouse a reader's disapproval of an object by ridicule. Satire is usually comedy that exposes errors with an eye to correct vice and folly. A classical form, satire is found in the verse of Alexander Pope or Samuel Johnson, the plays of Ben Jonson or Bernard Shaw, and the novels of Charles Dickens, Mark Twain, or Joseph Heller.

setting: The background to a story; the physical location of a play, story, or novel. The setting of a narrative will normally involve both time and place. The setting of *A Tale of Two Cities* is London and Paris at the time of the French revolution, but the setting of *Waiting for Godot* is impossible to pin down specifically.

simile: A directly expressed comparison; a figure of speech comparing two objects, usually with "like," "as," or "than." It is easier to recognize a simile that a metaphor because the comparison is explicit: my love is like a fever; my love is deeper than a well; my love is as dead as a doornail. The plural of "simile" is "similes," not "similies."

Strategy (or rhetorical strategy): The management of language for a specific effect. The strategy or rhetorical strategy of a poem is the planned placing of elements to achieve an effect. For example, Shakespeare's sonnet 29, "When, in disgrace with fortune and men's eyes," spends the first nine lines describing the speaker's discontent, then three describing the happiness the thought of the loved-one brings, all in a single sentence.

The effect of this contrast is to intensify the feelings of relief and joy in lines 10–12. The rhetorical strategy of most love poems is deployed to convince the loved-one to return the speaker's love. By appealing to the loved-one's sympathy ("If you don't return my love, my heart will break."), or by flattery ("How could I not love someone as beautiful as you?"), or by threat ("When you're old, you'll be sorry you refused me."), the lover attempts to persuade the loved-one to love in return.

structure: The arrangement of materials within a work; the relationship of the parts of a work to the whole; the logical divisions of a work. The most common principles of structure are series (A, B, C, D, E), contrast (A vs. B, C vs. D, E vs. A), and repetition (AA, BB). The most common units of structure are — play: scene, act; novel: chapter; poem: line, stanza.

style: The mode of expression in language; the characteristic manner of expression of an author. Many elements contribute to style, and if a question calls for a discussion of style or of "stylistic techniques," you can discuss diction, syntax, figurative language, imagery, selection of detail, sound effects, and tone, using the ones that are appropriate. Notice that there are several phrases used in the essay questions that invite you to choose among several possible topics: "devices of style," "narrative techniques," "rhetorical techniques," "stylistic techniques," and "resources of language" are all phrases that call for a consideration of more than one technique but do not specify what techniques you must discuss. Usually one of the two essay questions on a set passage will use one of these phrases, while the other question will specify the tasks by asking for "diction, imagery, and syntax" or a similar three or four topics.

symbol: Something that is simultaneously itself and a sign of something else. Winter, darkness, and cold are real things, but in literature they are also likely to be used as symbols of death. A paper lantern and a light bulb are real things, but in "A Streetcar Named Desire," they are also symbols of Blanche's attempt to escape from reality and reality itself. Yorick's skull is a symbol of human mortality, and Melville's white whale is certainly a symbol, but exactly what it symbolizes has yet to be agreed upon.

syntax: The structure of a sentence; the arrangement of words in a sentence. A discussion of syntax in your essay could include such considerations as the length or brevity of the sentences, the kinds of sentences (questions, exclamations, declarative sentences, rhetorical questions — or periodic or loose; simple, complex, or compound). Syntax is often an issue on the English language exam. It has also been used frequently in recent essay questions on the AP literature exams, because it is clear that many students are not prepared to write about syntax. Until this defect has been repaired, syntax questions will continue to appear regularly in both the multiple-choice and essay sections of the test.

theme: The main thought expressed by a work. Essay questions may ask for discussion of the theme or themes of a work or may use the words "meaning" or "meanings." The open question frequently asks you to relate a discussion on one subject to a "meaning of the work as a whole." When preparing the novels and plays you might use on the open question, be sure to consider what theme or themes you would write about if you are asked to talk about a "meaning of the work." The question is much harder to answer for some works than others. I'm not sure what I would say is the meaning of *Hamlet, Wuthering Heights*, or *Waiting for Godot*. But I have much less trouble defining a theme in works like *Brave New World* or *Animal Farm*.

tone: The manner in which an author expresses his or her attitude; the intonation of the voice that expresses meaning. Tone is described by adjectives, and the possibilities are nearly endless. Often a single adjective will not be enough, and tone may change from chapter to chapter or even line to line. Tone is the result of allusion, diction, figurative language, imagery, irony, symbol, syntax, and style to cite only the relevant words on this list. In the Wordsworth passage on the 1992 exam, the tone moves from quiet to apprehensive to confident to exuberant to terrified to panicked to uncertain to restive in only twenty-five lines.

Exercise on Terms Used in Essay Instructions

Read carefully the following well-known sonnet "On First Looking into Chapman's Homer" by John Keats. The title alludes to Keats's first reading of the sixteenth-century poet George Chapman's translation of Homer's Iliad.

> Much have I travell'd in the realms of gold,
> And many goodly states and kingdoms seen;
> Round many western islands have I been
> Which bards in fealty to Apollo hold.
> (5)   Oft of one wide expanse had I been told
> That deep-brow'd Homer ruled as his demesne;
> Yet did I never breathe its pure serene

Till I heard Chapman speak out loud and bold:
Then felt I like some watcher of the skies
(10)   When a new planet swims into his ken;
Or like stout Cortez when with eagle eyes
He stared at the Pacific — and all his men
Look'd at each other with a wild surmise —
Silent, upon a peak in Darien.

In the following four lines, five words or phrases lettered A, B, C, D, and E have been under-lined. Determine which of the following terms are appropriate to describe each word or phrase. In several cases, more than one of the terms should be cited:

Much <u>have I travell'd</u> in <u>the realms of gold,</u>
      A   B

And many <u>goodly states and kingdoms</u> seen;
              C

Round many <u>western islands</u> have I been
          D

Which bards in fealty to <u>Apollo</u> hold.
              E

1. allusion   A.
2. figurative language   B.
3. imagery   C.
4. irony   D.
5. metaphor   E.
6. simile
7. symbol

Which of the same seven terms are illustrated by the words or phrases in this passage?

Then felt I <u>like some watcher of the skies</u>
              F

When a new planet <u>swims</u> into his ken;
              G

Or <u>like stout Cortez</u> when with <u>eagle eyes</u>
     H   I

He stared at the Pacific — and all his men

Look'd at each other with a wild surmise —

<u>Silent, upon a peak in Darien.</u>
  J

1. allusion   F.

2. figurative language   G.

3. imagery   H.

4. irony   I.

5. metaphor   J.

6. simile

7. symbol

Answers

A. **"have I travell'd"** — 2, 3, and 5. The poet is speaking of his readings and compares reading to traveling. This is an example of figurative language, of imagery, and of a metaphor.

B. **"the realms of gold"** — 2, 3, and 5. The figure is continued: reading = traveling; the realms of gold = the works of literature the poet has read. Like A, this is a metaphor. The phrase "realms of gold" is also a metaphor for fine poetry, the value of gold equated with the worth of art.

C. **"goodly states and kingdoms"** — 2, 3, and 5. The figure comparing books or poems to realms is here altered to states and kingdoms.

D. **"western islands"** — 2, 3, and 5. The comparison now likens poems to islands; bards devoted to Apollo have written the poems.

E. **"Apollo"** — 1 and 7. The allusion is to the Greek god of poetry. Because we assume that Apollo represents poetry, we can also call this a symbol.

F. **"like some watcher of the skies"** — 2, 3, and 6. The figure or image here compares the poet to an astronomer. This is a simile, using "like." His discovery of Chapman's Homer is like the discovery of a new planet.

G. **"swims"** — 2, 3, and 5. The metaphor compares motion through water with the motion of a planet as seen by a telescope.

H. **"stout Cortez"** — 1, 2, 3, and 6. The allusion, though Keats confuses Cortez and Balboa, is to a Spanish explorer.

I. **"eagle eyes"** — 2, 3, and 5. The metaphor compares Cortez's eyes to those of an eagle.

J. **"Silent, upon a peak in Darien"** — 1 and 3. The allusion is to the mountain in Panama; the phrase presents an image.

The poem does not use irony.

Terms Used in Multiple-Choice Questions

The following terms have been used in multiple-choice questions and answers. The more important ones are marked with an asterisk.

allegory: A story in which people, things, and events have another meaning. Examples of allegory are Bunyan's *Pilgrim's Progress*, Spenser's *Faerie Queene*, and Orwell's *Animal Farm*.

ambiguity: Multiple meanings a literary work may communicate, especially two meanings that are incompatible.

*apostrophe: Direct address, usually to someone or something that is not present. Keats's "Bright star! Would I were steadfast" is an apostrophe to a star, and "To Autumn" is an apostrophe to a personified season.

*connotation: The implications of a word or phrase, as opposed to its exact meaning (denotation). Both China and Cathay denote a region in Asia, but to a modern reader, the associations of the two words are different.

*convention: A device of style or subject matter so often used that it becomes a recognized means of expression. For example, a lover observing the literary love conventions cannot eat or sleep and grows pale and lean. Romeo, at the beginning of the play is a conventional lover, while an overweight lover in Chaucer is consciously mocking the convention.

*denotation: The dictionary meaning of a word, as opposed to connotation.

didactic: Explicitly instructive. A didactic poem or novel may be good or bad. Pope's "Essay on Man" is didactic; so are the novels of Ayn Rand.

digression: The use of material unrelated to the subject of a work. The interpolated narrations in the novels of Cervantes or Fielding may be called digressions, and *Tristram Shandy* includes a digression on digressions.

epigram: A pithy saying, often using contrast. The epigram is also a verse form, usually brief and pointed.

euphemism: A figure of speech using indirection to avoid offensive bluntness, such as "deceased" for "dead" or "remains" for "corpse."

grotesque: Characterized by distortions or incongruities. The fiction of Poe or Flannery O'Connor is often described as grotesque.

*hyperbole: Deliberate exaggeration, overstatement. As a rule, hyperbole is self-conscious, without the intention of being accepted literally. "The strongest man in the world" and "a diamond as big as the Ritz" are hyperbolic.

jargon: The special language of a profession or group. The term jargon usually has pejorative associations, with the implication that jargon is evasive, tedious, and unintelligible to outsiders. The writings of the lawyer and the literary critic are both susceptible to jargon.

*literal: Not figurative; accurate to the letter; matter of fact or concrete.

lyrical: Songlike; characterized by emotion, subjectivity, and imagination.

*oxymoron: A combination of opposites; the union of contradictory terms. Romeo's line "feather of lead, bright smoke, cold fire, sick health" has four examples of the device.

parable: A story designed to suggest a principle, illustrate a moral, or answer a question. Parables are allegorical stories.

*paradox: A statement that seems to be self-contradicting but, in fact, is true. The figure in Donne's holy sonnet that concludes I never shall be "chaste except you ravish me" is a good example of the device.

parody: A composition that imitates the style of another composition normally for comic effect. Fielding's *Shamela* is a parody of Richardson's *Pamela*. A contest for parodies of Hemingway draws hundreds of entries each year.

*personification: A figurative use of language that endows the nonhuman (ideas, inanimate objects, animals, abstractions) with human characteristics. Keats personifies the nightingale, the Grecian urn, and autumn in his major poems.

*reliability: A quality of some fictional narrators whose word the reader can trust. There are both reliable and unreliable narrators, that is, tellers of a story who should or should not be trusted. Most narrators are reliable (Fitzgerald's Nick Carraway, Conrad's Marlow), but some are clearly not to be trusted (Poe's "Tell-Tale Heart," several novels by Nabokov). And there are some about whom readers have been unable to decide (James's governess in *The Turn of the Screw*, Ford's *The Good Soldier*).

*rhetorical question: A question asked for effect, not in expectation of a reply. No reply is expected because the question presupposes only one possible answer. The lover of Suckling's "Shall I wasting in despair / Die because a lady's fair?" has already decided the answer is no.

*soliloquy: A speech in which a character who is alone speaks his or her thoughts aloud. A monologue also has a single speaker, but the monologuist speaks to others who do not interrupt. Hamlet's "To be, or not to be" and "O! what a rogue and peasant slave am I" are soliloquies. Browning's "My Last Duchess" and "Fra Lippo Lippi" are monologues, but the hypocritical monk of his "Soliloquy of the Spanish Cloister" cannot reveal his thoughts to others.

*stereotype: A conventional pattern, expression, character, or idea. In literature, a stereotype could apply to the unvarying plot and characters of some works of fiction (those of Barbara Cartland, for example) or to the stock characters and plots of many of the greatest stage comedies.

syllogism: A form of reasoning in which two statements are made and a conclusion is drawn from them. A syllogism begins with a major premise ("All tragedies end unhappily.") followed by a minor premise ("Hamlet is a tragedy.") and a conclusion (Therefore, "Hamlet ends unhappily.").

thesis: The theme, meaning, or position that a writer undertakes to prove or support.

Metrical Terms

The following have been used in the questions or answers of the multiple-choice questions about the metrics of a passage. Those marked with an asterisk are the more important terms; the others appeared only as wrong answers.

*alliteration: The repetition of identical or similar consonant sounds, normally at the beginning of words. "Gnus never know pneumonia" is an example of alliteration, because despite the spellings, all four words begin with the "n" sound.

*assonance: The repetition of identical or similar vowel sounds. "A land laid waste with all its young men slain" repeats the same "a" sound in "laid," "waste," and "slain."

ballad meter: A four-line stanza rhymed abcb with four feet in lines one and three and three feet in lines two and four.

> O mother, mother make my bed.
> O make it soft and narrow.
> Since my love died for me today,
> I'll die for him tomorrow.

*blank verse: Unrhymed iambic pentameter.

> Men called him Mulciber; and how he fell
> From heaven, they fabled, thrown by angry Jove
> Sheer o'er the crystal battlements: from morn
> To noon he fell, from noon to dewy eve.

Blank verse is the meter of most of Shakespeare's plays, as well as that of Milton's *Paradise Lost*.

dactyl: A metrical foot of three syllables, an accented syllable followed by two unaccented syllables.

*end-stopped: A line with a pause at the end. Lines that end with a period, comma, colon, semicolon, exclamation point, or question mark are end-stopped lines.

*free verse: Poetry which is not written in a traditional meter but is still rhythmical. The poetry of Walt Whitman is perhaps the best know example of free verse.

*heroic couplet: Two end-stopped iambic pentameter lines rhymed aa, bb, cc with the thought usually completed in the two-line unit.

> When those fair suns shall set, as set they must,
> And all those tresses shall be laid in dust,
> This lock, the Muse shall consecrate to fame,
> And 'midst the stars inscribe Belinda's name.

hexameter: A line containing six feet.

*iamb: A two-syllable foot with an unaccented syllable followed by an accented syllable. The iamb is the most common foot in English poetry.

internal rhyme: Rhyme that occurs within a line, rather than at the end.

> "God save thee, ancient Mariner!
> From the friends, that plague thee thus! —
> Why look'st thou so?" — With my crossbow
> I shot the Albatross.

Line three contains the internal rhyme of "so" and "bow."

onomatopoeia: The use of words whose sound suggests their meaning. Examples are "buzz," "hiss," or "honk."

*pentameter: A line containing five feet. The iambic pentameter is the most common line in English verse written before 1950.

rhyme royal: A seven-line stanza of iambic pentameter rhymed ababbcc, used by Chaucer and other medieval poets.

*sonnet: Normally a fourteen-line iambic pentameter poem. The conventional Italian, or Petrachan, sonnet is rhymed abba, abba, cde, cde; the English, or Shakespearean, sonnet is rhymed abab, cdcd, efef, gg.

*stanza: Usually a repeated grouping of three or more lines with the same meter and rhyme scheme.

terza rima: A three-line stanza rhymed aba, bcb, cdc. Dante's *Divine Comedy* is written in terza rima.

*tetrameter: A line of four feet.

Grammatical Terms

antecedent: That which goes before, especially the word, phrase, or clause to which a pronoun refers. In the sentence "The witches cast their spells," the antecedent of the pronoun "their" is the noun "witches."

clause: A group of words containing a subject and its verb that may or may not be a complete sentence. In the sentence "When you are old, you will be beautiful," the first clause ("When you are old") is a dependent clause and not a complete sentence. "You will be beautiful" is an independent clause and could stand by itself.

ellipsis: The omission of a word or several words necessary for a complete construction that is still understandable. "If rainy, bring an umbrella" is clear though the words "it is" and "you" have been left out.

imperative: The mood of a verb that gives an order. "Eat your spinach" uses an imperative verb.

modify: To restrict or limit in meaning. In the phrase "large, shaggy dog," the two adjectives modify the noun; in the phrase "very shaggy dog," the adverb "very" modifies the adjective "shaggy" which modifies the noun "dog."

parallel structure: A similar grammatical structure within a sentence or within a paragraph. Winston Churchill's "We shall fight on the beaches, we shall fight on the landing grounds, we shall fight in the fields" speech or Martin Luther King's "I have a dream" speech depend chiefly on the use of parallel structure.

periodic sentence: A sentence grammatically complete only at the end. A loose sentence is grammatically complete before the period. The following are (1) periodic and (2) loose sentences.

1. When conquering love did first my heart assail, / Unto mine aid I summoned every sense.

2. Fair is my love, and cruel as she's fair.

Periodic sentences complete the important idea at the end, while loose sentences put the important idea first. Neither is a better sentence. Good writers use both.

syntax: The structure of a sentence.

Previous Text Used and Recommended Authors to Study for the Exam

The point of your AP English class is to teach you to read and write about literature well. This, not your exam score, should be your chief concern. Don't become preoccupied with what has been or what will be on the exam. Don't spend too much time writing practice exams, especially if doing so simply increases your anxiety.

Still, you must be aware of what the exam experience is like. Three hours is a long time to devote to intense concentration without a break, and many students find it is more exhausting than they had imagined. You should spend some time practicing writing using the questions from old exams. You will learn from them the level of difficulty of the texts and exactly what kinds of tasks are set for you to write about. Copies of the essay questions on old exams can be ordered from the Advanced Placement Program, P.O. Box 6670, Princeton, New Jersey 08541-6670.

Texts Used in Past Multiple-Choice Exams

The essay topics on the AP English Literature exams are released each year, but the multiple-choice questions are not. A complete exam that includes the multiple-choice passages and questions is made public only once every four or five years. An additional small selection of previously used multiple-choice questions is included in the annually published English Advanced Placement Course Description.

The following are the texts in English and American literature on which the released multiple-choice questions have been based in the past. They will give you an idea of the range and the level of difficulty of the prose and poetry that appear on the exam.

Poetry

Sixteenth and Seventeenth Century

Abraham Cowley: "My Picture"

George Herbert: "The Collar," "Church Monuments"

Ben Jonson: selection from *Volpone*

Andrew Marvell: "A Dialogue Between the Soul and Body"

William Shakespeare: "Like As the Waves" (Sonnet 60), soliloquies from *Richard II* and *Richard III*

Sir Thomas Wyatt: "They Flee from Me"

Eighteenth Century

Thomas Gray: "Hymn to Adversity"
Alexander Pope: selection from "Imitations of Horace"

Nineteenth Century

Samuel Taylor Coleridge: "The Eolian Harp"
Emily Dickinson: "I Dreaded that First Robin So"
Gerard Manley Hopkins: "The Habit of Perfection"
William Wordsworth: "There Was a Boy," "Elegiac Stanzas"

Twentieth Century

Elizabeth Bishop: "Sestina"
Amy Clampitt: "A Whippoorwill in the Woods"
Robert Frost: "The Most of It"
Yusef Komunyakaa: "Facing It"
May Sarton: "Lady with a Falcon"
Richard Wilbur: "Beasts," "Advice to a Prophet"

Prose

Sixteenth and Seventeenth Century

John Donne: selection from *Sermons*

Eighteenth Century

Henry Fielding: selection from *Tom Jones*
Edward Gibbon: selection from *The Decline and Fall of the Roman Empire*

Nineteenth Century

Charlotte Brontë: selection from *Shirley*
Charles Dickens: selection from *Hard Times*
John Stuart Mill: selection from *Autobiography*
William Makepeace Thackeray: selection from *Vanity Fair*
Henry David Thoreau: selection from *Walden*
Oscar Wilde: selection from "The Decay of Lying"

Twentieth Century

James Baldwin: selection from *Go Tell It on the Mountain*

Joseph Conrad: selection from *The Secret Agent*

Don DeLillo: selection from *White Noise*

T.S. Eliot: selection from "Tradition and the Individual Talent"

Mary Wilkins Freeman: selection from "A New England Nun"

Zora Neale Hurston: selection from *Their Eyes Were Watching God*

Mary McCarthy: selection from *Cast a Cold Eye*

Virginia Woolf: selection from *Mrs. Dalloway*

Essay Passages

The following pages list the authors and the works that have been used as the basis of essay questions on past exams.

Prose Questions

1970   George Meredith: from the novel *The Ordeal of Richard Feverel*

1971   George Orwell: from the essay "Some Thoughts on the Common Toad"

1972   James Joyce: "Eveline" — complete short story from *Dubliners*

1973   Charles Dickens: from the novel *Hard Times* and E. M. Forster: from the novel *A Passage to India*

1974   Henry James: from the novel *What Maisie Knew*

1975   Pär Lagerkvist: "Father and I" — complete short story

1976   John Gardner: from the verse novel *Jason and Medeia*

1977   No prose passage questions

1978   Samuel Johnson: from a review of Soame Jenyns's "A Free Enquiry into the Nature and Origin of Evil"

1979   Quentin Bell: from the biography *Virginia Woolf*

1980   Ralph Ellison: from the novel *Invisible Man* and Henry James: from an essay in Lippincott's Magazine

1981   George Bernard Shaw: from a letter on the death of his mother

1982   Adlai Stevenson: a letter to the Senate of the Illinois General Assembly

1983   Thomas Carlyle: from the political lectures *Past and Present*

1984   Jane Austen: from the novel *Emma*

1985   Ernest Hemingway: from the novel *A Farewell to Arms*

1986   Charles Dickens: from the novel *Dombey and Son*

1987   George Eliot: from the novel *Adam Bede*

1988   John Cheever: "Reunion" — complete short story

1989   Joseph Conrad: from the novella *Typhoon*

1990   Joan Didion: from the essay "On Self-Respect"

1991   James Boswell: from the biography *The Life of Samuel Johnson*

1992   Tillie Olsen: from the short story "I Stand Here Ironing"

1993   Lytton Strachey: from "Florence Nightingale" in *Eminent Victorians*

1994   Sarah Orne Jewett: from the short story "A White Heron"

1995   Sandra Cisneros: "Eleven" a complete short story

1996   Nathaniel Hawthorne: from the novel *The Marble Faun*

1997   Joy Kogawa: from the novel *Obasan*

1998   George Eliot: from the novel *Middlemarch*

1999   Cormac McCarthy: from the novel *The Crossing*

2000   Joseph Addison: from *The Spectator* (1712)

Seventeen of the prose passages have come from twentieth-century writers and twelve from nineteenth-century authors. Four questions have used complete short stories, one-third from nonfictional prose.

Poetry Questions

In the five years missing in the following list, no essay question was based on a poetry passage. It is very unlikely that the exam will repeat the omission of a question based on a verse text. The following poems or excerpts from the following poems have appeared on the exams.

1966   Emily Dickinson: "I never lost as much but twice"

1967   No poetry question

1968   Sir Edward Dyer: "The lowest trees have tops"

1969   W. B. Yeats: "The Wild Swans at Coole"

1970   Theodore Roethke: "Elegy for Jane"

1971   W. H. Auden: "The Unknown Citizen"

1972   No poetry question

1973   No poetry question

1974   Thomas Kinsella: from "Prologue: Downstream"

1975 No poetry question

1976 Philip Larkin: "Poetry of Departures"

1977 D. H. Lawrence: "Piano"

1978 W. H. Auden: "Law Like Love"

1979 Louise Gluck: "For Jane Meyers" and William Carlos Williams: "Spring and All"

1980 Elizabeth Bishop: "One Art"

1981 Adrienne Rich: "Storm Warnings"

1982 Richard Eberhart: "The Groundhog"

1983 W. H. Auden: "As I Walked Out One Evening"

1984 No poetry question

1985 William Wordsworth: "There Was a Boy" and Robert Frost: "The Most of It"

1986 E. K. Brathwaite: "Ogun"

1987 Sylvia Plath: "Sow"

1988 John Keats: "Bright Star" and Robert Frost: "Choose something like a star"

1989 John Updike: "The Great Scarf of Birds"

1990 William Shakespeare: "How many of my subjects . . ." from Henry IV, Part II, Act III

1991 Emily Dickinson: "The Last Night that She Lived"

1992 William Wordsworth: "One summer evening, led by her" from *The Prelude*, Book I

1993 May Swenson: "The Centaur"

1994 Edgar Allan Poe: "To Helen" and H.D.: "Helen"

1995 John Donne: "The Broken Heart"

1996 Anne Bradstreet: "The Author to Her Book"

1997 Richard Wilbur: "The Death of a Toad"

1998 Eavan Boland: "It's a Woman's World"

1999 Seamus Heaney: "Blackberry Picking"

2000 Margaret Atwood: "Siren Song" and a passage from *Odyssey*

Since 1966, twentieth-century authors have written most of the poems used on the exam, though five have been chosen from the sixteenth and eighteenth centuries, and six from nineteenth-century poets. Since 1980, many of the prose and poetry questions have been based on works by women and by minority writers.

Open Questions

In the past, the open question called for an essay discussing

1971 (using two works) the technical devices used to reveal the meanings of their titles

1972 the use of the opening scene or chapter to introduce significant themes of the play or novel

1973 no essay on drama or fiction

1974 the relevance to the present of a literary work written before 1900

1975 the use of a stereotyped character

1976 the moral meanings of a work in which an individual opposed his or her society

1977 a characters response to the past as a source of meaning in the work

1978 the relation of an implausible incident or character to the realistic aspects of the work

1979 an ostensibly evil character to whom the reader responds with some sympathy or understanding

1980 a character whose private passion is in conflict with his or her moral obligations

1981 a work in which the use of allusion (to myth or the Bible, for example) is significant

1982 the function in a work of a scene of violence

1983 a villain, the nature of villainy, and the relation of the character to meaning

1984 the relation of a single memorable line of poetry or scene in a play or novel to the whole work (an unusual and unsuccessful question)

1985 the cause of feelings of both pleasure and disquietude in a literary work

1986 the effect of an author's manipulation of time in a novel, epic, or play

1987 an author's techniques used to change a reader's attitudes, especially toward social ills

1988 an author's making internal or psychological events exciting

1989 the use of distortion in a literary work

1990 the significance in a work of a parent-child conflict

1991 the significance of two contrasting places in a play or novel

1992 the function of a confidant(e) in a play or novel

1993 a work that evokes "thoughtful laughter," why the laughter is thoughtful, and how it relates to meaning

1994 the function of a character who appears only briefly or not at all in a work

1995 how an alienated character reveals the assumptions and moral values of a society

1996 the significance in a work of an ending that shows a spiritual reassessment or moral reconciliation

1997 the contribution to the meaning of a work of a scene of a social occasion such as a wedding, funeral, or party

1998 how uncivilized, free, and wild thinking is central to the value of a work

1999 how a character's struggle with powerful conflicting forces is related to the meaning of the work

2000 how the investigation of a mystery in a novel or a play throws light on the meaning of the work

Suggested Authors

Based on the examinations of the last twenty years, the following is a list of the authors, plays, and novels that have been suggested for use on the open essay question and that students have chosen to write about. There are a handful of other titles that have appeared on the lists (Melville's novel *Redburn*, for example) that hardly anyone wrote about, and these names have been omitted. Over the years, the most frequently chosen novels have been Conrad's *Heart of Darkness*, Hawthorne's *The Scarlet Letter*, Fitzgerald's *The Great Gatsby*, and Mark Twain's *The Adventures of Huckleberry Finn*. The plays that students write about most often are Miller's *Death of a Salesman*, Williams' *The Glass Menagerie*, and Shakespeare's *Hamlet*. There have, of course, also been hundreds of other appropriate novels and plays that were not on the lists of suggested titles. A reading of this tabulation will give you a good idea of the range of the works that are probably the most widely taught in AP literature classes.

Chinua Achebe: *Things Fall Apart*

Aeschylus: the *Oresteia*

Aristophanes: *Lysistrata*

Jane Austen: *Pride and Prejudice*

Samuel Beckett: *Waiting for Godot*

Bertolt Brecht: *Mother Courage and Her Children*

Charlotte Brontë: *Jane Eyre*

Emily Brontë: *Wuthering Heights*

Albert Camus: *The Stranger*

Anton Chekhov: *The Cherry Orchard*

Kate Chopin: *The Awakening*

Joseph Conrad: *Heart of Darkness, Lord Jim, Victory*

Daniel Defoe: *Moll Flanders*

Charles Dickens: *David Copperfield, Great Expectations, Hard Times, A Tale of Two Cities*

Feodor Dostoevski: *Crime and Punishment*

Theodore Dreiser: *An American Tragedy, Sister Carrie*

Ralph Ellison: *Invisible Man*

Euripides: *Medea*

William Faulkner: *As I Lay Dying, Light in August, The Sound and the Fury*

Henry Fielding: *Joseph Andrews*

F. Scott Fitzgerald: *The Great Gatsby*

Gustave Flaubert: *Madame Bovary*

E. M. Forster: *A Passage to India*

William Golding: *Lord of the Flies*

Thomas Hardy: *Jude the Obscure, Tess of the D'Urbervilles*

Nathaniel Hawthorne: *The Scarlet Letter*

Joseph Heller: *Catch-22*

Lillian Hellman: *The Little Foxes*

Ernest Hemingway: *The Sun Also Rises*

Zora Neale Hurston: *Their Eyes Were Watching God*

Aldous Huxley: *Brave New World*

Henrik Ibsen: *A Doll's House, An Enemy of the People, Hedda Gabler, The Wild Duck*

Henry James: *The Turn of the Screw, Washington Square*

James Joyce: *A Portrait of the Artist as a Young Man*

Franz Kafka: *Metamorphosis, The Trial*

D. H. Lawrence: *Sons and Lovers*

Sinclair Lewis: *Main Street*

Gabriel García Márquez: *One Hundred Years of Solitude*

Herman Melville: *Billy Budd, Moby Dick*

Arthur Miller: *All My Sons, The Crucible, Death of a Salesman*

Toni Morrison: *Beloved, Song of Soloman*

Flannery O'Connor: *Wise Blood*

Eugene O'Neill: *The Hairy Ape, Long Day's Journey into Night*

George Orwell: *Animal Farm, 1984*

Alan Paton: *Cry, the Beloved Country*

Jean Rhys: *Wide Sargasso Sea*

Jean-Paul Sartre: *No Exit*

William Shakespeare: *Hamlet, Julius Caesar, King Lear, Macbeth, The Merchant of Venice, A Midsummer Night's Dream, Othello, Romeo and Juliet, Twelfth Night*

George Bernard Shaw: *Major Barbara, Man and Superman, Mrs. Warren's Profession, Pygmalion*

Mary Shelley: *Frankenstein*

Sophocles: *Antigone, Oedipus Rex*

John Steinbeck: *The Grapes of Wrath*

Tom Stoppard: *Rosencrantz and Guildenstern Are Dead*

August Strindberg: *Miss Julie*
Jonathan Swift: *Gulliver's Travels*
Leo Tolstoi: *Anna Karenina*
Mark Twain: *The Adventures of Huckleberry Finn*
Voltaire: *Candide*
Kurt Vonnegut: *Slaughterhouse Five*
Alice Walker: *The Color Purple*
Evelyn Waugh: *The Loved One*
Edith Wharton: *Ethan Frome, The House of Mirth*
Oscar Wilde: *The Importance of Being Earnest*
Thornton Wilder: *Our Town*
Tennessee Williams: *The Glass Menagerie, A Streetcar Named Desire*
Virginia Woolf: *To the Lighthouse*
Richard Wright: *Native Son*

Once in a while, an open question allows for the choice of a poem rather than a novel or play. The following poems have been included in the list of works on the exam:

Robert Browning: "My Last Duchess"
T. S. Eliot: "The Love Song of J. Alfred Prufrock," "The Waste Land"
Homer: the *Iliad*, the *Odyssey*
Milton: *Paradise Lost*
Pope: "The Rape of the Lock"

Do not write on one of these works if the question calls for a novel or play.

PART III

SIX FULL-LENGTH PRACTICE TESTS

A Note About the Essay Questions

The exam committee chooses the essay and multiple-choice questions to reflect as wide a range of English and American literature as possible. The choice of passages on the free-response section of the exam is, in part, determined by what appears in the multiple-choice section. Each exam uses passages by female and/or minority writers, and more often than not, at least one of the essay questions is about a poem or prose passage by a minority or female author. The passages on these practice exams reflect the kind of distribution you'll find in the real test. They include works by minority and women writers and passages from the sixteenth, seventeenth, eighteenth, nineteenth, and twentieth centuries.

If you are planning to test yourself by writing essays on the practice test topics, be sure that you do not read the discussion of the essay topics and the sample student essays (in the Answers and Explanations sections following each practice test) until after you have written your own essays for that test.

Answer Sheet for Practice Test 1

(Remove This Sheet and Use it to Mark Your Answers)

1 Ⓐ Ⓑ Ⓒ Ⓓ Ⓔ	21 Ⓐ Ⓑ Ⓒ Ⓓ Ⓔ	41 Ⓐ Ⓑ Ⓒ Ⓓ Ⓔ
2 Ⓐ Ⓑ Ⓒ Ⓓ Ⓔ	22 Ⓐ Ⓑ Ⓒ Ⓓ Ⓔ	42 Ⓐ Ⓑ Ⓒ Ⓓ Ⓔ
3 Ⓐ Ⓑ Ⓒ Ⓓ Ⓔ	23 Ⓐ Ⓑ Ⓒ Ⓓ Ⓔ	43 Ⓐ Ⓑ Ⓒ Ⓓ Ⓔ
4 Ⓐ Ⓑ Ⓒ Ⓓ Ⓔ	24 Ⓐ Ⓑ Ⓒ Ⓓ Ⓔ	44 Ⓐ Ⓑ Ⓒ Ⓓ Ⓔ
5 Ⓐ Ⓑ Ⓒ Ⓓ Ⓔ	25 Ⓐ Ⓑ Ⓒ Ⓓ Ⓔ	45 Ⓐ Ⓑ Ⓒ Ⓓ Ⓔ
6 Ⓐ Ⓑ Ⓒ Ⓓ Ⓔ	26 Ⓐ Ⓑ Ⓒ Ⓓ Ⓔ	46 Ⓐ Ⓑ Ⓒ Ⓓ Ⓔ
7 Ⓐ Ⓑ Ⓒ Ⓓ Ⓔ	27 Ⓐ Ⓑ Ⓒ Ⓓ Ⓔ	47 Ⓐ Ⓑ Ⓒ Ⓓ Ⓔ
8 Ⓐ Ⓑ Ⓒ Ⓓ Ⓔ	28 Ⓐ Ⓑ Ⓒ Ⓓ Ⓔ	48 Ⓐ Ⓑ Ⓒ Ⓓ Ⓔ
9 Ⓐ Ⓑ Ⓒ Ⓓ Ⓔ	29 Ⓐ Ⓑ Ⓒ Ⓓ Ⓔ	49 Ⓐ Ⓑ Ⓒ Ⓓ Ⓔ
10 Ⓐ Ⓑ Ⓒ Ⓓ Ⓔ	30 Ⓐ Ⓑ Ⓒ Ⓓ Ⓔ	50 Ⓐ Ⓑ Ⓒ Ⓓ Ⓔ
11 Ⓐ Ⓑ Ⓒ Ⓓ Ⓔ	31 Ⓐ Ⓑ Ⓒ Ⓓ Ⓔ	51 Ⓐ Ⓑ Ⓒ Ⓓ Ⓔ
12 Ⓐ Ⓑ Ⓒ Ⓓ Ⓔ	32 Ⓐ Ⓑ Ⓒ Ⓓ Ⓔ	52 Ⓐ Ⓑ Ⓒ Ⓓ Ⓔ
13 Ⓐ Ⓑ Ⓒ Ⓓ Ⓔ	33 Ⓐ Ⓑ Ⓒ Ⓓ Ⓔ	53 Ⓐ Ⓑ Ⓒ Ⓓ Ⓔ
14 Ⓐ Ⓑ Ⓒ Ⓓ Ⓔ	34 Ⓐ Ⓑ Ⓒ Ⓓ Ⓔ	54 Ⓐ Ⓑ Ⓒ Ⓓ Ⓔ
15 Ⓐ Ⓑ Ⓒ Ⓓ Ⓔ	35 Ⓐ Ⓑ Ⓒ Ⓓ Ⓔ	
16 Ⓐ Ⓑ Ⓒ Ⓓ Ⓔ	36 Ⓐ Ⓑ Ⓒ Ⓓ Ⓔ	
17 Ⓐ Ⓑ Ⓒ Ⓓ Ⓔ	37 Ⓐ Ⓑ Ⓒ Ⓓ Ⓔ	
18 Ⓐ Ⓑ Ⓒ Ⓓ Ⓔ	38 Ⓐ Ⓑ Ⓒ Ⓓ Ⓔ	
19 Ⓐ Ⓑ Ⓒ Ⓓ Ⓔ	39 Ⓐ Ⓑ Ⓒ Ⓓ Ⓔ	
20 Ⓐ Ⓑ Ⓒ Ⓓ Ⓔ	40 Ⓐ Ⓑ Ⓒ Ⓓ Ⓔ	

CUT HERE

Practice Test 1

Section 1: Multiple-Choice Questions

Time: 60 Minutes

54 Questions

Directions: This section contains selections from two passages of prose and two poems with questions on their content, style, and form. Read each selection carefully. Choose the best answer of the five choices.

Questions 1–13. Read the passage carefully before you begin to answer the questions.

Of Superstition

It were better to have no opinion of God at all, than such an opinion as is unworthy of him: for the one is unbelief, the other is contumely: and certainly su-
(5) perstition is the reproach of the Deity. Plutarch saith well to that purpose: *Surely* (saith he) *I had rather a great deal men should say there was no such man at all as Plutarch, than that they*
(10) *should say that there was one Plutarch that would eat his children as soon as they were born*; as the poets speak of Saturn. And as the contumely is greater towards God, so the danger is greater to-
(15) wards men. Atheism leaves a man to sense, to philosophy, to natural piety, to laws, to reputation; all which may be guides to an outward moral virtue, though religion were not, but supersti-
(20) tion dismounts all these, and erecteth an absolute monarchy in the minds of men. Therefore atheism did never perturb states; for it makes men wary of themselves, as looking no further: and we see
(25) the times inclined to atheism (as the time of Augustus Caesar) were civil times. But superstition hath been the confusion of many states, and bringeth in a new *primum mobile,* that ravisheth
(30) all the spheres of government. The master of superstition is the people; and in all superstition wise men follow fools; and arguments are fitted to practice, in a reversed order. It was gravely said by
(35) some of the prelates in the Council of Trent, where the doctrine of the Schoolmen bare great sway, *that the Schoolmen were like astronomers, which did feign eccentrics and epicy-*
(40) *cles, and such engines of orbs, to save the phenomena,*[1] *though they knew there were no such things*; and in like manner, that the Schoolmen had framed a number of subtle and intricate axioms and
(45) theorems to save the practice of the Church. The causes of superstition are: pleasing and sensual rites and ceremonies; excess of outward and pharisaical holiness; overgreat reverence of
(50) traditions, which cannot but load the Church; the stratagems of prelates for their own ambition and lucre; the favoring too much of good intentions, which

GO ON TO THE NEXT PAGE

openeth the gate to conceits and novel-
(55) ties; the taking an aim at divine matters
by human, which cannot but breed mixture of imaginations; and lastly, barbarous times, especially joined with
calamities and disasters. Superstition,
(60) without a veil, is a deformed thing; for,
as it addeth deformity to an ape to be so
like a man, so the similitude of superstition to religion makes it the more deformed. And as wholesome meat
(65) corrupteth to little worms, so good forms
and orders corrupt into a number of petty
observances. There is a superstition in
avoiding superstition, when men think
to do best if they go furthest from the su-
(70) perstition formerly received: therefore
care would be had that (as it fareth in ill
purgings) the good be not taken away
with the bad; which commonly is done,
when the people is the reformer.

¹eccentrics...phenomena: irregularities and secondary orbits (of
the heavenly bodies) invented by astronomers to account for
astronomical facts.

1. The passage is an example of the

   A. short story
   B. essay
   C. novel
   D. epistle
   E. oration

2. According to the passage, the atheist is

   A. incapable of morality
   B. more likely to be immoral than a believer
   C. influenced to act morally
   D. likely to be indifferent to reputation
   E. a danger to the harmony of the state

3. The phrase "though religion were not" (line 19) can be best understood to mean

   A. even if religion is lacking
   B. as religion cannot do
   C. although religious people believe differently
   D. in spite of religion
   E. if religious belief were untrue

4. In line 20, the word "dismounts" is

   A. an auxiliary verb
   B. a plural form of a noun
   C. a participle modifying "superstition"
   D. a transitive verb
   E. an intransitive verb

5. The figure of speech in lines 29–30 ("*primum mobile* . . . government") is based upon

   A. law
   B. political economy
   C. astronomy
   D. solid geometry
   E. history

6. Which of the following is an example of what lines 33–34 call "arguments . . . fitted to practice, in a reversed order"?

   A. "*astronomers, which did feign eccentrics and epicycles*" (lines 38–40)
   B. "pleasing and sensual rites and ceremonies" (lines 47–48)

C. "excess of outward and pharisaical holiness" (lines 48–49)

D. "the taking an aim at divine matters by human" (line 55–56)

E. "calamities and disasters" (line 59)

7. Lines 38–42 compare the Schoolmen to astronomers because both

A. depend upon logical arguments in their studies

B. are highly educated in abstruse subjects

C. are free from superstitious belief

D. are uniquely committed to intellectual pursuits

E. invent data to suit their conclusions

8. According to the passage, at which of the following times is superstition most likely to flourish?

A. a time of prosperity

B. a time of scientific discovery

C. a time of political change

D. a time of solar and lunar eclipse

E. a time of famine and flood

9. The sentence "And as wholesome meat . . . petty observances" (lines 64–67) is an example of

A. metaphor

B. paradox

C. understatement

D. simile

E. *ad hominem* argument

10. The danger described in the conclusion of the passage (lines 67–74) is that

A. superstition may blind men to the truth of religion

B. superstition may lead men to presume knowledge of the supernatural

C. the attempt to suppress superstition may lead to injustice

D. the reformation of an evil may disrupt the stability of the state

E. the recurrence of superstition is most likely when people believe it has been suppressed

11. The author's condemnation of superstition is conveyed by the words of all the following EXCEPT

A. "wary of themselves" (lines 23–24)

B. "confusion" (line 28)

C. "pharisaical holiness" (lines 48–49)

D. "lucre" (line 52)

E. "mixture of imaginations" (lines 56–57)

12. All of the following phrases employ figurative language EXCEPT

A. "erecteth an absolute monarchy" (lines 20–21)

B. "the stratagems of prelates for their own ambition" (lines 51–52)

C. "which openeth the gate to conceits and novelties" (lines 53–55)

D. "without a veil" (line 60)

E. "as it fareth in ill purgings" (lines 71–72)

GO ON TO THE NEXT PAGE

13. For which of the following reasons can it be argued that the style of the passage differs from that of most modern informal prose composition?

  I.   The paragraph is much longer.

  II. The syntax is more complex.

  III. The allusions are more obscure.

A. I only

B. I and II only

C. I and III only

D. II and III only

E. I, II, and III

Questions 14–29. Read the following poem carefully before you begin to answer the questions.

Love's Diet

To what a cumbersome unwieldiness
And burdenous corpulence my love had grown
   But that I did, to make it less
   And keep it in proportión,
(5) Give it a diet, made it feed upon
That which love worst endures, discretión.

Above one sigh a day I allowed him not,
Of which my fortune and my faults had part;
   And if sometimes by stealth he got
(10)   A she sigh from my mistress' heart
And thought to feast on that, I let him see
'Twas neither very sound, nor meant to me.

If he wrung from me a tear, I brined it so
With scorn or shame that him it nourished not;
(15)   If he sucked hers, I let him know
   'Twas not a tear which he had got;
His drink was counterfeit as was his meat;
For eyes which roll towards all weep not, but sweat.

Whatever he would dictate, I writ that,
(20) But burnt my letters. When she writ to me,
   And that that favor made him fat,
   I said, if any title be
Conveyed by this, ah, what doth it avail
To be the fortieth name in an entail?

(25) Thus I reclaimed my buzzard love to fly
At what, and when, and how, and where I choose;
   Now negligent of sport I lie,
   And now as other falc'ners use,
I spring a mistress, swear, write, sigh, and weep;
(30) And the game killed or lost, go talk, and sleep.

14. The extended metaphor of stanzas 1–4 compares love to

  A. an unwilling dieter

  B. an illness

  C. an unruly child

  D. a prisoner in jail

  E. a lawyer

15. In line 2, the verb "had grown" would be written by a modern prose writer as

  A. grew

  B. has grown

  C. would have grown

  D. did grow

  E. has been growing

GO ON TO THE NEXT PAGE

16. The figure of speech used through stanzas 1–4 is an example of

    A. simile

    B. personification

    C. irony

    D. ambiquity

    E. apostrophe

17. In the last line of the second stanza, the speaker suggests that

    A. the lady is deeply in love

    B. only men, not women, sigh for love

    C. the lady does not sigh for him

    D. the sighs of the lady are more genuine than his

    E. true love cannot feast on sighs

18. According to the second and third stanzas, the food and drink by which love grows are

    A. faults and fortunes

    B. scorn and shame

    C. the heart and the eyes

    D. sighs and tears

    E. stealth and counterfeiting

19. The metaphor of lines 22–24 compares winning the lady's favor with

    A. finishing in the fortieth position in a race

    B. being obligated to work for forty days

    C. inheriting a fortune

    D. waiting until middle age to be married

    E. being placed very low on a long list

20. According to the poem, which of the following is not a potentially fattening food?

    A. sighs

    B. a man's tears

    C. a lady's tears

    D discretion

    E. love letters

21. The word "Thus" which begins the last stanza of the poem refers to

    A. "entail" (line 24)

    B. lines 19 and 20

    C. stanza 1

    D. stanza 4

    E. lines 1–24

22. In lines 27–28, the repeated "Now" . . . "now" would be phrased in modern English

    A. sometimes . . . other times

    B. now . . . then

    C. both . . . and

    D. if now . . . then

    E. once . . . now

23. In the next-to-last line of the poem, the three verbs "sigh," "weep," and "write" are used to

    I. recall the events of stanzas 2, 3, and 4

    II. show how deeply the speaker now feels about love

    III. recount the expected behavior of a lover

    A. II only

    B. I and II only

    C. I and III only

    D. II and III only

    E. I, II, and III

24. In stanza 5, all the following words are part of the central metaphor EXCEPT

    A. "fly" (line 25)

    B. "negligent" (line 27)

    C. "spring" (line 29)

    D. "game" (line 30)

    E. "killed" (line 30)

25. In the final stanza of the poem, the speaker

    A. has changed and now accepts the possibility of a genuine love

    B. is more respectful of women than he was at the beginning of the poem

    C. has become pessimistic about the love of women

    D. is self-congratulating, cynical, and content

    E. is divided in his mind — wanting to believe in love but afraid of commitment

26. Which of the following best describes the logical organization of the poem?

    A. Stanza 1 — stanzas 2, 3, 4 — stanza 5

    B. Stanza 1 — stanzas 2, 3 — stanzas 4, 5

    C. Stanzas 1, 2 — stanza 3 — stanzas 4, 5

    D. Stanzas 1, 2, 3 — stanzas 4, 5

    E. Stanza 1 — stanza 2 — stanzas 3, 4, 5

27. The poem draws its imagery from all the following EXCEPT

    A. falconry

    B. law

    C. eating

    D. drinking

    E. music

28. Of the following words, which best suggest by their sound and length the qualities that they denote?

    A. "cumbersome unwieldiness and burdenous corpulence" (lines 1–2)

    B. "A she sigh" (line 10)

    C. "that that favor made him fat" (line 21)

    D. "the fortieth name in an entail" (line 24)

    E. "buzzard love" (line 25)

GO ON TO THE NEXT PAGE

29. The poem alludes to all the following conventional ideas about how a lover should behave EXCEPT

   A. the lover is unable to sleep

   B. the lover is melancholy and often weeps

   C. the lover sits alone thinking about the loved one

   D. the lover is so distracted by love that his clothes are disheveled

   E. the lover writes tender love letters to the beloved

Questions 30–42. Read the following passage carefully before you begin to answer the questions.

Falsehood is so easy, truth so difficult. The pencil is conscious of a delightful facility in drawing a griffin — the longer the claws, and the larger the wings, the
(5) better; but that marvellous facility which we mistook for genius is apt to forsake us when we want to draw a real unexaggerated lion. Examine your words well, and you will find that even when you
(10) have no motive to be false, it is a very hard thing to say the exact truth, even about your immediate feelings — much harder than to say something fine about them which is *not* the exact truth.
(15) It is for this rare, precious quality of truthfulness that I delight in many Dutch paintings, which lofty-minded people despise. I find a source of delicious sympathy in these faithful pictures of a mo-
(20) notonous homely existence, which has been the fate of so many more among my fellow-mortals than a life of pomp or of absolute indigence, of tragic suffering or of world-stirring actions. I turn,
(25) without shrinking, from cloud-borne angels, from prophets, sibyls, and heroic warriors, to an old woman bending over her flowerpot, or eating her solitary din-
(30) ner, while the noonday light, softened perhaps by a screen of leaves, falls on her mob-cap, and just touches the rim of her spinning-wheel, and her stone jug, and all those cheap common things
(35) which are the precious necessaries of life to her; — or I turn to that village wedding, kept between four brown walls, where an awkward bridegroom opens the dance with a high-shouldered,
(40) broad-faced bride, while elderly and middle-aged friends look on, with very irregular noses and lips, and probably with quart-pots in their hands, but with an expression of unmistakable content-
(45) ment and good-will. "Foh!" says my idealistic friend, "what vulgar details! What good is there in taking all these pains to give an exact likeness of old women and clowns? What a low phase
(50) of life! — what clumsy, ugly people!"
But bless us, things may be lovable that are not altogether handsome, I hope? I am not at all sure that the majority of the human race have not been

(55) ugly, and even among those "lords of their kind," the British, squat figures, ill-shapen nostrils, and dingy complexions are not startling exceptions. Yet there is a great deal of family love amongst us. I (60) have a friend or two whose class of features is such that the Apollo curl on the summit of their brows would be decidedly trying; yet to my certain knowledge tender hearts have beaten for them, and (65) their miniatures — flattering, but still not lovely — are kissed in secret by motherly lips. I have seen many an excellent matron, who could never in her best days have been handsome, and yet (70) she had a packet of yellow love-letters in a private drawer, and sweet children showered kisses on her sallow cheeks. And I believe there have been plenty of young heroes, of middle stature and fee-(75) ble beards, who have felt quite sure they could never love anything more insignificant than a Diana, and yet have found themselves in middle life happily settled with a wife who waddles. Yes! thank (80) God; human feeling is like the mighty rivers that bless the earth: it does not wait for beauty — it flows with resistless force and brings beauty with it.

30. In the first paragraph, the author is primarily concerned with the

    A. superiority of truth to fiction

    B. difficulty of expressing the truth

    C. vagaries of mythological illustration

    D. definitions of truth and fiction

    E. impossibility of ever reaching the truth

31. The griffin, as it is used in the first paragraph, is parallel to which of the following in the second paragraph?

    A. "Dutch paintings" (lines 16–17)

    B. "lofty-minded people" (line 17)

    C. "cloud-borne angels,...prophets, sibyls" (lines 25–26)

    D. "the rim of her spinning-wheel, and her stone jug" (lines 32–33)

    E. "old women and clowns" (line 49)

32. In the second paragraph, the author refers to "lofty-minded people" in order to

    A. claim kinship with them

    B. demonstrate her own humility

    C. give the reader an ally to identify with

    D. call their ideas into question

    E. give an equal amount of consideration to views that differ from her own

33. In line 43, the reference to "quart-pots" in the hands of the wedding guests

    A. suggests that women's work continued even at a wedding party

    B. shows how overcrowded the wedding table had become

    C. alludes to gifts of plants brought to the wedding

    D. reveals that guests are chiefly concerned with eating

    E. indicates that the guests are drinking ale or beer

GO ON TO THE NEXT PAGE

34. Which of the following terms are used in the second paragraph to refer to those whose ideas the speaker does NOT share?

  I.   "lofty-minded people" (line 17)

  II. "my fellow-mortals" (line 22)

 III. "my idealistic friend" (line 46)

  A. I only

  B. I and II only

  C. I and III only

  D. II and III only

  E. I, II, and III

35. Which of the following describes the relationship of the third paragraph to the second?

  I.   The third paragraph gives additional examples of a "monotonous homely existence."

  II. The third paragraph replies to the objections raised at the end of the second paragraph.

 III. The third paragraph reaches a philosophical conclusion about the subject of the second paragraph.

  A. I only

  B. I and II only

  C. I and III only

  D. II and III only

  E. I, II, and III

36. In the third paragraph, second sentence, "even among those 'lords of their kind,' the British, squat figures, ill-shapen nostrils, and dingy complexions are not startling exceptions" (lines 55–58), is an example of

  A. understatement

  B. personification

  C. paradox

  D. simile

  E. syllogism

37. In the phrase "young heroes, of middle stature and feeble beards," (lines 74–75), which of the following words is used ironically?

  A. "young"

  B. "heroes"

  C. "middle"

  D. "stature"

  E. "feeble"

38. In the third paragraph, the "friend or two" (line 60), the "excellent matron" (lines 67–68), and the "wife" (line 79) have in common that they are

  A. no longer beautiful

  B. secretly in love

  C. loved regardless of their looks

  D. people the author has observed in real life

  E. the objects of corrosive satire

39. In line 82, the pronoun "it" ("it flows") refers to

A. God

B. human feeling

C. rivers

D. earth

E. beauty

40. The passage argues that ugliness is

 I. more common than handsomeness

 II. lovable

 III. made beautiful by feeling

A. III only

B. I and II only

C. I and III only

D. II and III only

E. I, II, and III

41. If the author of this passage were a novelist, her novels would probably be described as

A. experimental

B. romantic

C. stream-of-consciousness

D. realistic

E. symbolic

42. With which of the following statements would the author of this passage be most likely to agree?

A. The most important quality of a painting is its accuracy in rendering life.

B. The novel must teach the love of virtue and the hatred of vice.

C. The poor are closer to reality than the rich.

D. The greatest of painters are the Dutch.

E. Human sympathy will create beauty.

GO ON TO THE NEXT PAGE

Questions 43–54. Read the following poem carefully before you begin to answer the questions.

A Description of the Morning

Now hardly here and there an hackney-coach
Appearing, showed the ruddy morn's approach.
Now Betty from her master's bed had flown,
And softly stole to discompose her own;
(5)   The slip-shod 'prentice from his master's door
Had pared the dirt, and sprinkled round the floor.
Now Moll had whirled her mop with dext'rous airs,
Prepared to scrub the entry and the stairs.
The youth with broomy stumps began to trace
(10)   The kennel-edge, where wheels had worn the place.
The small-coal man was heard with cadence deep,
Till drowned in shriller notes of chimney-sweep:
Duns at his lordship's gate began to meet;
And brickdust Moll had screamed through half a street.
(15)   The turnkey now his flock returning sees,
Duly let out a-nights to steal for fees:
The watchful bailiffs take their silent stands,
And schoolboys lag with satchels in their hands.

43. Given the title of the poem, which of the following might a reader expect but not find?

    A. an account of the sounds of the morning

    B. an account of the countryside at daybreak

    C. a reference to children on the way to school

    D. an account of the early activity indoors

    E. a picture of urban life in the morning

44. The focus of the poem is on

    A. working class men and women

    B. aristocrats

    C. children

    D. white-collar workers

    E. the unemployed

45. The speaker of the poem does NOT

    A. live in the city

    B. understand the implication of lines 3–4

    C. approve of Moll (lines 7–8)

    D. make overt moral judgments

    E. perceive the intention of the bailiffs (line 17)

46. The social range of the poem encompasses all the following EXCEPT the

  A. aristocrat

  B. servant

  C. clergyman

  D. apprentice

  E. peddler

47. In line 4, Betty discomposes her bed

  A. as part of her duties as a maidservant

  B. in preparation for the laundry

  C. to give the appearance she has slept in it

  D. because the beds are made of straw

  E. because she is unable to sleep

48. In line 13, "Duns" are

  A. salesmen

  B. out-of-work lawyers

  C. fools

  D. upper servants

  E. bill collectors

49. In line 15, the metaphor compares the turnkey to a

  A. shepherd

  B. farmer

  C. ticket-taker

  D. cobbler

  E. butcher

50. In line 15, the "flock" is returning to a

  A. pub

  B. factory

  C. barn

  D. slaughterhouse

  E. prison

51. The word "Duly" in line 16 can be understood to mean

  I. fitly, appropriately

  II. punctually, on time

  III. day after day

  A. I only

  B. II only

  C. III only

  D. I and II only

  E. II and III only

52. If successful, the "watchful bailiffs" in line 17 will provide additions to the

  A. duns at his lordship's gate

  B. worn kennel-edge

  C. army and the navy

  D. turnkey's flock

  E. laggard schoolboys

GO ON TO THE NEXT PAGE

53. The poem is an example of which of the following verse forms?

   A. blank verse

   B. couplet

   C. terza rima

   D. ballad meter

   E. free verse

54. Compared to most poetry, this poem is notable for infrequently using

   A. rhyme

   B. figurative language

   C. realistic detail

   D. syntax

   E. meter

IF YOU FINISH BEFORE TIME IS CALLED, CHECK YOUR WORK ON THIS SECTION ONLY. DO NOT WORK ON ANY OTHER SECTION IN THE TEST.

Section II: Essay Questions

Time: 2 Hours

3 Questions

Question 1

(Suggested time — 40 minutes. This question accounts for one-third of the total essay section score.)

Directions: The following passage is the conclusion of Samuel Johnson's "Life of Savage," an account of the eighteenth-century writer Richard Savage, who died in great poverty in 1743.

Read the passage carefully. Write a well-organized essay in which you discuss Johnson's evaluation of Savage and the resources of language Johnson employs to communicate his opinions effectively.

For his life, or for his writings, none who candidly consider his fortune will think an apology either necessary or difficult. If he was not always sufficiently

(5) instructed in his subject, his knowledge was at least greater than could have been attained by others in the same state. If his works were sometimes unfinished, accuracy cannot reasonably be exacted

(10) from a man oppressed with want, which he has no hope of relieving but by a speedy publication. The insolence and resentment of which he is accused, were not easily to be avoided by a great mind,

(15) irritated by perpetual hardships, and constrained hourly to return the spurns of contempt, and repress the insolence of prosperity; and vanity surely may be readily pardoned in him, to whom life

(20) afforded no other comforts than barren praises, and the consciousness of deserving them.

Those are no proper judges of his conduct who have slumbered away their

(25) time on the down of plenty; nor will any wise man presume to say, "Had I been in Savage's condition, I should have lived or written better than Savage."

This relation will not be wholly with-

(30) out its use, if those who languish under any part of his sufferings shall be enabled to fortify their patience, by reflecting that they feel only those afflictions from which the abilities of Savage did

(35) not exempt him; or those, who, in confidence of superior capacities or attainments, disregard the common maxims of life, shall be reminded that nothing will supply the want of prudence, and that

(40) negligence and irregularity, long continued, will make knowledge useless, wit ridiculous, and genius contemptible.

GO ON TO THE NEXT PAGE

Question 2

(Suggested time — 40 minutes. This question counts toward one-third of the total essay section score.)

Directions: Read the following poem carefully. Then write a cohesive essay in which you show how the language of each stanza reveals the perceptions and feelings of the speaker.

The birds began at four o'clock,
Their period for dawn,
A music numerous as space
But neighboring as noon.

(5)   I could not count their force,
Their voices did expend
As brook by brook bestows itself
To multiply the pond.

Their witnesses were not
(10)   Except occasional man,
In homely industry arrayed
To overtake the morn.

Nor was it for applause
(That I could ascertain)
(15)   But independent ecstasy
Of deity and men.

By six, the flood had done.
No tumult there had been
Of dressing, or departure,
(20)   And yet the band was gone.

The sun engrossed the east,
The day controlled the world,
The miracle that introduced
Forgotten, as fulfilled.

Question 3

(Suggested time — 40 minutes. This question counts toward one-third of the total essay section score.)

Directions: An eating scene is common in drama and fiction. It may be a simple meal or a banquet, a holiday party or ordinary family dinner, but the work would not be quite the same without it.

Choose a play, epic, or novel which contains such a scene of eating, and write an essay in which you discuss what the scene reveals, how the scene is related to the meaning of the work as a whole, and by what means the author makes the scene effective.

Focus your essay on only ONE scene. Do not summarize the plot. You may write on one of the following works or any other novel, epic, or play of your choice of equivalent literary merit.

A Portrait of the Artist as a Young Man

Beowulf

Little Dorrit

Great Expectations

Jane Eyre

Wuthering Heights

The Great Gatsby

the Iliad

the Odyssey

The Tempest

Macbeth

The Mayor of Casterbridge

Pride and Prejudice

Invisible Man

The Birthday Party

The Three Sisters

Mrs. Dalloway

To the Lighthouse

Ethan Frome

A Passage to India

The Importance of Being Earnest

Our Town

Lord of the Flies

The Joy Luck Club

IF YOU FINISH BEFORE TIME IS CALLED, CHECK YOUR WORK ON THIS SECTION ONLY. DO NOT WORK ON ANY OTHER SECTION IN THE TEST.

Answer Key

Section I: Multiple-Choice Questions

First Prose Passage	First Poem
1. B	**14.** A
2. C	**15.** C
3. A	**16.** B
4. D	**17.** C
5. C	**18.** D
6. A	**19.** E
7. E	**20.** D
8. E	**21.** E
9. D	**22.** A
10. C	**23.** C
11. A	**24.** B
12. B	**25.** D
13. E	**26.** A
	27. E
	28. A
	29. D

Second Prose Passage

30. B
31. C
32. D
33. E
34. C
35. E
36. A
37. B
38. C
39. B
40. E
41. D
42. E

Second Poem

43. B
44. A
45. D
46. C
47. C
48. E
49. A
50. E
51. D
52. D
53. B
54. B

Practice Test 1 Scoring Worksheet

Use the following worksheet to arrive at a probable final AP grade on Practice Test 1. While it is sometimes difficult to be objective enough to score one's own essay, you can use the sample essay answers that follow to approximate an essay score for yourself. You may also give your essays (along with the sample essays) to a friend or relative to score if you feel confident that the individual has the knowledge necessary to make such a judgment and that he or she will feel comfortable in doing so.

Section I: Multiple Choice

$$\underset{\substack{\text{right} \\ \text{answers}}}{\rule{2.5cm}{0.4pt}} - (1/4 \text{ or } .25 \times \underset{\substack{\text{wrong} \\ \text{answers}}}{\rule{2cm}{0.4pt}}) = \underset{\substack{\text{multiple-choice} \\ \text{raw score}}}{\rule{2.5cm}{0.4pt}}$$

$$\underset{\substack{\text{multiple-choice} \\ \text{raw score}}}{\rule{3cm}{0.4pt}} \times 1.25 = \underset{\substack{\text{multiple-choice} \\ \text{converted score}}}{\rule{3cm}{0.4pt}} \text{(of possible 67.5)}$$

Section II: Essay Questions

$$\underset{\substack{\text{question 1} \\ \text{raw score}}}{\rule{2cm}{0.4pt}} + \underset{\substack{\text{question 2} \\ \text{raw score}}}{\rule{2cm}{0.4pt}} + \underset{\substack{\text{question 3} \\ \text{raw score}}}{\rule{2cm}{0.4pt}} = \underset{\text{essay}}{\rule{2cm}{0.4pt}}$$

$$\underset{\substack{\text{essay} \\ \text{raw score}}}{\rule{3cm}{0.4pt}} \times 3.055 = \underset{\substack{\text{essay} \\ \text{converted score}}}{\rule{3cm}{0.4pt}} \text{(of possible 82.5)}$$

Final Score

$$\underset{\substack{\text{multiple-choice} \\ \text{converted score}}}{\rule{3cm}{0.4pt}} + \underset{\substack{\text{essay} \\ \text{converted score}}}{\rule{3cm}{0.4pt}} = \underset{\substack{\text{final} \\ \text{converted score}}}{\rule{3cm}{0.4pt}} \text{(of possible 150)}$$

Probable Final AP Score

Final Converted Score	Probable AP Score
150–100	5
99–86	4
85–67	3
66–0	1 or 2

Answers and Explanations for Practice Test 1

Section I: Multiple-Choice Questions

First Prose Passage

1. **B.** An essay is a short composition on a single subject. This is Francis Bacon's essay "Of Superstition," written late in the sixteenth century. Most students would find this prose more difficult to read than the other tests in this multiple-choice section. If you do find a first passage hard to deal with, go on to the others and come back to the first section later. Your score is based on the total number of right answers, and you don't want to waste too much time on one passage at the expense of the rest of the exam. "Of Superstition" is non-fiction, so the two fiction forms, short story (**A**) and novel (**C**), can be eliminated. An epistle (**D**) is a letter, but this passage is not addressed to a specific person. An oration (**E**) is a formal, public speech.

2. **C.** Choices **A**, **B**, **D**, and **E** contradict the passage. Lines 15–21 argue that the atheist is less dangerous to civil order than the superstitious person, because the atheist may be guided to a natural moral virtue by philosophy and sense and by a respect for law and reputation.

3. **A.** Though none of these paraphrases is ideal, the best of the five choices is **A**. Remember that the instructions call only for the "best" answer of the five, not the "right," "correct," or "ideal" answer. The idiom "were not" of three hundred years ago is now expressed by "there were no." With questions like this one, you must rely on what has been said already and the immediate context of the phrase.

4. **D.** Though the common modern use of the verb "to dismount" is as an intransitive verb (a verb without a direct object), as in to dismount from a horse or from gymnastics apparatus, the verb here clearly has an object, "these." Be sure to look carefully at the text before answering a question like this one. The word "dismounts" could be a plural form of a noun (**B**) or an intransitive verb (**E**), and you can discover the right answer only from the context in the passage.

5. **C.** The allusion is to medieval astronomy in which the outermost sphere of the universe (the *primum mobile*) was believed to control the motions of the other spheres. Even if you are unfamiliar with the notion of the *primum mobile*, the use of "spheres" should suggest astronomy. Choice **D** is nasty because "spheres" also is a term of solid geometry. The passage uses another analogy from astronomy later on.

6. **A.** To answer this question, you must first understand the meaning of line 33. The phrase refers to the practice of the superstitious of inventing data to fit events that have already happened. If I spill my soup on Monday and get a parking ticket on Tuesday, I may superstitiously claim that spilling soup leads to parking tickets. The astronomers referred to in

lines 38–42, who wished to confirm what they believed were the orbits of heavenly bodies, invented other motions of the bodies to explain away what did not fit their preconceived ideas.

7. **E.** Bacon accuses the Schoolmen (the medieval university teachers of philosophy and theology) of being "like astronomers, which did feign . . . ," that is, both invented data ("eccentrics and epicycles," "intricate axioms and theorems") to fit conclusions they had reached already. Choices **A, B, C,** and **D** denote an approval of the astronomers and Schoolmen, just the opposite of what the essay says.

8. **E.** In the list of the causes of superstition (lines 46–59), the conclusion is "barbarous times, especially joined with calamities and disasters." It is possible that a time of political change would be a time of calamity, but "famine and flood" are clearly more explicit examples of disasters.

9. **D.** The sentence is a simile, a comparison with "like" or "as" expressed. The author here uses "as . . . so." The same figure as a metaphor would be "Good forms are wholesome meats corrupted." An *ad hominem* argument **E** is one that attacks an opponent rather than discusses the issues.

10. **C.** The passage warns against a "superstition in avoiding superstition," that is, going too far in the *other* direction in order to avoid an error of superstition. This error may sacrifice the "good" as well as the "bad." The most plausible of the five answers is **C**, which describes a good (justice) that may be lost by an overzealous suppression of the bad (superstition). Notice that the incorrect answers are not of themselves untrue. They are ideas that are plausible but simply are not relevant to this question. Good wrong answers in multiple-choice exams are often sensible or even profound. Don't let the ring of moral truth distract you from exactly what the question has asked you.

11. **A.** To answer a question like this, you must look at each of these phrases in context. In this case, the first option, "wary of themselves" in lines 23–24, is used to describe an effect of atheism, which makes men "wary of themselves." A shrewd test taker would realize that this must be the right answer, because it describes the atheist, not the superstitious. To go through the passage examining options **B, C, D,** and **E** would waste time. There are some questions where you can't avoid checking on all five answers. When you find one that you can answer without wasting time, be glad of the discovery and go on to the next question. Unfortunately, the right answer is not always the first one you come to. A mean test writer would put the correct answer here as **E**.

12. **B.** In this phrase, "stratagems," "prelates," and "ambition" are all used literally to refer to the deceitful practices of ambitious churchmen. Choice **E** is a simile using "as." Choices **A, C,** and **D** are metaphors, using "monarchy," "gate," and "veil" figuratively. A real monarchy cannot exist in the mind, a real gate does not lead to conceits, and superstition cannot wear a real veil.

13. **E.** All three describe differences between Bacon's essay and modern informal prose. Bacon has clearly not had the advantages of modern instruction in the craft of paragraphing, because his whole essay has only one. His sentences are much longer and often more complex than is usual in modern prose. His allusions — to Plutarch, Saturn, astronomy, Roman history, and medieval philosophy, for example — are likely to be unfamiliar to many modern readers.

First Poem

The poem is John Donne's "Love's Diet."

14. **A.** The first four stanzas imagine a speaker and his love for a woman as two distinct people. The speaker forces the personified love to go on a diet so it will not grow out of his control. This first question of the set is an easy one, and the exam normally begins a set of questions with one of the easier questions. The *conceit* (an ingenious metaphor) of love as a reluctant dieter is the basis of the poem's title and the chief figure of the first four stanzas.

15. **C.** Lines 1–5 can be paraphrased as follows: Unless I had put my love on a diet to decrease its size and keep it manageable, it would have grown gigantic and uncontrollable. The sentence is conditional, and the verb "had grown" is a subjunctive meaning "would have grown," though it looks like a past perfect tense of an indicative verb. The point is that the speaker saw the danger and put love on a diet before it grew too fat.

16. **B.** The figure, or conceit, is a metaphor, not a simile. The comparison of a thing, quality, or idea to a human is also an example of personification. Notice that the pronouns for this love/person are "it," "he," or "him."

17. **C.** To enjoy this poem, we must accept the unlikely situation of a man who does not want to be in love arguing with his personified love for a woman. The speaker hopes to disenchant love by finding fault with the lady. Here, though he admits that lady has sighed, he argues that the sigh is unsound, impaired, or invalid, and not meant for him anyway. Choice **E** contradicts the figure of this stanza; love *can* feed on sighs. The more the lovers sigh, the greater their love will grow. But the speaker argues that her sigh cannot be fattening because it is meant for someone else. The speaker's own sighs are also calorie-free because they are not for love, but sighs for his own faults and fortune.

18. **D.** As stanza 2 is based on the notion of the sigh as the food of lovers, stanza 3 assumes that tears are the drink of lovers. The idea of a lover's sighing and weeping are commonplace in love poetry, as the Romeo of Act I of *Romeo and Juliet* demonstrates. Stanza 3 argues that the salt water on the lady's face is not a tear but sweat. She has been so actively rolling her eyes at every man who passes that her eyes are sweating, not weeping.

19. **E.** The metaphor compares the value of the lady's letters to being "the fortieth name in an entail." An "entail" is the sequence of heirs in a will. If the speaker were fortieth, thirty-nine others would have to die before he would inherit the estate, which is to say that her love letters are of no more value than her sighs or tears. Love will not get fat on them.

20. **D.** Though the poem devalues the sighs, letters, and tears of the lady here, all of them, as well as the man's sighs, are potentially means of increasing love. Discretion, on the other hand, is the worst thing in the world for love, what it "worst endures" (line 6). The basic notion of the poem is that love is irrational, but cold, reasonable behavior can keep it in check.

21. **E.** "Thus" in line 25 refers back to the first four stanzas of the poem. These stanzas describe how the speaker has prevented love from growing, how he has asserted his power by controlling love's diet. The metaphor in line 25 changes from a personified love on a restricted diet to a "buzzard love," love as a bird he has trained by these means (that is, by what lines 1–24 describe). The transition from the diet figure to the bird image will seem

less abrupt if we are aware that falcons were and are trained to hunt by strictly controlling their diet. The word "reclaimed" in line 25 is still listed in dictionaries with its obsolete meaning "to tame or subdue, as a hawk." This meaning was not obsolete when this poem was written.

22. A With his love wholly in his control, the speaker can do as he pleases, now (that is, sometimes) indifferent to the game of love, and now (that is, at other times) pursuing women just like other predatory men.

23. C The speaker does not feel deeply about love (II); it is a game to him that he can take or leave. The three verbs recall the events of stanzas 2, 3, and 4, and their use here is another structural link between the last stanza and the first part of the poem. The verbs also denote the expected behavior of a lover (III), which this man will use because he knows how the game is to be played but not because he is really in love.

24. B "Negligent" refers to the speaker's indifference to love. The four other words, "fly," "spring" (to cause birds to break from their cover), "game," and "killed" all allude to falconry. The verb "reclaimed" could also be added to the list of words in the stanza that refer to falconry.

25. D The speaker is cynical and complacent throughout the poem. The whole poem is his boast about how clever he is, how fully he has mastered his emotions. If the poem were the first act of a play, we could expect him to fall in love in act two, like Benedict in Shakespeare's "Much Ado About Nothing."

26. A You should see at once that the basic organization of the poem is stanzas 1–4 (the diet) and stanza 5 (the falcon). Any organizational scheme that does not separate stanza 5 from the rest of the poem should be eliminated at once. On further consideration, we can see that stanza 1 introduces the idea of the diet and stanzas 2, 3, and 4 deal with a different component of the diet. Much the best description of the organization, then, is 1–2, 3, 4–5.

27. E. Falconry is used in the last stanza. The entail figure in lines 22–24 is drawn from law. The images of stanzas 2 and 3 are from eating and drinking, but there are no images from music.

28. A. Look at the size of these words, all with three or four syllables. Try to say them fast. Their sound and length reflect the size and awkwardness the words denote.

29. D. Though it mocks many of the conventions of love poetry, this poem depends for its comic effect on the reader's recognizing how a conventional lover will behave. The central idea of a calorie-counting love in danger of gaining too much weight was probably suggested by the conventional notion of the lean and pale lover so in love that he cannot eat. Donne may have noticed that as the lover grows thinner, love grows larger. He alludes to the convention of the sleepless lover (A) in the last line. This lover has no trouble sleeping, whether or not his love-quest is successful. This lover weeps (B) and sighs but not for love. He does not sit alone (C) but socializes ("go talk," line 30). His letters, like his tears, do not increase his love (E). Choice D is also a conventional notion about lovers but *not* one that Donne exploits in this poem.

Second Prose Passage

The passage is from George Eliot's novel *Adam Bede*.

30. B. The thesis of the paragraph is expressed in its first sentence: "Falsehood is so easy, truth so difficult." The idea is reasserted in the long last sentence of the paragraph. The paragraph does not claim that truth is superior to fiction (**A**), only that it is more difficult. Nor does it attempt to define truth and fiction (**D**) or to claim that truth cannot be attained (**E**).

31. C. In the first paragraph, the griffin represents the fanciful, the untrue that is so much easier to draw than the reality of the lion. In the second paragraph, the angels, prophets, sibyls, and heroic warriors are parallel images of figures larger than life that the author finds less precious than the truth of Dutch paintings (**A**) with their spinning wheels (**D**) and old women and clowns (**E**).

32. D. The "lofty-minded" people of the second paragraph are those who snobbishly reject the truthful paintings that the speaker prefers. The author refers to the "lofty-minded" in order to criticize their rejection of the unglamorous truth in art. She would not claim kinship with them and is not concerned to appear to be either humble or fair.

33. E. British English uses "pot" to refer to a vessel for holding a drink, especially beer or ale. In the paintings of village weddings such as this one, the guests would probably be drinking beer or ale from quart pots.

34. C. The passage opposes the speaker and others who welcome the truth of the commonplace in art to those who prefer the idealized, the lofty, the beautiful. The speaker claims kinship with her "fellow mortals" who have lived homely lives. Her antagonists are the "lofty-minded" who despise the truthfulness of Dutch paintings and the "idealistic friend" whose disgust with the painting of the vulgar truth of ordinary village life is expressed at the end of the paragraph.

35. E. Lines 59–79 ("I have a friend...who waddles.") give three examples of people whose existence is "homely" but who are no less cherished. It replies to the complaint at the end of the second paragraph that these clumsy, ugly people are not fit subjects for art with the argument that what is lovable is not always handsome and that more humans are plain than are beautiful. The paragraph concludes with a generalization about beauty and human feeling.

36. A. That the "lords of their kind" should include some squat and ill-shapen men is not quite a *paradox* (an apparent self-contradiction), and there is no personification, simile, or syllogism in the phrase. But by using "even" and the double negative of "not startling exceptions," the author understates what she really believes. The less-than-handsome is, in fact, not the rare exception but the rule.

37. B. The *ironic* word is the one whose intended meaning is the opposite of what is stated. Here "young," "middle," "stature," and "feeble" all mean what they say. These are not "heroes," however; they are ordinary young men who do not marry goddesses but still live happily.

38. C. The series lists three examples of people who are loved although they are not beautiful. Choice **A** is incorrect; the point is that they never were beautiful. The "friend" and "matron" have been observed, but the "wife" is not identified as someone the speaker has known or seen. They are not the objects of satire, for the speaker's point is that love is more important than physical beauty.

39. B. All three of the pronouns (it) in the sentence refer to human feeling. You can eliminate the noun "rivers" immediately because the pronoun is singular.

40. E. The last paragraph makes all three of these points. The speaker tentatively suggests that the majority of the human race may have been ugly. There are several examples of the less-than-beautiful people who are beloved, and the passage ends with the paean to human feeling, whose irresistible flow brings beauty with it.

41. D. As it happens, the author of this passage is a novelist, the great nineteenth-century British realist George Eliot. The passage is outspoken in its preference of "truth," the "un-exaggerated," the "real," praising "faithful pictures of a monotonous homely existence." There is nothing in the passage to suggest a taste for the experimental or the romantic or the symbolic and nothing in the ordered progress of the argument to suggest an interest in a stream-of-consciousness technique.

42. E. All these choices present ideas that the author may endorse, but because it is explicitly stated in the last sentence of the passage ("human feeling...brings beauty with it."), **E** is the best choice. The writer expresses her admiration of the realism of Dutch painting but stops short of saying this is a painting's "most important quality." Though George Eliot may agree with **B**, it is certainly not in this passage, which never alludes to the novel. We cannot prove **C** or **D** wrong from the passage, but we also cannot support either convincingly. The Dutch painters are praised but not judged as "greater" or "greatest."

Second Poem

The poem is by Jonathan Swift and was written in 1709. You should see right away that this is a much shorter and much less complex poem than the Donne lyric on this exam. Most readers would agree that this is the easiest of the four passages. Try to budget your time in the multiple-choice section so that you don't have to skip an easier passage because you've spent too much time on a harder or longer one. Get a sense of the whole exam before you begin to answer the questions.

43. B. Conditioned as most readers of poetry are by the English romantic poets or American poets of nature like Emerson or Frost, we may be surprised to find a poetic description of the morning without a single flower or birdsong. Swift's poem does give us the "ruddy morn," but its focus is entirely urban, not rural.

44. A. The poem does allude to an aristocrat's gate besieged by bill collectors, to reluctant schoolboys and a youth, and to the inmates of the debtor's prison, but it gives more examples of working class men and women: Betty, the apprentice, Moll, the youth, the coal seller, and the chimney-sweep.

45. D. Another unusual aspect of this poem is the author's refusal to make moral judgments. He simply describes the scene and the people with no overt evaluations.

46. C. Though Swift was a clergyman, he has included none in this poem. We have an aristocrat ("his lordship"), a servant ("Betty"), an apprentice, and a peddler (the coal man).

47. C. Line 3 tells that Betty has spent the night in her master's bed but left it at dawn to sneak back to "discompose her own." We are obliged to infer that Betty is disturbing her own bed to give the impression that she spent the night in her own room.

48. E. To dun is to demand payment from a debtor. The noun refers to either an insistent request for payment of a debt or, as is the case here, a person who collects debts. The word is used today as it was in the eighteenth century.

49. A. The turnkey is the jailer at the debtors' prison, who is compared here to a shepherd; the returning prisoners are his flock. Rather than feeding his flock, this good shepherd releases his each night so they can find the money to pay the fees that were charged for room and board at their prison.

50. E. The "flock" of released prisoners returns at daybreak to the debtors' prison.

51. D. Swift employs two meanings of the word "duly" here. The custom of releasing prisoners to enable them to find some money is "duly" observed, and the prison officials no doubt regard the practice as fitting. The time of the release, "a-nights," is also duly observed, that is, punctually.

52. D. A bailiff is an officer of the court, a process-server. The watchful bailiffs here are probably on the lookout for debtors who have defaulted, and if they find their prey, the turnkey's flock will grow larger.

53. B. Like many of the poems of the eighteenth century, this is written in couplets. Line 1 rhymes with line 2, line 3 with line 4, and so on. Nine couplets make up this eighteen-line poem.

54. B. Normally, poetry is distinguished by its use of figurative language. This poem, however, uses hardly any (although there is the "flock" figure in line 15 and the common use of "drowned" in line 12). Rhyme, on the other hand, is used in every line. The poem is made up of a number of realistic details. The meter of the poem, a regular iambic pentameter, is used in every line. Unless one writes gibberish, it is hard not to use syntax.

Section II: Essay Questions

Question 1: Samuel Johnson

This question calls for a reading of Johnson's "evaluation of Savage" and a discussion of the "resources of language" he uses. The phrase "resources of language" allows students to decide what stylistic devices they want to write about; the plural indicates that they must write about more than one. This is, in fact, another example of the archetypal essay question: discuss X's evaluation of Y and the stylistic devices X uses. An essay of three well-developed paragraphs that discusses Johnson's attitude in the first paragraph and deals specifically with two or more stylistic techniques in the second and third paragraphs would do the job well.

Part III: Six Full-Length Practice Tests

The passage is remarkable for its balance in both content and style. Johnson's sympathy with Savage does not blind him to his defects, and in almost every sentence, Johnson balances praise and blame. He sees, for example, that Savage's works are sometimes inaccurate, or uninformed, or unfinished, but he also sees that Savage's knowledge was greater than what others could have attained and that his poverty forced him to write too quickly. Similarly, though he grants that Savage may have been insolent, resentful, and vain, he understands these faults as the response of a great mind under constant and intolerable stress.

The most obvious resources of language to discuss in this passage are probably its diction and its syntax. Almost every sentence offers examples of the balance of words that praise with words that dispraise. The syntax usually employs a parallel construction. To cite just one example, the conclusion of the third paragraph suggests Savage's defects by using words and phrases like "want of prudence," "negligence," and "irregularity" and his strengths by using words like "knowledge," "wit," and, most significantly, "genius." The parallel phrasing of the concluding series ("knowledge useless," "wit ridiculous," "genius contemptible") is characteristic of the entire passage, which for its first phrases ("For his life, or for his writings") also employs parallel constructions.

The following two student essays on this question give you a better idea of the kind of answer this topic will elicit.

Student Essay 1

Samuel Johnson expressed admiration and sympathy for Richard Savage in the conclusion of his work "Life of Savage." Using his language resources effectively, Johnson manages to defend Savage from his critics, helping them to understand the hardships in life that Savage endured.

Johnson begins this passage by explaining something of Savage's background, as well as how his poverty affected his work. "If he was not always sufficiently instructed in his subject, his knowledge was at least greater than could have been attained by others in the same state. If his works were sometimes unfinished, accuracy cannot be reasonably exacted from a man oppressed by want, which he has no hope of relieving but by a speedy publication." Savage was trapped in a cycle of inability to complete works due to dire poverty, yet only could he begin to escape that poverty by sending completed works to the publisher. Johnson understood this cycle of poverty and helplessness, and wrote so that other authors and intellectuals of that time might appreciate Savage's works, as well as his misfortune.

Johnson continues on to rebut criticisms of Savage's character in a direct and solid manner. "The insolence and resentment of which he is accused, were not easily to be avoided by a great mind, irritated by perpetual hardships, and constrained hourly to return the spurns of contempt, and repress the insolence of prosperity; and vanity surely may be readily pardoned in him, to whom life afforded no other comforts than barren praises, and the consciousness of deserving them." All at once, Johnson removes questions and accusations about Savage's character with his straightforward style.

Finally, Johnson questions the validity of the critics' allegations toward Savage. "Those are no proper judges of his conduct who have slumbered away their time on the down of

136

plenty; nor will any wise man presume to say, 'Had I been in Savage's condition, I should have lived or written better than Savage.'" In doing so, Johnson eradicates all charges against Savage simply by reminding readers and critics not to judge Savage's actions and attitudes, because those actions were a result of his singularly unfortunate experience as a poverty-stricken scholar and writer in the midst of wealthy writers.

Samuel Johnson employs direct language, thoughtful understanding, and a straightforward manner to gain understanding and acceptance for the life and works of Richard Savage in his account "Life of Savage."

Student Essay 2

Samuel Johnson admonishes those who would belittle Savage without taking into account the extreme poverty which continually wore on him. His evaluation of Savage is of a man who did the best he could with his talent, fighting adverse conditions, and emerged an inspirational figure despite the problems plaguing him. He endured. A latter day Briton might have said he "muddled through." But Johnson portrays him as doing more than muddling; despite his faults, he led a remarkable life.

Johnson has a style that is scholarly, almost erudite. He writes with elegance putting the best face on a man (Savage) who was apparently much maligned. Always Johnson uses delicacy in detailing Savage's perceived faults. Savage was not ignorant, he "was not always sufficiently instructed in his subject . . ." Accuracy at times suffered in Savage's work, but scarcely has Johnson conceded this than he adds that exacting standards cannot be set for a man "oppressed with want." His intent seems not so much to foster reader sympathy with Savage as to excuse his perceived failings, to make readers admire and respect a man who has fought hard in a cruel world.

Johnson's diction is fundamental to his evaluation. As he addresses each of Savage's flaws, he uses similar words to describe the onus of poverty and misfortune weighing on the writer. Resentment and insolence "could not be avoided" because Savage was "irritated." His hardships were not incidental, but "perpetual." He was "constrained hourly . . . life afforded no other comforts than barren praises." Johnson's evaluation, then, is irretrievably intertwined with the hardships Savage faced; Savage can ultimately be understood only in the context of his life's circumstances.

Finally, Johnson turns the lens of his scrutiny on the reader. He contrasts the probable conditions of the reader's life with those of Savage to demonstrate the inability of most readers to make an empathetic criticism of the writer. Critics, Johnson alleges, have "slumbered away their time on the down of plenty." Yet they, in Savage's circumstances, could have done no better — would have probably done far worse. Johnson ends his work on a similar note: Those who are similarly disadvantaged can take heart in the successes, the brilliance of Richard Savage, who persevered and prevailed in the face of trouble and criticism; Those confident and successful should extract a lesson from Johnson's portrayal, should understand that fundamental qualities of "prudence" and conscientiousness cannot be superceded by material prosperity. Without those qualities of Richard Savage, that will to do the best that he could, "knowledge [would be] useless, wit ridiculous, and genius contemptible."

The success of Johnson's persuasion arises largely from his final focus on the faults of the general public. Putting readers on the defensive by criticizing their anticipated criticism. Johnson gives them pause, effectively causing them to look at Savage in a different light than they would have had Savage's faults been illuminated but Johnson merely argued that they lacked significance.

Response to Student Essay 1

This essay is a good example of a competently written five-paragraph essay that would score no higher than a five and might well fall a point lower on the nine-point scoring scale. The writer clearly understands the meaning of the selection, though the essay overstates its effect ("Johnson eradicates all charges"). The real problem here is that almost all of the essay is either direct quotation (about one-third) or paraphrase. The quotations are well chosen, and the paraphrase is, largely, accurate, but the essay never deals with the "resources of language" half of the question. It twice calls Johnson's style "direct" and "straightforward" but makes no other comment on the language of the passage. Neither "direct" nor "straightforward" is an appropriate term to describe this prose, with its frequent double negatives, periodic sentences, and a final paragraph that comprises only one sentence eighty-seven words long.

Response to Student Essay 2

The second essay is a much better response to the question. Notice how the student quotes only words or phrases to support specific points. The third paragraph deals with Johnson's diction, and the comments on Johnson's style are accurate. The quality falls off somewhat in the fourth paragraph, which misinterprets part of Johnson's conclusion. The essay would, no doubt, be improved if the writer discussed another "resource of language." Remember that when a question calls for a discussion of "style," or "devices," or "resources" with no more specific demands, shrewd students use in their essays such terms as "diction," "point of view," "imagery," and the like. Your reader is then sure that you know just what "resources of language" are. This essay would receive at least a seven on the nine-point scale.

Question 2: Emily Dickinson

The question here takes a very permissive form, simply asking for a discussion of how language reveals the speaker's perceptions and feelings. The phrase "of each stanza" should tell you that you must say something about each of the six stanzas in the poem. By asking only for a discussion of "language," the question allows students to select their topics, but because the diction and imagery of the poem are so unusual and important, a successful essay would probably have to deal with both. Another topic that few would choose, but which the poem especially invites, is syntax. Just the briefest mention of the omission of words that we expect or the odd word order ("independent ecstasy of deity and men" instead of "ecstasy independent of deity and men," for example) would make a favorable impression.

In a paragraph about the first stanza of the poem, you could discuss the ambiguity and richness of the first two lines. Does "period" have only its obvious meaning of "portion of time" and refer to the four o-clock time period, or does it have its meaning as a musical term, "a group of measures that form a statement"? Is it in apposition to four o'clock or the direct object of the verb "began"? This music is described by two remarkable adjectives and two curious similes: "numerous as space" and "neighboring as noon." The first surprises because we think music exists in time not space, and though we speak of the numerous voices of a choir, we would not transfer the adjective to describe music itself.

Stanza two concludes the description of the early song of the birds. A discussion of diction might cite the word "force" (the size of their forces or the large number of birds but also the power of the song), and a discussion of images might refer to "expend," "bestow," and "multiply" as part of a financial figure. The simile of lines 5–8 that compares the songs of the birds to brooks that fill a pond will be recalled in the fifth stanza's use of "flood."

Stanzas three and four ask why the birds sing. For whose benefit? For what listeners? The speaker's feelings are especially clear in the choice of the word "ecstasy" to describe an exalted joy with no regard for the deity or man. The poem reaches its climactic assertion in these lines. In stanzas five and six, it recedes.

Stanza five describes the end of the song. In line 20, "band" is probably another word with several meanings, the group and the more specific group of instrumentalists. Though the sun and the day take over in stanza six, one last key word reveals the poet's feelings about the birds: "miracle."

This poem by Emily Dickinson is so rich and suggestive and the question so unspecific that the range of essays it would produce is enormous. Here are two samples.

Student Essay 1

Language is used carefully and meaningfully in each stanza of this poem, revealing the perceptions of the speaker after experiencing the chorus of birds at dawn.

In the first stanza the speaker describes the timing of the birds' songs in the early hours as "A music as numerous as space/ But neighboring as noon." Although the birds begin their chorus at four o'clock, according to the speaker it is a music as powerful and as lively as music that would be familiar during the daylight hours of civilization.

The speaker continues in the second stanza to portray the awesome power of the birds' songs, comparing the separate notes that form a song of hundreds to the insignificant brooks that flow together to become a pond. Here, the speaker is clearly impressed by the birds' strength and observes, "I could not count their force,/ Their voices did expend . . ."

In the third stanza the speaker recounts the birds' domination of those first morning hours, when cities and factories and other symbols of human civilization are unimportant, and nature reigns. Few people are fortunate enough to witness this scene of music and energy as the birds "In homely industry arrayed/ To overtake the morn." In this stanza the speaker particularly emphasizes the essential power of being as belonging solely to the birds, who are completely unaware of humanity.

Again stressing the birds' absolute autonomy from mankind, stanza four describes the song of the birds as an expression of exhilaration and freedom. "Nor was it for applause/ . . . But independent ecstasy/ Of deity and men." The speaker describes how unnecessary mankind is to the cycle of nature and the earth, proven in this wondrous song.

Stanzas five and six depict the end of this bird chorus, and the awakening of the human world as the cities and homes come back to life. The speaker realizes how rich the natural world is and how oblivious the human world is to its beauty. "The sun engrossed the east,/ The day controlled the world,/ The miracle that introduced/ forgotten, as fulfilled." In these final stanzas the speaker reveals how separate nature and humanity truly are, as the birds' concert ends and the human day begins.

The speaker of this poem uses language thoughtfully as he expresses the beauty of the birds and their song of energy, as well as their complete independence and isolation from mankind.

Student Essay 2

In this selection about the birds singing in the waning of the night, much is revealed about the poet's attitude and feelings. The reader gets the impression that the poet has great respect and love for the wonders that he wakes early to appreciate. Immediately the poet makes clear the intimate connection he feels with the birds and the awe in which he holds them. He writes, "A music numerous as space/ But neighboring as noon." He feels the music as infinite, like the dark cosmos, and yet as close and easy for him to relate to as "neighboring," as the midday sun. Thus the poet quickly conveys much about himself and his desire to commune with the enigmas of nature, enigmas with which, numerous though they be, he feels a certain connection.

Next the poet embellishes earlier implications about their numbers, comparing them to the myriad brooks that run into a pond. Each brook is an artery to the poet, a connection to a pond that is the repository of his spirituality. Here diction is key: The brook "bestows" itself to make the pond. So the morning birds are bestowing their song; the poet regards it as a gift, perhaps a gift too often gone unnoticed and unappreciated. Indeed, in the following stanza the poet addresses the aloofness of most men, sleeping through the birds' song in contented oblivion. But what is important here is less the numbers of those who observe, but rather the relative insignificance of the work of man juxtaposed with the more holy labor of the singing birds. The work of such early rising men is "homely," their duties not so vital as they believe them to be.

The poet notes the selfless impression imparted by the birds. He writes, "Nor was it for applause/ But independent ecstasy/ Of deity and men." Implicit in such lines is the poet's approval of the birds' independence and lack of concern for the approval of others — a vaguely nonconformist stance, almost transcendental. Obviously, the writer places great weight upon such self-confidence and lack of inhibition; again, his critique of the birds is a tacit exploration of human qualities and characteristics.

As quickly as they appear, the birds are gone, without ceremony or fanfare. The poet seems gently approving of this as well, pleased that "No tumult there had been." An apparent paradox is at play, for in the line previous, the poet refers to the morning's singing as a "flood." This flood then, since it is without tumult (and presumably spared of flotsam and fear), must be perceived by the writer as a good occurrence, requiring not an Ark, but rather an opening of the heart to receive the floodwaters. The dawn is then described in terms of a taking of power, a usurpation and nullification of the birds and their song. The sun "engrosses," the day "controls." The clearest indication yet of the poet's perception of the birds is given. Their song is nothing short of a "miracle." And yet, the writer is not saddened; though the birdsong that ushered in the day is forgotten, it has also been fulfilled. The miracle has seen fruition in the glory of a new day.

The reader has learned of the poet's reverence toward nature, his sense of childlike wonder, and his perception of things not often noticed as being miraculous. More than the birds now, one knows he who penned the poem.

Response to Student Essays 1 and 2

Though the first of these two papers avoids the occasional overwriting of the second and presents a competent reading of the poem, it lacks the specificity of the second. It paraphrases the poem adequately but does not deal fully enough with what the language actually accomplishes. The second essay gives a much more specific account of the perceptions and feelings of the poet. It also deals in detail with the effects of single words or phrases, with figures of speech, and accurately identifies those which are the most powerful in the poem. The first essay would probably be scored a six and the second an eight.

Question 3: Open Question

On the open essay question, your choice of work is crucial. Do *not* decide what novel or play you will write about before you have thought carefully about the question. Even if you like and know one work better than another, the work you prefer may not suit the question nearly as well as the other. With this question, you may well know three or four plays and books with eating scenes in them. Think about all three parts of the question before you decide which one to use. For which can you give good answers to all three tasks? You may, for example, know the dinner scene in *To the Lighthouse* and the banquet scene in *Macbeth*. On which of the two can you say more about the meaning of the scene and its relation to the meaning of the work? Can you discuss Woolf's or Shakespeare's means of making the scene effective? The easiest part of this question is the issue of what the scene reveals, but to get a top score, you would have to deal equally well with the other parts of the question.

Before you begin to write your essay, make absolutely sure you know exactly what the tasks are. In this case, after you've chosen a work with an eating scene, there are three tasks:

1. Discuss what the scene reveals.

2. Discuss how the scene is related to the meaning of the work.

3. Discuss the means by which the author makes the scene effective.

Many AP students would select Joyce's *A Portrait of the Artist as a Young Man* and write about the Christmas dinner scene in chapter one. The book is widely read in AP classes, and most students do not lose interest in it until chapter five.

A sensible organization would simply follow the order of the question. The first two tasks call for an interpretation of meaning, while the third asks for a discussion of the techniques ("means") Joyce uses in the scene. There is, of course, no single right answer to any of the essay questions, and the open question always produces the widest range of responses.

The scene presents Stephen at a time in his early childhood when his family is still prosperous. They live in a comfortable home in Bray; there are servants in the house and no lack of food and drink. Ireland at this time is still torn by the dissension that followed the death of Parnell. The young Stephen Dedalus is already puzzled by the conflict of the adults around him, in this scene notably, Mr. Casey and Mrs. Riordan (Dante), who violently attack and defend the Church's role in the downfall of Parnell. Stephen is already intensely conscious of language and wonders about the several meanings of a word like "turkey" or how the phrase "tower of ivory" can refer to a woman.

An essay dealing with the second task of this question could discuss how the Church, Irish politics, and Stephen's sensitivity to language are related to meaning in the novel. The book is centrally about Stephen's development to the brink of his career as an artist. He can continue to develop only after he has come to terms with his religious belief and with his loyalties to his family and to his homeland. This Ireland, he discovers, would ensnare him with the "nets" of nationality, language, and religion, and to become himself, to become an artist, Stephen must escape from these "nets." His assertion of independence is to deny the Church and to leave Ireland. The Christmas dinner scene presents the antagonism of two forces that would hold him captive. At the end of the book, Stephen perceives that both are dangerous to his freedom and determines to reject them.

The list of technical devices that Joyce uses to make the scene effective can be very long. The more precisely you can recall the scene you write about, the more specific and impressive your handling of this part of the question will be. You could, for example, discuss point of view in this scene. Though Joyce uses the third person, the point of view in the scene is Stephen's. Much of the scene is dialogue, the increasingly heated interchange between Simon Dedalus, Mr. Casey, and Mrs. Riordan, who defiantly defends the Church. There are also short passages of Stephen's interior monologue, and we see the action of his mind as well as the external action. The language of the passage encompasses racy, Irish vernacular, a comic story, formal description, and pious quotation from the Old and New Testaments. The effectiveness of the scene is to a large extent due to the vigor of the conflict it dramatizes. The scene begins quietly, but tempers flare and are calmed only to flare again more violently. The scene ends theatrically with Dante's enraged exit, Mr. Casey's sobbing breakdown, and Stephen's baffled contemplation of his father's tear-stained face.

The two student essays that follow answer the question using different books, the first with Joyce's *Portrait* and the second with Golding's *Lord of the Flies*.

Student Essay 1

Family meal time — whether a fancy dinner party or an everyday meal — is often included in a written work to show how the main characters communicate with each other, as well as to indicate the intricate, complicated nature of familial relationships. In James Joyce's <u>Portrait of the Artist as a Young Man</u>, Joyce employs the family eating scene as a means to display Stephen's family and their inter-woven relationships, as well as a symbolic tie to Ireland, her politics and history.

The Christmas dinner described by Joyce occurs when Stephen — not much more than six or seven — is home on holiday from school. The dinner begins as a happy, relaxed occasion for all the members but soon the atmosphere changes. As the conversation turns away from pleasantries and begins to include extremely different viewpoints, the meal becomes more and more uncomfortable for Stephen. Originally a discussion on differing religious views and political radicals, the atmosphere becomes heated and soon Stephen's father and aunt are engaged in a shouting match across the table. Stephen does not understand what the conversation is about or what the reason for arguing is. While Stephen's mother tries to calm everyone down, Stephen is left wondering who Charles Parnell is and why his family is fighting about him. This is the first major introduction to Stephen's family that Joyce gives the reader, and it is indicative not only of the political atmosphere but it is also foreshadowing Stephen's future.

The basic idea of a family arguing during a holiday occasion is somewhat shocking. Stephen feels disconcerted and upset as well; and that Joyce depicts a family who cannot discuss different viewpoints without screaming at each other indicates how opinionated and proud they are. On an elementary level, this eating scene demonstrates the Dedalus family's inability to communicate as thinking, rational adults. It shows the reader the lack of affection and respect the family members have for each other. This is an unfortunate situation which contrasts sharply with the theme of holiday joy and caring.

That the family is arguing about religion and political figures, two volatile subjects, reinforces the theme of Irish history and politics. Charles Parnell is mentioned often throughout the book, a symbol of Ireland's explosive political atmosphere. This argument is the beginning of several similar arguments that Stephen will observe and participate in, in school and in his home. This idea of political unrest and debate that shakes the nation of Ireland is a persistent theme that Joyce employs.

This dinner scene is also a method of foreshadowing. At the dinner table Stephen feels confused and no one will explain the argument to him. This major theme of isolation is expanded upon during Christmas dinner. Stephen feels upset and alienated, and it is possible for the reader to begin to see a rift between the generations present at the table. This rift continues as Stephen grows older and further away from his parents emotionally. At this meal, Stephen is unable to relate to the family's discussion, a pattern that continues later in his life as he is unable to relate to his parents and siblings. At this meal Joyce begins the alienation of Stephen, a motif that continues during his school years, and perhaps the most impressive theme of the novel.

James Joyce uses a family holiday meal to create the beginnings of several themes that reappear throughout the book. Foreshadowing, symbolism, and the idea of isolation are apparent in this commotion, which Joyce utilizes effectively to tie this scene to the work as a whole.

Student Essay 2

Eating ranks among the most primal and sensual activities of mankind. No drive is more primitive or essential, more able to push men to fight or kill. William Golding addresses that primitive nature with the barbaric feast scene in Lord of the Flies. The meal becomes part of a primeval ritual that begins in defiance and ends in violent death. The feast represents the point of no return for the boys on the isle, the moment when most of them descend into irredeemable savagery. Golding metaphorically represents the depths to which the boys have sunk and the power of their instinctual drives in the eating scene.

The castaways have yet to recognize the true identity of the beast they fear. Ignorant of their own innate evil, they hunt and kill, perpetually on the lookout for some horrid demon. Wild boars become ritualistic targets, and they roast the pigs on spits over the fire, crazy with crude salivary lust. When messianic Simon enters the circle of the boys' feverish tribal dance he is devoured as well. The Christ-figure, who has seen the truth about the boys' rejection of reason and civilization, who indeed has seen the face of evil incarnate as characterized by the Lord of the Flies, is not literally eaten, but the result is similar. Like the roasting pigs on the spit, the wild boys pounce upon him and tear him apart. Their hunger, the hunger of fear and desperation in the face of a shadowy figure they fail to recognize, is the same fear with which they devour the meal.

The boys have failed to acknowledge their savior, sealing their own doom in the process. By joining Jack's lawless tribe and rejecting Ralph and Piggy, the boys have reverted to the darker side of human nature. The feast, as well as being the dramatic high point of the novel (and arguably its climax), is a visceral scene of ravenous impulses central to the theme. Nowhere is the boys' reversion to beastliness more evident than in the feast scene, as they pounce upon the meat and upon their comrade.

Golding makes use of readers' senses to describe the scene, evolving archetypal images of fire and storm, chanting and thunder. The feast is melodramatic, not just because of the power-struggle between Ralph and Jack, but because of the setting. The boys dance around an enormous fire on the beach, even as the clouds gather and thunder crashes in the night sky. The storm builds, the suspense mounts, and the boys descend into amorality. When Simon appears from the brush, he is a pitiful figure, strong of character but weak of body. The boys attack, and the results are chilling. As the corpse drifts out to sea, the martyr is food for the fish; another corrupt feast ensues.

The eating scene is indispensable to Lord of the Flies, and through the feast Golding addresses some of his most significant and topical ideas. Both aesthetically and symbolically, the ritual proves crucial to the novel.

Response to Student Essays 1 and 2

There are several problems with the Joyce essay. The first is its inaccurate recollection of the book. Mr. Casey is not a relative. Dante is not Stephen's aunt and not a relative of the Dedalus family, so the argument that the scene demonstrates the family's lack of affection and respect is simply untrue. At this point in the book, the Dedalus family is affectionate. The essay does too little with the role religion is to play in the novel. Its chief defect is its failure to deal with the third task (the "means" by which the author makes the scene effective).

The essay on the Golding novel, on the other hand, is much more convincing. It deals fully and clearly with all three parts of the question, and though it is much shorter than the Joyce essay, it tells us much more about the meaning of the novel and the techniques by which Golding makes this scene so powerful. Inaccurate and incomplete, the Joyce essay would probably be scored a five, while the Golding essay would receive a seven or eight.

Answer Sheet for Practice Test 2

(Remove This Sheet and Use it to Mark Your Answers)

1 Ⓐ Ⓑ Ⓒ Ⓓ Ⓔ	21 Ⓐ Ⓑ Ⓒ Ⓓ Ⓔ	41 Ⓐ Ⓑ Ⓒ Ⓓ Ⓔ
2 Ⓐ Ⓑ Ⓒ Ⓓ Ⓔ	22 Ⓐ Ⓑ Ⓒ Ⓓ Ⓔ	42 Ⓐ Ⓑ Ⓒ Ⓓ Ⓔ
3 Ⓐ Ⓑ Ⓒ Ⓓ Ⓔ	23 Ⓐ Ⓑ Ⓒ Ⓓ Ⓔ	43 Ⓐ Ⓑ Ⓒ Ⓓ Ⓔ
4 Ⓐ Ⓑ Ⓒ Ⓓ Ⓔ	24 Ⓐ Ⓑ Ⓒ Ⓓ Ⓔ	44 Ⓐ Ⓑ Ⓒ Ⓓ Ⓔ
5 Ⓐ Ⓑ Ⓒ Ⓓ Ⓔ	25 Ⓐ Ⓑ Ⓒ Ⓓ Ⓔ	45 Ⓐ Ⓑ Ⓒ Ⓓ Ⓔ
6 Ⓐ Ⓑ Ⓒ Ⓓ Ⓔ	26 Ⓐ Ⓑ Ⓒ Ⓓ Ⓔ	46 Ⓐ Ⓑ Ⓒ Ⓓ Ⓔ
7 Ⓐ Ⓑ Ⓒ Ⓓ Ⓔ	27 Ⓐ Ⓑ Ⓒ Ⓓ Ⓔ	47 Ⓐ Ⓑ Ⓒ Ⓓ Ⓔ
8 Ⓐ Ⓑ Ⓒ Ⓓ Ⓔ	28 Ⓐ Ⓑ Ⓒ Ⓓ Ⓔ	48 Ⓐ Ⓑ Ⓒ Ⓓ Ⓔ
9 Ⓐ Ⓑ Ⓒ Ⓓ Ⓔ	29 Ⓐ Ⓑ Ⓒ Ⓓ Ⓔ	49 Ⓐ Ⓑ Ⓒ Ⓓ Ⓔ
10 Ⓐ Ⓑ Ⓒ Ⓓ Ⓔ	30 Ⓐ Ⓑ Ⓒ Ⓓ Ⓔ	50 Ⓐ Ⓑ Ⓒ Ⓓ Ⓔ
11 Ⓐ Ⓑ Ⓒ Ⓓ Ⓔ	31 Ⓐ Ⓑ Ⓒ Ⓓ Ⓔ	51 Ⓐ Ⓑ Ⓒ Ⓓ Ⓔ
12 Ⓐ Ⓑ Ⓒ Ⓓ Ⓔ	32 Ⓐ Ⓑ Ⓒ Ⓓ Ⓔ	52 Ⓐ Ⓑ Ⓒ Ⓓ Ⓔ
13 Ⓐ Ⓑ Ⓒ Ⓓ Ⓔ	33 Ⓐ Ⓑ Ⓒ Ⓓ Ⓔ	53 Ⓐ Ⓑ Ⓒ Ⓓ Ⓔ
14 Ⓐ Ⓑ Ⓒ Ⓓ Ⓔ	34 Ⓐ Ⓑ Ⓒ Ⓓ Ⓔ	54 Ⓐ Ⓑ Ⓒ Ⓓ Ⓔ
15 Ⓐ Ⓑ Ⓒ Ⓓ Ⓔ	35 Ⓐ Ⓑ Ⓒ Ⓓ Ⓔ	55 Ⓐ Ⓑ Ⓒ Ⓓ Ⓔ
16 Ⓐ Ⓑ Ⓒ Ⓓ Ⓔ	36 Ⓐ Ⓑ Ⓒ Ⓓ Ⓔ	56 Ⓐ Ⓑ Ⓒ Ⓓ Ⓔ
17 Ⓐ Ⓑ Ⓒ Ⓓ Ⓔ	37 Ⓐ Ⓑ Ⓒ Ⓓ Ⓔ	
18 Ⓐ Ⓑ Ⓒ Ⓓ Ⓔ	38 Ⓐ Ⓑ Ⓒ Ⓓ Ⓔ	
19 Ⓐ Ⓑ Ⓒ Ⓓ Ⓔ	39 Ⓐ Ⓑ Ⓒ Ⓓ Ⓔ	
20 Ⓐ Ⓑ Ⓒ Ⓓ Ⓔ	40 Ⓐ Ⓑ Ⓒ Ⓓ Ⓔ	

Practice Test 2

Section I: Multiple-Choice Questions

Time: 60 Minutes

56 Questions

Directions: This section contains selections from two passages of prose and two poems with questions on their content, style, and form. Read each selection carefully. Choose the best answer of the five choices.

Questions 1–16. Read the poem carefully before you begin to answer the questions.

> When men shall find thy flower, thy glory pass,
> And thou, with careful brow sitting alone,
> Received hast this message from thy glass,
> That tells thee truth, and says that all is gone,
> (5) Fresh shalt thou see in me the wounds thou madest,
> Though spent thy flame, in me the heat remaining,
> I that have loved thee thus before thou fadest;
> My faith shall wax, when thou art in thy waning.
> The world shall find this miracle in me,
> (10) That fire can burn when all the matter's spent;
> Then what my faith hath been thyself shall see,
> And that thou wast unkind thou mayst repent.
> Thou mayst repent that thou has scorned my tears,
> When winter snows upon thy golden hairs.

1. The speaker and the person addressed in the poem are probably

    A. an old man speaking to an old woman

    B. an old woman speaking to another old woman

    C. a young man speaking to an old woman

    D. a young man speaking to a young woman

    E. a young man speaking to himself

2. Setting aside considerations of rhythm and rhyme, a modern writer would probably replace the verb form "pass" in line 1 with

    A. passing

    B. is passing

    C. to pass

    D. will have passed

    E. to have passed

3. The word "glass" in line 3 means
   A. tumbler
   B. mirror
   C. crystal ball
   D. decanter
   E. window

4. The "miracle" referred to in line 9 is
   A. his continuing love
   B. his suffering
   C. her beauty
   D. her remaining beautiful in old age
   E. her returning his love

5. In line 10, "all the matter's spent" can be best rephrased as
   A. all cares are over
   B. all my reasons for living have vanished
   C. all the fuel is gone
   D. all difficulties have been ended
   E. the subject has been closed completely

6. In line 14, "winter" is a symbol of
   A. love rejected
   B. isolation
   C. old age
   D. indifference
   E. death

7. Which of the following are arguments of the poem?
   I. When you are old, you will be sorry you ignored my love.
   II. Poetry will preserve your beauty despite the passage of time.
   III. No matter how you look, I will still love you.
   A. II only
   B. I and II only
   C. I and III only
   D. II and III only
   E. I, II, and III

8. On which of the following constructions does the poem implicitly or explicitly most rely?
   A. Both . . . and
   B. When . . . then
   C. If . . . then
   D. If . . . but
   E. Since . . . therefore

9. One meaning of the word "glory" is a halo; if this meaning is intended in line 1, the image recurs in
   A. line 2
   B. line 5
   C. line 9
   D. line 11
   E. line 14

10. The poem deliberately repeats all the following words and phrases EXCEPT

   A. "spent"
   B. "in me"
   C. "fire"
   D. "repent"
   E. "faith"

11. All the following words and phrases are used to represent the beauty of the woman EXCEPT

   A. "flower" (line 1)
   B. "glory" (line 1)
   C. "thy flame" (line 6)
   D. "miracle" (line 9)
   E. "golden hairs" (line 14)

12. All the following are used to represent the continuing love of the speaker EXCEPT

   A. "truth" (line 4)
   B. "wounds" (line 5)
   C. "heat" (line 6)
   D. "faith" (line 8)
   E. "miracle" (line 9)

13. The rhetorical purpose of the speaker of the poem is to

   A. convince the lady to return his love now
   B. inform the lady about what the future will bring
   C. warn the lady of the consequences of vanity

   D. convince himself to give up a useless pursuit
   E. convince the lady of the superiority of poetry to passion

14. Which of the following contrasts does the poem employ?

   I. Youth vs. age
   II. Growth vs. decline
   III. Permanence vs. transience
   IV. Truth vs. lie

   A. I and III only
   B. I, III, and IV only
   C. II, III, and IV only
   D. I, II, and III only
   E. I, II, III, and IV

15. The poem employs religious diction in all the following words EXCEPT

   A. "faith" (line 8)
   B. "miracle" (line 9)
   C. "faith" (line 11)
   D. "repent" (line 12)
   E. "scorned" (line 13)

16. The form of this poem is a

   A. Shakespearean sonnet
   B. Petrarchan sonnet
   C. Romantic ode
   D. Ballad
   E. Villanelle

GO ON TO THE NEXT PAGE

Questions 17–28. Read the following passage carefully before you begin to answer the questions.

Dombey sat in the corner of the darkened room in the great arm-chair by the bedside, and Son lay tucked up warm in a little basket bedstead, carefully disposed on a low settee immediately in front of the fire and close to it, as if his constitution were analogous to that of a muffin, and it was essential to toast him brown while he was very new.

(10) Dombey was about eight-and-forty years of age. Son about eight-and-forty minutes. Dombey was rather bald, rather red, and though a handsome well-made man, too stern and pompous in appearance to be prepossessing. Son was very bald, and very red, and though (of course) an undeniably fine infant, somewhat crushed and spotty in his general effect, as yet. On the brow of Dombey,

(20) Time and his brother Care had set some marks, as on a tree that was to come down in good time — remorseless twins they are for striding through their human forests, notching as they go — while the

(25) countenance of Son was crossed and recrossed with a thousand little creases, which the same deceitful Time would take delight in smoothing out and wearing away with the flat part of his scythe,

(30) as a preparation of the surface for his deeper operations.

Dombey, exulting in the long-looked-for event, jingled and jingled the heavy gold watch-chain that depended from

(35) below his trim blue coat, whereof the buttons sparkled phosphorescently in the feeble rays of the distant fire. Son, with his little fists curled up and clenched, seemed, in his feeble way, to

(40) be squaring at existence for having come upon him so unexpectedly.

"The house will once again, Mrs. Dombey," said Mr. Dombey, "be not only in name but in fact Dombey and

(45) Son; Dom-bey and Son!"

The words had such a softening influence that he appended a term of endearment to Mrs. Dombey's name (though not without some hesitation, as being a

(50) man but little used to that form of address) and said, "Mrs. Dombey, my — my dear."

A transient flush of faint surprise overspread the sick lady's face as she

(55) raised her eyes towards him.

"He will be christened Paul, my — Mrs. Dombey — of course."

She feebly echoed, "Of course," or rather expressed it by the motion of her

(60) lips, and closed her eyes again.

"His father's name, Mrs. Dombey, and his grandfather's! I wish his grandfather were alive this day!" And again he said "Dom-bey and Son," in exactly the

(65) same tone as before.

Those three words conveyed the one idea of Mr. Dombey's life. The earth was made for Dombey and Son to trade in, and the sun and moon were made to

(70) give them light. Rivers and seas were formed to float their ships; rainbows gave them promise of fair weather; winds blew for or against their enterprises; stars and planets circled in their

(75) orbits to preserve inviolate a system of which they were the centre. Common abbreviations took new meaning in his eyes, and had sole reference to them: A.D. had no concern with anno Domini,

(80) but stood for anno Dombei — and Son.

17. The passage is probably taken from

A. a journal

B. an epistolary novel

C. a Victorian novel

D. a stream-of-consciousness novel

E. an essay

18. In lines 19–25 of the second paragraph, which of the following are compared?

I. Time is compared to a forester.

II. The brow is compared to a tree.

III. The lines on a face are compared to marks on a tree to be felled.

A. II only

B. I and II only

C. I and III only

D. II and III only

E. I, II, and III

19. In line 42, the "house" is

A. Parliament

B. a business firm

C. a place of residence

D. a family

E. a social unit

20. Dombey and Son is evidently a

A. trading company

B. law firm

C. retailer of domestic goods

D. religious denomination

E. ship-building company

21. In the lines dealing with Mrs. Dombey, she is characterized as all the following EXCEPT

A. passive

B. accustomed to her husband's stern demeanor

C. frail

D. loving

E. reticent

22. In lines 53–55, Mrs. Dombey is surprised because

A. she has not yet recovered from her labor

B. Mr. Dombey has spoken affectionately

C. she has misunderstood Mr. Dombey's words

D. Mr. Dombey has called her "Mrs. Dombey"

E. Mr. Dombey is delighted that the child is a son rather than a daughter

23. The central concern of Mr. Dombey's life is his

A. wife

B. child

C. riches

D. company

E. sense of well-being

24. In lines 74–76 ("stars and planets...centre"), the antecedent of the pronoun "they" is

A. "stars"

B. "planets"

C. both "stars" and "planets"

D. "orbits"

E. "Dombey and Son"

GO ON TO THE NEXT PAGE

25. The point of view expressed in the last paragraph of the passage is that of

- A. the narrator of the passage
- B. the author of the passage
- C. Dombey
- D. Mrs. Dombey
- E. Dombey and Son

26. The last paragraph of the passage uses all of the following EXCEPT

- A. repartee
- B. repetition
- C. blasphemous comparison
- D. parallel construction
- E. overstatement

27. Given the remarks on Time in the second paragraph and Mr. Dombey's obsession, we may infer that young Paul Dombey will

- A. become a successful man of business
- B. alienate his wife
- C. not become rich
- D. die young
- E. refuse to carry on the business

28. The use of irony in the passage is most apparent in the

- A. first paragraph
- B. second paragraph
- C. third paragraph
- D. dialogue between Mr. and Mrs. Dombey
- E. final paragraph

Questions 29–42. Read the following poem carefully before you begin to answer the questions.

Ode on the Death of a Favorite Cat

Drowned in a Tub of Goldfishes

1

'Twas on a lofty vase's side,
Where China's gayest art had dyed
The azure flowers that blow;
Demurest of the tabby kind,
(5)   The pensive Selima reclined,
Gazed on the lake below.

2

Her conscious tail her joy declared;
The fair round face, the snowy beard,
The velvet of her paws,
(10)   Her coat, that with the tortoise vies,
Her ears of jet, and emerald eyes,
She saw; and purred applause.

3

Still had she gazed; but 'midst the tide
Two angel forms were seen to glide,
(15)   The genii of the stream:
Their scaly armor's Tyrian hue
Through richest purple to the view
Betrayed a golden gleam.

4

The hapless nymph with wonder saw;
(20)   A whisker first and then a claw,
With many an ardent wish,
She stretched in vain to reach the prize.
What female heart can gold despise?
What cat's averse to fish?

5

(25)   Presumptuous maid! With looks intent
Again she stretched, again she bent,
Nor knew the gulf between.
(Malignant Fate sat by and smiled)
The slippery verge her feet beguiled,
(30)   She tumbled headlong in.

6

Eight times emerging from the flood
She mewed to every watery god,
Some speedy aid to send.
No dolphin came, no nereid stirred:
(35)   Nor cruel Tom, nor Susan heard.
A favorite has no friend!

7

From hence, ye beauties, undeceived,
Know, one false step is ne'er retrieved,
And be with caution bold.
(40)   Not all that tempts your wandering eyes
And heedless hearts is lawful prize;
Nor all that glisters gold.

29. Lines 1–3 describe

  A. a garden

  B. an embroidered dress

  C. a cat

  D. a china bowl

  E. an oriental painting

GO ON TO THE NEXT PAGE

30. The subject(s) of the sentence in lines 8–12 ("The fair . . . saw") is (are)

    A. "face"

    B. "coat"

    C. "jet"

    D. "face," "beard," "velvet," "coat," "ears," "eyes"

    E. "she"

31. In line 10, Selima's coat is said to vie "with the tortoise" because

    A. it is silky

    B. it is parti-colored

    C. the cat is lazy and slow moving

    D. the cat is attracted to water

    E. it is tinged with green

32. In the second stanza, Selima is purring applause

    A. because of the natural contentment of a cat at rest

    B. for her own reflection

    C. at the sight of the fishbowl

    D. at the sight of the fish

    E. at the sight of her tail

33. In line 13, "Still had she gazed" can be best paraphrased as

    A. quietly she stared

    B. she looked without stirring

    C. she would yet be watching

    D. nevertheless, she looked intently

    E. constantly she stared

34. In the third stanza, the poem employs elevated diction in all of the following EXCEPT

    A. "tide" (line 13)

    B. "glide" (line 14)

    C. "genii" (line 15)

    D. "armor's" (line 16)

    E. "Tyrian hue" (line 16)

35. The "hapless nymph" in stanza 4 is

    A. Selima

    B. the genii of stanza 3

    C. the goldfish

    D. the nereid of stanza 6

    E. Susan

36. In line 20, "claw" is the

    A. object of "saw"

    B. subject of its clause

    C. object of a preposition

    D. object of "stretched"

    E. object of "reach"

37. Line 34 alludes to the dolphin and nereid because they

    A. rescue drowning men in myth

    B. are decorations on the fish tub

    C. identify Tom and Susan

    D. are inhabitants of water

    E. are examples of watery gods

38. In stanza 6, the implication of the aphorism "A favorite has no friend" is

   I. the servants resent the pampered cat

  II. other cats in the house refuse to help Selima out of envy

 III. those who have been most fortunate have the most to lose

  A. I only

  B. III only

  C. I and III only

  D. II and III only

  E. I, II, and III

39. The metaphor developed through stanzas 1–6 compares

  A. the fate of a cat and the fate of beautiful women

  B. a cat and a goldfish

  C. a cat and an epic hero

  D. a cat and an epic heroine

  E. goldfish and epic heroes

40. The conclusions drawn in the final stanza are primarily intended to

  A. morally instruct the reader

  B prevent a reader from suffering a fate like Selima's

  C. amuse the reader

  D. warn against the lure of specious wealth

  E. warn against pride

41. The style of the poem as a whole may be best described as

  A. informal

  B. mock-heroic

  C. understated

  D. ironic

  E. impressionistic

42. In which of the following meters is the poem written?

   I. Iambic trimeter

  II. Iambic tetrameter

 III. Iambic pentameter

  A. III only

  B. I and II only

  C. I and III only

  D. II and III only

  E. I, II, and III

GO ON TO THE NEXT PAGE

Practice Test 2

Questions 43–56. Read the following passage carefully before you begin to answer the questions.

I mention the spawning of the toads because it is one of the phenomena of spring which most deeply appeal to me, and because the toad, unlike the skylark
(5) and the primrose, has never had much of a boost from the poets. But I am aware than many people do not like reptiles or amphibians, and I am not suggesting that in order to enjoy the spring you
(10) have to take an interest in toads. There are also the crocus, the missel thrush, the cuckoo, and the blackthorn, etc. The point is that the pleasures of spring are available to everybody, and cost noth-
(15) ing. Even in the most sordid street the coming of spring will register itself by some sign or other, if it is only a brighter blue between the chimney pots or the vivid green of an elder sprouting on a
(20) blitzed site. Indeed it is remarkable how Nature goes on existing unofficially, as it were, in the very heart of London. I have seen a kestrel flying over the Deptford gasworks, and I have heard a
(25) first-rate performance by a black-bird in the Euston Road. There must be some hundreds of thousands, if not millions, of birds living inside the four-mile radius, and it is rather a pleasing thought
(30) that none of them pays a half-penny of rent.

As for spring, not even the narrow and gloomy streets round the Bank of England are quite able to exclude it. It
(35) comes seeping in everywhere, like one of those new poison gases which pass through all filters. The spring is commonly referred to as "a miracle," and during the past five or six years this
(40) worn-out figure of speech has taken on a new lease of life. After the sort of winters we have had to endure recently, the spring does seem miraculous, because it has become gradually harder and harder
(45) to believe that it is actually going to happen. Every February since 1940 I have found myself thinking that this time winter is going to be permanent. But Persephone, like the toads, always rises
(50) from the dead at about the same moment. Suddenly towards the end of March, the miracle happens and the decaying slum in which I live is transfigured. Down in the square the sooty
(55) privets have turned bright green, the leaves are thickening on the chestnut trees, the daffodils are out, the wallflowers are budding, the policemen's tunic looks positively a pleasant shade of
(60) blue, the fishmonger greets his customers with a smile, and even the sparrows are quite a different color, having felt the balminess of the air and nerved themselves to take a bath, their first
(65) since last September.

43. From details in the passage, we can infer that it was written

- **A.** sometime in the mid-nineteenth century
- **B.** during World War I
- **C.** in the spring of 1925
- **D.** in 1945 or 1946
- **E.** sometime in the 1970s

44. In the opening sentence of the passage, the author refers to the "spawning of the toads" for which of the following reasons?

- I. He is interested in and informed about natural history.
- II. He wishes to be different from other writers.
- III. The reference will surprise his readers.

- **A.** I only
- **B.** I and II only
- **C.** I and III only
- **D.** II and III only
- **E.** I, II, and III

45. The diction of a phrase like "the toad . . . has never had much of a boost from the poets" can be best described as

- **A.** formal
- **B.** interpretive
- **C.** colloquial
- **D.** jargon-ridden
- **E.** reproachful

46. The author refers to the "crocus, the missel thrush, the cuckoo, and the blackthorn" (lines 11–12)

- **A.** as examples of birds and plants that are especially beautiful
- **B.** as examples of birds and plants that are not usually associated with early spring
- **C.** to demonstrate the range of his knowledge of the natural world
- **D.** as examples of the birds and plants he prefers to toads
- **E.** as examples of the birds and plants conventionally associated with spring

47. In a more conventionally written passage of expository prose, the sentence in lines 13–15 — "the pleasures of spring are available to everybody, and cost nothing" — would probably be

- **A.** edited out of the passage
- **B.** placed first as a topic sentence
- **C.** changed from a loose to a periodic sentence
- **D.** changed from a periodic to a loose sentence
- **E.** divided into two complete simple sentences

GO ON TO THE NEXT PAGE

48. All the following are figurative EXCEPT

- A. "boost from the poets" (line 6)
- B. "many people do not like reptiles or amphibians" (lines 7–8)
- C. "a first-rate performance by a black-bird" (lines 24–25)
- D. "new lease of life" (line 41)
- E. "like the toads" (line 49)

49. The author juxtaposes the natural world and the urban scene in all the following phrases EXCEPT

- A. "brighter blue between the chimney pots" (lines 17–18)
- B. "elder sprouting on a blitzed site" (lines 19–20)
- C. "kestrel flying over the Deptford gasworks" (lines 23–24)
- D. "a black-bird in the Euston Road" (lines 25–26)
- E. "leaves are thickening on the chestnut trees" (lines 56–57)

50. If nature exists in London "unofficially" (line 21), official London is best represented by

- A. "millions, of birds living inside the four-mile radius" (lines 27–29)
- B. "the narrow and gloomy streets round the Bank of England" (lines 32–34)
- C. "one of those new poison gases which pass through all filters" (lines 35–37)

- D. "winter" (line 48)
- E. "positively a pleasant shade of blue" on "the policeman's tunic" (lines 58–60)

51. In the sentence "this worn-out figure of speech has taken on a new lease of life" (lines 39–41), the author employs

- A. a worn-out figure of speech
- B. a simile based on real estate
- C. a common error in syntax
- D. a symbol
- E. poetic license

52. The most unconventional figure of speech used to describe spring in the passage is probably

- A. "it" (line 34)
- B. "one of those new poison gases" (lines 35–36)
- C. "miracle" (line 38)
- D. "Persephone . . . rises from the dead" (lines 49–50)
- E. "miracle" (line 52)

53. In the second paragraph, the idea of spring as a miracle is

   I. advanced tentatively at first, then boldly

   II. initially qualified by the use of "commonly referred to" and "does seem"

   III. intensified by the bleakness of the winter

   A. III only

   B. I and II only

   C. I and III only

   D. II and III only

   E. I, II, and III

54. In the last sentence of the passage (lines 54–65), the optimism of the description is undermined by which of the following words or phrases?

   A. "different"

   B. "balminess"

   C. "air"

   D. "nerved"

   E. "bath"

55. From the passage, we can infer that the author is

   A. eager to earn money

   B. poor

   C. unrealistic

   D. sympathetic to the capitalist system

   E. conservative

56. All the following adjectives could properly be used to describe the style and effect of this passage EXCEPT

   A. pedantic

   B. comic

   C. optimistic

   D. realistic

   E. spontaneous

Practice Test 2

IF YOU FINISH BEFORE TIME IS CALLED, CHECK YOUR WORK ON THIS SECTION ONLY. DO NOT WORK ON ANY OTHER SECTION IN THE TEST.

Section II: Essay Questions

Time: 2 Hours

3 Questions

Question 1

(Suggested time — 40 minutes. This question accounts for one-third of the total essay section score.)

Directions: Read the following passage carefully. Write an essay in which you discuss how the choice of detail, diction, and syntax are used to reveal the speaker's attitude to Sir Walter Elliot.

Sir Walter Elliot, of Kellynch Hall, in Somersetshire, was a man who, for his own amusement, never took up any book but the Baronetage; there he found
(5) occupation for an idle hour, and consolation in a distressed one; there his faculties were roused into admiration and respect by contemplating the limited remnant of the earliest patents; there any
(10) unwelcome sensations arising from domestic affairs changed naturally into pity and contempt as he turned over the almost endless creations of the last century; and there, if every other leaf were
(15) powerless, he could read his own history with an interest that never failed. This was the page at which the favourite volume was always opened: —
Elliot of Kellynch Hall.
(20) "Walter Elliot, born March 1, 1760, married July 15, 1784, Elizabeth, daughter of James Stevenson, Esq., of South Park, in the City of Gloucester; by which lady (who died 1800) he has is-
(25) sue, Elizabeth, born June 1, 1785; Anne, born August 9, 1787; a stillborn son, November 5, 1789; Mary born November 20, 1791."

Precisely such had the paragraph orig-
(30) inally stood from the printer's hands; but Sir Walter had improved it by adding, for the information of himself and his family, these words, after the date of Mary's birth: — "Married December 16,
(35) 1810, Charles, son and heir of Charles Musgrove, Esq., of Uppercross, in the county of Somerset," and by inserting most accurately the day of the month on which he had lost his wife.
(40) Then followed the history and rise of the ancient and respectable family in the usual terms; how it had been first settled in Cheshire, how mentioned in Dugdale, serving the office of high sheriff, repre-
(45) senting a borough in three successive parliaments, exertions of loyalty, and dignity of baronet, in the first year of Charles II with all the Marys and Elizabeths they had married; forming altogether two
(50) handsome quarto pages, and concluding

with the arms and motto: — "Principal seat, Kellynch Hall, in the country of Somerset," and Sir Walter's handwriting again in this finale: —

(60)   "Heir presumptive, William Walter Elliot, Esq., great-grandson of the second Sir Walter."

Vanity was the beginning and end of Sir Walter Elliot's character: vanity of (65) person and of situation. He had been remarkably handsome in his youth, and at fifty-four was still a very fine man. Few women could think more of their (70) personal appearance than he did, nor could the valet of any new-made lord be more delighted with the place he held in society. He considered the blessing of beauty as inferior only to the blessing of a baronetcy; and the Sir Walter Elliot, who united these gifts, was the constant object of his warmest respect and devotion.

Question 2

(Suggested time — 40 minutes. This question accounts for one-third of the total essay section score.)

Directions: Read the following poem by the Jamaican-born writer Claude McKay carefully. Then write an essay in which you discuss the ways in which the author's style (diction, imagery, selection of detail) reveals his feeling about what he recalls and cannot remember about his youth.

Flame-Heart

So much have I forgotten in ten years,
So much in ten brief years! I have forgot
What time the purple apples come to juice,
And what month brings the shy forget-me-not.
(5)   I have forgot the special, startling season
Of the pimento's flowering and fruiting;
What time of year the ground doves brown the fields
And fill the noonday with their curious fluting.
I have forgotten much, but still remember
(10)   The poinsettia's red, blood-red in warm December.

I still recall the honey-fever grass,
But cannot recollect the high days when
We rooted them out of the ping-wing path
To stop the mad bees in the rabbit pen.
(15)   I often try to think in what sweet month
The languid painted ladies used to dapple
The yellow by-road mazing from the main,
Sweet with the golden threads of the rose-apple.
I have forgotten — strange — but quite remember
(20)   The poinsettia's red, blood-red in warm December.

GO ON TO THE NEXT PAGE

What weeks, what months, what time of the mild year
We cheated school to have our fling at tops?
What days our wine-thrilled bodies pulsed with joy
Feasting upon blackberries in the copse?
(25) Oh, some I know! I have embalmed the days,
Even the sacred moments when we played,
All innocent of passion, uncorrupt,
At noon and evening in the flame-heart's shade.
We were so happy, happy, I remember
(30) Beneath the poinsettia's red in warm December.

Question 3

(Suggested time — 40 minutes. This question accounts for one-third of the total essay section score.)

Directions: Many plays and novels that focus upon the courtship or marriage of a man and a woman include a second pair who help to define the central figures. Write a well-organized essay in which you discuss how the secondary man and woman illuminate the central characters of the work.

You may write on one of the following works or any other play or novel of your choice of equivalent literary merit.

The Merchant of Venice
Twelfth Night
She Stoops to Conquer
The Way of the World
Hedda Gabler
Mrs. Warren's Profession
Man and Superman
The Three Sisters
The Importance of Being Earnest
The Little Foxes
A Doll's House
Macbeth
Who's Afraid of Virginia Woolf?
Pride and Prejudice
Emma
Wuthering Heights

Jane Eyre
Adam Bede
Middlemarch
Hard Times
Great Expectations
The Return of the Native
The Mayor of Casterbridge
The House of Mirth
The Great Gatsby

IF YOU FINISH BEFORE TIME IS CALLED, CHECK YOUR WORK ON THIS
SECTION ONLY. DO NOT WORK ON ANY OTHER SECTION IN THE TEST.

Answer Key

Section I: Multiple-Choice Questions

First Poem

1. D
2. E
3. B
4. A
5. C
6. C
7. C
8. B
9. E
10. C
11. D
12. A
13. A
14. D
15. E
16. A

First Prose Passage

17. C
18. E
19. B
20. A
21. D
22. B
23. D
24. E
25. C
26. A
27. D
28. E

Second Poem

29. D
30. E
31. B
32. B
33. C
34. B
35. A
36. D
37. A
38. A
39. D
40. C
41. B
42. B

Second Prose Passage

43. D
44. D
45. C
46. E
47. B
48. B
49. E
50. B
51. A
52. B
53. E
54. D
55. B
56. A

Practice Test 2 Scoring Worksheet

Use the following worksheet to arrive at a probable final AP grade on the Practice Test 2. While it is sometimes difficult to be objective enough to score one's own essay, you can use the sample essay answers that follow to approximate an essay score for yourself. You may also give your essays (along with the sample essays) to a friend or relative to score if you feel confident that the individual has the knowledge necessary to make such a judgment and that he or she will feel comfortable in doing so.

Section I: Multiple-Choice Questions

$$\underline{\hspace{2cm}} - (^1/_4 \text{ or } .25 \times \underline{\hspace{2cm}}) = \underline{\hspace{2cm}}$$

right   wrong multiple-choice
answers   answers raw score

$$\underline{\hspace{2cm}} \times 1.25 = \underline{\hspace{2cm}} (\text{of possible } 67.5)$$

multiple-choice   multiple-choice
raw score   converted score

Section II: Essay Questions

$$\underline{\hspace{2cm}} + \underline{\hspace{2cm}} + \underline{\hspace{2cm}} = \underline{\hspace{2cm}}$$

question 1 question 2 question 3 essay
raw score raw score raw score

$$\underline{\hspace{2cm}} \times 3.055 = \underline{\hspace{2cm}} (\text{of possible } 82.5)$$

essay   essay
raw score   converted score

Final Score

$$\underline{\hspace{2cm}} + \underline{\hspace{2cm}} = \underline{\hspace{2cm}} (\text{of possible } 150)$$

multiple-choice   essay   final
converted score converted score converted score

Probable Final AP Score

Final Converted Score	Probable AP Score
150–100	5
99–86	4
85–67	3
66–0	1 or 2

Answers and Explanations for Practice Test 2

Section I: Multiple-Choice Questions

First Poem

Unlike the other practice exams, this one begins with a relatively easy passage, especially for students with some experience of Renaissance poetry. The poem is short and carefully patterned, so once you've seen its point, most of the details will fall into place. This is a text you'll certainly want to work with right away, leaving the more difficult prose and the other poem to be handled in order.

1. **D.** The poem, part of a sequence of sonnets by Samuel Daniel, was written in the late sixteenth century. The speaker is probably a young man and the person addressed a young woman. The poem looks ahead to a future when both of them are old. At the time of the poem, the lady is still beautiful (line 7) and her hair is still golden (line 14).

2. **E.** The poet is imagining a future when the woman's beauty will have faded. The expected form of the verb is "to have passed." The rest of the verbs in the sentence are unremarkable. The poem uses "pass" because it is part of a sequence of sonnets where the last line of one poem is, in part, repeated by the first line of the following poem, and the poem before this has ended with "her flower, her glory, pass." Though you are not expected to know this fact, you should see that the verb form is odd in its context.

3. **B.** Though in other contexts "glass" may mean "tumbler" or even "barometer," here, as is often the case in Renaissance poetry, it means "mirror" or "looking glass." Her mirror will in time reveal the fact that her beauty has faded.

4. **A.** The "miracle" here is his continuing to love her despite her cruel treatment of him and despite the fact that she has grown old and is no longer beautiful.

5. **C.** Line 10 explains by metaphor what the miracle is. The fire can continue to burn although there is no fuel to feed it. That is, his love will be just as ardent although the beauty that inspired his love has gone.

6. **C.** Though "winter" may be a symbol of any of these choices in other works, the details here point to "old age." Throughout the poem, the speaker has looked to a future when the lady is old and no longer beautiful. Here he speaks of winter's snowing upon her golden hairs, the turning of the blond hair to white in old age.

7. C. Although the idea of the poem's preserving the beauty of the lady despite time's passing is a common notion in the sonnets of this period, in Spenser's and Shakespeare's, for example, the concept does not appear here. Lines 12–13 warn that she may be sorry she spurned his love, while lines 5–11 assert that he will love her despite the loss of her beauty.

8. B. Like many lyrics of the period, this poem uses the "when. . . then" construction. The "when" is explicit in line 1 and introduces the clause of lines 1–4. The "then" is implicit as the beginning of the completion of this sentence (lines 5–8). In lines 13–14, the order is reversed, the "then" implied in line 13 and the "when" explicit in line 14.

9. E. If the "glory" of line 1 is an image of the lady's hair that once surrounded her head like the golden halos in pictures of the saints, the figure is recalled in the last line of the poem. The "glory" that has passed away in line 1 becomes the "golden hairs" that have turned white in line 14.

10. C. The word "fire" is used only once. The number of repetitions is an indication of how carefully crafted this poem is. The repetitions are "spent" (lines 6 and 10), "in me" (lines 5, 6, and 9), "repent" (lines 12 and 13), and "faith" (lines 8 and 11).

11. D. The woman's beauty is represented by the metaphors of "flower," "glory," and "flame" and by "golden hairs." The man, not the lady, performs the miracle.

12. A. The "truth" of line 4 is the loss of beauty in old age. The lover's "wounds" are his continued suffering for love of the lady, the "heat" is the ardency of his love, the "faith" is his always-growing devotion to her, and the "miracle" is the continuation of his love into her old age.

13. A. The rhetorical purpose is the real reason for the poem, the argument that the speaker most wants to express. Probably 95 percent of all the world's love poetry has the same intention: to convince the beloved to return the love of the speaker. Though choices **C**, **D**, and **E** appear at times in love poetry, they are not issues in this sonnet. The poem does warn the lady of what the future will bring (**B**), but that is not its rhetorical purpose. The poet is arguing that if the lady returns his love now, she can avoid the regret and guilt that he predicts she will feel when she is old.

14. D. The poem contrasts the woman's and the lover's present (youth) with the future (old age). It contrasts the growth of his love ("wax," line 8) with her decline into age ("waning," line 8) and the permanence of his love in the face of human mutability. The poem uses the word "truth" in line 4 but does not oppose truth to lie.

15. E. The word "scorned" here has no religious overtone. It denotes the lady's indifference to the lover's suffering. There are religious associations, however, with the words "faith," "miracle," and "repent."

16. A. The poem is a Shakespearean, or English, sonnet. It is written in iambic pentameter and rhymed abab, cdcd, efef, gg.

First Prose Passage

17. C. Because the passage presents a narrative about related characters, we can infer that it is not from a journal, a day-to-day personal record, or from an essay, a nonfictional personal account of a single subject. We must choose among three forms of the novel. It is not epistolary (in letters), and it is not a stream-of-consciousness technique (presented through the thoughts of one of the characters). The only choice remaining is Victorian novel. You don't have to be able to distinguish a Victorian novel from a novel of another period to answer this question, because the other four options can be eliminated. The AP exam won't ask you questions about dates that can't be inferred from the passage or the answer choices. This passage is from *Dombey and Son,* written by Charles Dickens in 1848.

18. E. All three figures are used. Time is compared to a forester "striding through . . . forests" and notching the trees to be felled. Time's marks have been set on Dombey's brow, and these notches signify a tree "to come down in good time."

19. B. The "house" is the firm of Dombey and Son. The last paragraph speaks of Dombey and Son's trading ventures, ships, and enterprises.

20. A. The details of the last paragraph indicate that the company is engaged in international trade.

21. D. In the few sentences that deal with Mrs. Dombey, she is characterized as passive, frail, and reticent. She is surprised by her husband's unaccustomed tenderness. Whether or not she is loving is unsaid.

22. B. She is startled because her husband, who usually addresses her as Mrs. Dombey, has used the words "my dear." By producing a son, she has greatly pleased him. He almost uses the affectionate phrase a second time (line 56) but thinks better of it. Mr. Dombey, clearly, is a very cold fish.

23. D. As lines 66–67 state, the "one idea" of Mr. Dombey is the firm Dombey and Son. His first words in this passage are about the business, and he repeats its name like an incantation.

24. E. The last paragraph elaborates on the importance of Dombey and Son to Mr. Dombey. The "them" in line 70 and the "their" in line 71 also refer to Dombey and Son in line 68.

25. C. The point of view is that of Mr. Dombey. It is only he who believes his company is the center of the universe. The author of the passage (Dickens) and the narrator (an invention of the author) do not share Mr. Dombey's view that, for example, A.D. stands for "anno Dombei — and Son."

26. A. Repartee is witty and surprising dialogue, not a talent of Mr. Dombey's and not in evidence in this paragraph. The replacement of "Domini" by "Dombei" is a striking example of blasphemous comparison and overstatement. The repetition of words like "was made," "were made," "were formed," or the pronouns "them" and "their" and the series of passive clauses in lines 66–72 are examples of parallel construction.

27. D. This question calls for an inference, that is, something not explicit in the passage. The question points us to the paragraph on time, and that paragraph speaks of preparation for death. Nothing in that paragraph has any relation to Paul's business abilities or marital situation, so the best inference is that he will die young. Dombey and Son is, in fact, a novel about Dombey and daughter.

28. E. The author does not, like Mr. Dombey, believe in the all-importance of Dombey and Son. All the assertions here are the opposite of what the writer really thinks. Nowhere else in the passage is the irony so clear.

Second Poem

The poem is by Thomas Gray.

29. D. The lines describe a china bowl filled with water in which goldfish are swimming. It is probably blue and white porcelain.

30. E. The word order in this stanza is inverted. The series of nouns in lines 8–11 are all the direct objects of the verb "saw" (line 12). The subject of the sentence is "she" (line 12), that is, the cat, Selima. The cat is looking at her reflection in the water of the goldfish tub.

31. B. In this context, the word "tortoise" refers to tortoise shell, the hard, variegated material used to make combs or eyeglass frames. Tortoise shell, in its mottled yellow and brown colors, is like a tabby cat.

32. B. Because the poem denotes the purring as "applause" (line 12), the cat is celebrating her own appearance, which is reflected in the water of the bowl.

33. C. To answer this question, you must look at the whole sentence, which goes on to say, "but . . . two . . . forms were seen to glide." This construction with the conjunction "but" makes it clear that "had stared" is a subjunctive verb, not an indicative past perfect tense. In this context, "still" has the meaning of "yet," "even now."

34. B. The use of the verb "glide" to describe the motion of goldfish is not unusual. To describe motion of the water of a goldfish bowl, even a very large one, as "tide" is elevated diction. So is to speak of goldfish as "genii" or their scales as a "scaly armor" or their color as a "Tyrian hue." This inflated diction to describe ordinary things exemplifies the poem's mock-heroic language.

35. A. The hapless (unlucky) nymph is the cat, Selima, who is about to drown.

36. D. There is a semicolon after "saw" in line 19. That sentence is complete. In lines 20–22, the subject and verb of the sentence are "She stretched," and the objects of the verb are "whisker" and "claw."

37. A. If they are decorations (**B**), the verbs "came" and "stirred" make no sense. Tom and Susan are servants in the house (**C**). Nereids are watery gods, but dolphins are not (**E**). They are inhabitants of water (**D**), but that does not explain the line. In classical myth, dolphins or nereids may be the rescuers of drowning men, as in the myth of Arion. Notice that this question can be answered by the process of elimination and by common sense. It is easier, of course, for the student with some familiarity with Greek myth. Because no mythical rescuers come to her aid, Selima will drown.

38. A. Selima gets no supernatural or human help from Tom or Susan. The use of adjective "cruel" for Tom followed by the remark about a "favorite" suggests that the servants resent the cat.

39. D. The metaphor of the six stanzas compares the cat with an epic heroine. She is demure, pensive, fair, with eyes of emerald, a hapless nymph, a presumptuous maid who meets her fate when the gods fail to intervene to save her. The goldfish may be like epic heroes, because they do wear armor, but the metaphor is not developed through stanzas 1–6.

40. C. The improving advice of the last stanza cannot be taken seriously, though the death of the cat is ingeniously turned into a lesson for beautiful women. Nonetheless, the primary intention of stanza 7 is not moral instruction. This is a comic poem, well aware of the incongruity of this high moral tone set against the accidental death of a cat. The poem takes the death of the cat too seriously to be serious.

41. B. The terms "informal," "understated," and "impressionistic" are not at all suitable. Though there is irony in the poem, mock-heroic is the better choice. The mock-heroic style uses an elevated language to treat a trivial subject in an apparently serious manner.

42. B. Although iambic pentameter is the most common meter in English poetry, this poem uses only iambic trimeter and tetrameter. In each stanza, lines 1, 2, 4, and 5 are iambic tetrameter (four feet), while lines 3 and 6 are iambic trimeter (three feet).

Second Prose Passage

43. D. The passage was written by George Orwell. It was first published in April, 1946. We can infer from the passage that it must have been written near the end of or shortly after World War II. The first paragraph refers to a "blitzed site." The second paragraph refers specifically to every "February since 1940" and "the past five or six years."

44. D. His uncertainty about whether toads are reptiles or amphibians does not suggest that the speaker is especially interested in or well informed about natural history. It is much more likely that he chooses to favor the toad for an effect of originality and surprise. If he had said that his favorite sign of spring was the robin, many readers would not go on. The toad is the first of several surprises in this passage.

45. C. This phrase, and indeed the whole passage, is colloquial. Many dictionaries still list "boost" as colloquial, and the idea of poets as boosters is another of the passage's small surprises. Formal (**A**) is exactly the wrong word to describe Orwell's prose in this passage. Nor is it interpretive (**B**), reproachful (**E**), or jargon-ridden (too dependent on a specialized vocabulary and idiom).

46. E. These plants and birds are those that have had a boost from the poets as signs of spring — for example, by Shakespeare (the cuckoo), Rossetti (the blackthorn), and Hopkins (the thrush). The casual "etc." at the end of the list indicates Orwell's lack of enthusiasm for these conventional signs of spring.

47. B. In the formula essay, this sentence would probably begin the paragraph — the topic sentence. By not using it first, Orwell can get away with this less-than-original assertion without losing his reader. Imagine how different this paragraph would be if this sentence came first instead of the sentence about the spawning of toads. Next time someone tells you to begin all paragraphs with a topic sentence, show him or her this passage.

48. **B.** The line "many people do not like reptiles or amphibians" is literal. It means exactly what it says. Choices **A**, **C**, and **D** are all metaphors. The metaphors are in the words "boost," "performance," and "lease." "Like the toads" is a simile.

49. **E.** One of the techniques Orwell uses several times to present the coming of spring to London is to place a detail from the urban scene next to something from the natural world. Each of the first four options here places nature (blue sky, elder in leaf, flying kestrel, blackbird) next to a part of the cityscape (Chimney pots, blitzed site, Deptford gasworks, Euston Road). Choice **E** describes a natural scene but has no detail of the city.

50. **B.** Like a scene from Dickens, the passage suggests that the city has its own life and is at odds with nature, which pays no rent. The narrow and gloomy streets near the Bank of England, the commercial heart of the city, are presented as trying their best but failing to keep spring out.

51. **A.** One of the jokes of the passage is Orwell's using the cliché ("new lease of life") in a sentence that speaks of another cliché ("miracle") as a "worn-out figure of speech." The allusion may be to real estate (**B**), but the phrase is a metaphor, not a simile. It is not an error in syntax, a symbol, or an example of poetic license.

52. **B.** This is certainly the most unexpected comparison for spring I have read; spring is like a poison gas. The Persephone and the miracle figures are old hat. In line 34, "it" is simply a pronoun, not a figure of speech.

53. **E.** The paragraph begins by putting quotation marks around "a miracle" and calling the term a worn-out figure of speech for spring. Others, the author suggests, may use this word, but not me. Because the winters have been so terrible, spring does "seem miraculous." Notice the hedge is still there in "seem." Finally, several lines later, all hesitation disappears, and "the miracle happens."

54. **D.** Though the air is "warm," that the sparrows must "nerve" themselves to take a bath serves to control the optimism of the passage. The image of the bird with six months of accumulated London grime is characteristic of the unique approach to spring of this passage.

55. **B.** A few details suggest that the author is unsympathetic to capitalism (**D**). No details support choices **A**, **C**, or **E**. We can infer his poverty from the description of his home as a "decaying slum."

56. **A.** The passage is never pedantic. It is, at times, comic, optimistic, realistic, and spontaneous.

Section II: Essay Questions

Question 1: Jane Austen

Unlike the question on the passage by Dr. Johnson in the first practice test, this one lists three specific techniques to be discussed: choice of detail, diction, and syntax. Because it would be hard to misread the author's contemptuous attitude to Sir Walter, the scores on this question would be determined chiefly by the answers on technique. Most students will be able to deal with diction well; more will have some trouble in handling choice of detail; a huge number will leave out any discussion of syntax. Others will use the word but never talk about it. The few who know what the word means and find something to say about it will score very well.

If you wrote your own essay for this question, compare it to the two student essays that follow. If you did not write an answer for this particular question, you should still read the passage carefully and plan how you would answer the question. In either case, ask yourself the following questions: What are the strengths and weaknesses of the first essay? Of the second? Which of the two is better? Was yours or would yours have been better than these?

Student Essay 1

Sir Walter Elliot appears to be a man profoundly impressed with himself. The author describes a man who is his own biggest fan, a pompous blueblood enthralled with his lineage, wholly self-centered and reverent toward himself. Elliot is not openly criticized in the passage: rather, the author "plays it straight," allowing readers to form their own impressions based on the depiction of the baron. This method is far more effective than a lecture from the author describing in general terms Elliot's arrogance and self-absorption. Readers will put together the details of her description, come to their own conclusions, and inevitably be far more satisfied with the results.

Narcissism is delineated by the author through careful diction. Sir Walter looks at the Baronetage's writings from the past with "pity and contempt." He is a man concerned primarily with "his own amusement." Rather than reading, as some do, to learn or enrich himself, Sir Walter reads so that he may revel in a character he deems already perfect. No possibility of the need for enrichment exists in Elliot's self-conception; reading the Baronetage is the amusement of an idle hour, and the impression that results is that of an idle man. The author's most impacting phrase comes not when it is plainly stated that Elliot is vain in both character and situation. The final sentence, drenched in irony, presents the definitive portrait of Elliot in the reader's mind: "Sir Walter Elliot . . . was the constant object of his warmest respect and devotion." While referring to Elliot as someone capable of warmth and caring, the author subtextually belies the apparent meaning of the sentence. Of course Elliot is brimming with good feeling — but for himself.

The author also has a skillful command of detail, using specifics to further flesh out Elliot's character. Most grieving husbands or proud parents would be forgiven for amending a volume in which they appeared, so that it included the significant episodes of their lives. Indeed, this would even be admirable were it done for posterity, for the information of future generations and the historical record. Yet one gets the impression that Elliot is little concerned with such matters, that his revision of the history is intended for the present, exclusively for the sake of his own enjoyment. The joy comes to Elliot not in seeing the record set down accurately, but in the revision itself, the act of embellishing his own life even as the baron's impression of himself is repeatedly embellished by his own ever-expanding respect for his good looks and noble bearing. The image of Elliot, needing to have the last word over the printer, sitting in his study improving the volume, seems the best indication of the author's attitude toward Elliot.

Elliot's final amendment to the book is telling as well. He takes great pride in setting down the name of his future heir. This indicates the paramount importance and pride with which he regards his own position; he feels he will be giving over something truly great.

Through such effective details and diction, the author makes clear the nature of Sir Walter's character. The author's scornful attitude will surely be shared by the reader who meets with the vanity and snobbishness of Sir Walter Elliot.

Student Essay 2

Diction, syntax, and choice of detail are often important keys to understanding an author's attitude prevalent in his written works. In this excerpt, these elements of style demonstrate the author's writing style and amused tone to the reader.

The passage opens with a description of Sir Walter Elliot and his favorite form of amusement: reading the Baronetage. The author explains that this book serves not only as an enjoyable pastime for Elliot, but also as a comfort when life seems disagreeable to him. ". . . there he found occupation for an idle hour, and consolation in a distressed one; there his faculties were roused into admiration and respect . . ." The tone in the first paragraph of the passage is quite straightforward, and because of the author's objectivity and absolute wording, little is revealed about the writer's attitude.

The author continues to describe Elliot's extreme interest in the page that contained his personal family genealogy, and for the first time in this passage the reader is able to understand Elliot's self-absorbed nature better. "Precisely such had the paragraph [of his family's genealogy] originally stood from the printer's hands; but Sir Walter had improved

it by adding, for the information of himself and his family, these words . . ." This detail, chosen by the author, shows the reader Elliot's meticulous and almost obsessive nature about preserving his personal history. The author continues to describe the pages of Elliot family history and Elliot's absurd pride in perfectly recording the family's reputation for "serving the office of high sheriff, representing a borough in three successive parliaments, exertions of loyalty, and dignity of baronet . . . forming altogether two handsome quarto pages, and concluding with the arms and motto . . ." Here the author uses a satirical tone to express the silliness of Elliot's actions. Words such as "handsome pages," "loyalty," and "dignity" all communicate the writer's true feelings of amusement as he chooses to use irony to describe the Elliot family's feats, reinforcing the satirical tone. The author also continually refers to Elliot as "Sir Walter," a pretentious title and humorous use of satire. The last detail also contributes to the prevailing attitude of absurdity when the author notes that "Sir Walter's handwriting again in . . . finale . . ." edited the original document to correctly include his heir.

The final paragraph directly expresses the author's feelings as he clearly writes, "Vanity was the beginning and end of Sir Walter Elliot's character: vanity of person and of situation." Although the writer makes his opinion of Elliot obvious, he is not judgmental or condescending. The tone in the final paragraph is simple and direct, yet truthful. It is with amusement that the writer concludes, "He considered the blessing of beauty as inferior only to the blessing of a baronetcy; and the Sir Walter Elliot, who united these gifts, was the constant object of his warmest respect and devotion."

The author of this passage employs word choice, irony, and objective detail to express his attitude of gentle humor towards his subject, Sir Walter Elliot.

Comments on Question 1

The passage is the opening of Jane Austen's novel *Persuasion*, describing Sir Walter Elliot. Sir Walter is a baronet, the lowest of the British hereditary ranks (the ascending order is baronet, baron, viscount, earl, marquis, duke — if you should ever need to know), and the Baronetage, his favorite book, lists all the families who hold the title of baronet. If the pretesting of this question disclosed that many students were unable to determine what the Baronetage is from the passage, the word would be explained in a footnote. A modern equivalent to Sir Walter would be a successful man whose only recreational reading was his own biographical entry in *Who's Who in America*.

Response to Student Essay 1

The first student essay begins strongly but goes on to say that the passage does not "openly" criticize Sir Walter. The passage begins somewhat obliquely, but when it says, "Vanity was the beginning and end of Sir Walter Elliot's character," it is as direct as it could possibly be; this frontal assault continues when Sir Walter is said to be more pleased with his looks than almost any woman and as proud of his station as the valet of a man who has just been given a title. Inconsistently, the second paragraph of the essay says, "it is plainly stated that Elliot is vain in both character and situation." The treatment of detail in the third paragraph is plausible. Nothing is said about syntax. This essay would be scored in the middle of the scale, at five or possibly six.

Response to Student Essay 2

The second essay is also inaccurate and incomplete. Can anyone reading Jane Austen's first paragraph be in doubt about her attitude to Sir Walter? The paragraph tells us that the Baronetage is the only book he reads "for his own amusement," that he is contemptuous of those whose titles are not as old as his own, and that no matter how often he does so, nothing can give him pleasure equal to that of reading about himself.

The third paragraph has several errors. Jane Austen's paragraph that begins "Then followed the history" is indirectly repeating the words of the Baronetage, not what Sir Walter records. The references to Sir Walter as "Sir" are not "pretentious" or "satiric." "Sir" is simply the proper form of address for a baronet and is no more satirical than speaking of Sir Lawrence Olivier or

Lord Nelson. On the real exam, an error like the former, which is caused by careless reading of the passage, would be held against a paper, but an error like the second, due to the student's not knowing the protocol of British titles, would probably have little effect on the score of the essay.

Notice that though this essay's first words are "Diction, syntax, and choice of detail," the last sentence speaks of "word choice, irony, and objective detail." Somehow, syntax has disappeared. The inaccuracy and omissions of this paper would drop its score to the lower half of the scale at four.

Restudy the Jane Austen passage, taking notes only on its syntax. Put your notes together into a paragraph. Add this paragraph to the best things in the two student essays here, and you should have a good answer to this question.

Question 2: Claude McKay

A small sampling of student responses to the first and second practice tests suggests that the McKay poem is the easiest of the four questions on required texts. In the first test, the Emily Dickinson poem gave more trouble than the passage from Dr. Johnson. In this exam, the Jane Austen passage appears to be more difficult than the poem.

The question on McKay's "Flame-Heart," unlike the question on Emily Dickinson's poem, specifies a discussion of diction, imagery, and selection of detail. The three are interrelated, and an observant reader will notice that almost all the details of the poem come from the natural world: flowers, fruits, grasses, shrubs, birds, and bees. Only a few details are man-made (by-road, school, tops).

In the process of telling what has been forgotten, the poem also tells us what has been remembered. In stanza one, for example, if the speaker has forgotten what time the purple apples come to juice, he has not forgotten the purple apples, or the pimento's flowering, or the sight and sound of the ground doves. The poem is not about the loss of memory, but the loss of childhood. The child here was close to nature, surrounded by colors and richly fruitful plants. The time was "sweet," and life was "so happy" because the speaker was still innocent of passion. The adult, the poem implies, is no longer innocent, uncorrupt. The blood-red flame-heart, which sounds to us like a symbol of passion, was then just another splash of color in the warm December landscape.

The following student essay, an eight on the nine-point scale, exemplifies the good answers that this question should elicit.

Student Essay

Among the most poignant subjects of poetry has been that misty past of memory, as poets strive to comprehend and tenaciously cling to the past, to childhood innocence. In "Flame-Heart," Claude McKay addresses such memories, attempting to explain his youth in terms of memories still with him. He mourns the things he has forgotten, but takes note of the details he remembers. Despite ambivalence expressed in the first two stanzas, the poem is ultimately a celebration of youth revealing McKay's positive and affectionate feelings toward the past.

McKay claims to have forgotten much in the past decade. But it becomes clear that the things he has forgotten are ancillary details, matters of time and season rather than impressions of vibrant natural beauty. The poet conveys to readers the degree that he loved his youth by the way he associates it with flowers and other manifestations of natural beauty; he may regret what he has forgotten, but loves the details he does remember, of "purple apples come to juice . . . pimento's flowering and fruiting . . . honey fever grass . . . languid painted ladies dappl[ing]." Because he has forgotten the season of such beauties, because he lacks the context of their occurrence, McKay's memories are bittersweet. That he remembers specifics other than these perhaps indicates a difficulty in putting his past in perspective and understanding or accepting its place in the chronology of his life.

McKay's diction is as important as his imagery in gaining clues to his attitude toward the past. The terms in which he describes the natural wonders of his half-remembered childhood are terms of innocence and youth; because he has difficulty remembering when these memories imbedded themselves in his psyche, the implication is that he has lost his connection to such qualities. He has changed beyond recognition and is haunted by the ghosts of what he once was. The forget-me-nots are "shy," the ground doves' song is one of "curious fluting," the painted ladies dapple "languidly," and the "rose-apple" is sweet with . . . golden threads." That is, all that McKay is struggling to place, to secure in the solid soil of time and place, is tied closely to qualities of innocence and wonder. Indeed, in the third stanza, McKay writes of playing "All innocent of passion, uncorrupt."

The piece's most striking image is the repetitive motif of the poinsettias. McKay ends the first two stanzas of the lament with the qualification that he does remember "The poinsettia's red, blood-red in warm December." At once an unsettling, surreal image, its repetition sets the work's mood. In his frustrated remembrance, McKay compares the holiday flower's color to blood, and notes that the Decembers of his childhood were warm; in conjunction with "blood-red," the resulting image is disturbing.

The past is mournfully dead to McKay because of his aging. He leaves clues to the reason for his sorrow when he writes that he has "embalmed" his days of innocence. McKay's sadness stands in stark relief next to the joy of his childhood amidst the glory of nature. The one thing he does remember is that he used to be happy. When he was happy, he did not see the world in such a fatalistic light; the poinsettias were not "blood-red," nor does he describe them so in the last stanza. Remembering his former happiness amidst the dour mood of the present, McKay concludes: "We were so happy, happy, I remember./ Beneath the poinsettia's red in warm December."

"Flame-Heart" ends then on a note of hope, as McKay finally immerses himself in childhood happiness despite the loss of details. In a sense reconciling himself to their loss, he acknowledges that the times were good. His feelings of longing toward the past are thereby at least partially assuaged.

Question 3: Open Question

There are so many possible approaches to an open question like this that it is hard to know where to begin. There is only one task: to discuss how a secondary couple illuminates the central figures in a play or novel that focuses on courtship or marriage. Most of Shakespeare's comedies contain second and even third couples (Jessica and Lorenzo in *The Merchant of Venice,* Olivia and Sebastian or Toby and Maria in *Twelfth Night,* Celia and Oliver in *As You Like It,* any three of the four couples in *A Midsummer Night's Dream*). If you argue that *Othello* is about marriage, even Iago and Emilia would fit this question.

The nineteenth-century British and American novel from Scott to Hardy or Cooper to James provides many examples of a defining secondary pair. Many of these novels have a fair and a dark heroine, a fair hero and a dark villain, with the blond woman (inevitably presented as beautiful, conventional, chaste, and passive) married in the final chapters to an equally conventional, chaste, and handsome hero. The darker couple, on the other hand, are vital passionate beings. Figures like Emily Bronte's Edgar and Isabella Linton or George Eliot's Adam Bede and Dinah Morris are set against Heathcliff and Catherine Linton, Arthur Donnithorne and Hetty Sorrel. The genre reaches its Hollywood apotheosis with Melanie and Ashley and Rhet and Scarlett in Margaret Mitchell's *Gone with the Wind.*

This excellent student essay, an eight on the nine-point scale, on *Pride and Prejudice* will give you an idea of what might be done with this question. The essay shows how Jane and Bingley throw light on Elizabeth and Darcy and on the meaning of the title of the novel.

Student Essay

Courtship and marriage are often primary focuses in written works. In Jane Austen's *Pride and Prejudice*, Jane Bennet and Mr. Bingley are helpful in defining Elizabeth Bennet and Mr. Darcy.

For all her beauty, wit, and intelligence, Elizabeth's greatest fault is her nature to judge people too quickly. Her initial prejudice towards Darcy and her pride in her ability to judge people prevent her from knowing his true nature. Similarly, Darcy's pride and his inability to overcome his prejudice against some of the connections of Jane and Elizabeth deter his pursuit of Elizabeth. Jane and Bingley, on the other hand, have no pride and prejudice. They fall in love almost at first sight. Being without pride, they are also passive, and Bingley lets Darcy draw him away from Jane. Darcy, misled by Jane's placid behavior, genuinely believes she does not love Bingley, and Bingley accepts Darcy's view. If Darcy is too proud, Bingley is too modest to trust his own judgment. If Elizabeth is too quick to find faults, Jane is too nice and can see only the best in people. For this reason, she fails to understand Caroline Bingley or to judge Darcy as harshly as Elizabeth does. Darcy and Elizabeth show the danger of too much pride and prejudice; Jane and Bingley show the danger of too little.

The two couples also illuminate each other's strong points, Darcy is interfering but also motivated by genuine concern for Bingley's well-being. Elizabeth's dislike of

Darcy is partly caused by her love for Jane. When Elizabeth realizes how proud and prejudiced she has been, she realizes more than ever before Jane's true strength and value. The wit of Elizabeth is set off by the kinder but far less interesting character of Jane, just as Darcy's greater depth, intelligence, and complexity is set off by contrast with the genial but bland Bingley.

Because of the roles that Jane and Bingley play, the characters of Elizabeth and Darcy are brought more clearly into focus. Jane Austen uses this secondary couple to clarify Elizabeth and Darcy's relationship, giving meaning to the title *Pride and Prejudice*.

Answer Sheet for Practice Test 3

(Remove This Sheet and Use it to Mark Your Answers)

1 Ⓐ Ⓑ Ⓒ Ⓓ Ⓔ	21 Ⓐ Ⓑ Ⓒ Ⓓ Ⓔ	41 Ⓐ Ⓑ Ⓒ Ⓓ Ⓔ
2 Ⓐ Ⓑ Ⓒ Ⓓ Ⓔ	22 Ⓐ Ⓑ Ⓒ Ⓓ Ⓔ	42 Ⓐ Ⓑ Ⓒ Ⓓ Ⓔ
3 Ⓐ Ⓑ Ⓒ Ⓓ Ⓔ	23 Ⓐ Ⓑ Ⓒ Ⓓ Ⓔ	43 Ⓐ Ⓑ Ⓒ Ⓓ Ⓔ
4 Ⓐ Ⓑ Ⓒ Ⓓ Ⓔ	24 Ⓐ Ⓑ Ⓒ Ⓓ Ⓔ	44 Ⓐ Ⓑ Ⓒ Ⓓ Ⓔ
5 Ⓐ Ⓑ Ⓒ Ⓓ Ⓔ	25 Ⓐ Ⓑ Ⓒ Ⓓ Ⓔ	45 Ⓐ Ⓑ Ⓒ Ⓓ Ⓔ
6 Ⓐ Ⓑ Ⓒ Ⓓ Ⓔ	26 Ⓐ Ⓑ Ⓒ Ⓓ Ⓔ	46 Ⓐ Ⓑ Ⓒ Ⓓ Ⓔ
7 Ⓐ Ⓑ Ⓒ Ⓓ Ⓔ	27 Ⓐ Ⓑ Ⓒ Ⓓ Ⓔ	47 Ⓐ Ⓑ Ⓒ Ⓓ Ⓔ
8 Ⓐ Ⓑ Ⓒ Ⓓ Ⓔ	28 Ⓐ Ⓑ Ⓒ Ⓓ Ⓔ	48 Ⓐ Ⓑ Ⓒ Ⓓ Ⓔ
9 Ⓐ Ⓑ Ⓒ Ⓓ Ⓔ	29 Ⓐ Ⓑ Ⓒ Ⓓ Ⓔ	49 Ⓐ Ⓑ Ⓒ Ⓓ Ⓔ
10 Ⓐ Ⓑ Ⓒ Ⓓ Ⓔ	30 Ⓐ Ⓑ Ⓒ Ⓓ Ⓔ	50 Ⓐ Ⓑ Ⓒ Ⓓ Ⓔ
11 Ⓐ Ⓑ Ⓒ Ⓓ Ⓔ	31 Ⓐ Ⓑ Ⓒ Ⓓ Ⓔ	51 Ⓐ Ⓑ Ⓒ Ⓓ Ⓔ
12 Ⓐ Ⓑ Ⓒ Ⓓ Ⓔ	32 Ⓐ Ⓑ Ⓒ Ⓓ Ⓔ	52 Ⓐ Ⓑ Ⓒ Ⓓ Ⓔ
13 Ⓐ Ⓑ Ⓒ Ⓓ Ⓔ	33 Ⓐ Ⓑ Ⓒ Ⓓ Ⓔ	53 Ⓐ Ⓑ Ⓒ Ⓓ Ⓔ
14 Ⓐ Ⓑ Ⓒ Ⓓ Ⓔ	34 Ⓐ Ⓑ Ⓒ Ⓓ Ⓔ	54 Ⓐ Ⓑ Ⓒ Ⓓ Ⓔ
15 Ⓐ Ⓑ Ⓒ Ⓓ Ⓔ	35 Ⓐ Ⓑ Ⓒ Ⓓ Ⓔ	55 Ⓐ Ⓑ Ⓒ Ⓓ Ⓔ
16 Ⓐ Ⓑ Ⓒ Ⓓ Ⓔ	36 Ⓐ Ⓑ Ⓒ Ⓓ Ⓔ	
17 Ⓐ Ⓑ Ⓒ Ⓓ Ⓔ	37 Ⓐ Ⓑ Ⓒ Ⓓ Ⓔ	
18 Ⓐ Ⓑ Ⓒ Ⓓ Ⓔ	38 Ⓐ Ⓑ Ⓒ Ⓓ Ⓔ	
19 Ⓐ Ⓑ Ⓒ Ⓓ Ⓔ	39 Ⓐ Ⓑ Ⓒ Ⓓ Ⓔ	
20 Ⓐ Ⓑ Ⓒ Ⓓ Ⓔ	40 Ⓐ Ⓑ Ⓒ Ⓓ Ⓔ	

CUT HERE

Practice Test 3

Section I: Multiple-Choice Questions

Time: 60 Minutes

55 Questions

Directions: This section contains selections from two passages of prose and two poems with questions on their content, style, and form. Read each selection carefully. Choose the best answer of the five choices.

Questions 1–12. Read the following passage carefully before you begin to answer the questions.

Meditation

We say that the world is made of sea and land, as though they were equal; but we know that there is more sea in the western than in the eastern hemisphere.
(5) We say that the firmament is full of stars, as though it were equally full; but we know that there are more stars under the northern than under the southern pole. We say the elements of man are misery
(10) and happiness, as though he had an equal proportion of both, and the days of man vicissitudinary, as though he had as many good days as ill, and that he lived under a perpetual equinoctial, night and
(15) day equal, good and ill fortune in the same measure. But it is far from that; he drinks misery, and he tastes happiness; he mows misery, and he gleans happiness; he journeys in misery, he does but
(20) walk in happiness; and, which is worst, his misery is positive and dogmatical, his happiness is but disputable and problematical. All men call misery misery, but happiness changes the name by the taste
(25) of man. In this accident that befalls me, now that this sickness declares itself by

spots to be a malignant and pestilential disease, if there be a comfort in the declaration that thereby the physicians see
(30) more clearly what to do, there may be as much discomfort in this, that the malignity may be so great as that all that they can do shall do nothing; that an enemy declares himself then when he is able to
(35) subsist and to pursue and to achieve his ends is no great comfort. In intestine conspiracies, voluntary confessions do more good than confessions upon the rack; in these infections, when nature
(40) herself confesses and cries out by these outward declarations which she is able to put forth of herself, they minister comfort; but when all is by the strength of cordials, it is but a confession upon the
(45) rack, by which, though we come to know the malice of that man, yet we do not know whether there be not as much malice in his heart then as before his confession; we are sure of his treason, but not
(50) of his repentance; sure of him, but not of his accomplices. It is a faint comfort to know the worst when the worst is remediless, and a weaker than that to

GO ON TO THE NEXT PAGE

know much ill and not to know that that (55) is the worst. A woman is comforted with the birth of her son, her body is eased of a burden; but if she could prophetically read his history, how ill a man, perchance how ill a son he would prove, she should (60) receive a greater burden into her mind. Scarce any purchase that is not clogged with secret encumbrances; scarce any happiness that hath not in it so much of the nature of false and base money as (65) that the allay is more than the metal. Nay, is it not so (at least much towards it) even

in the exercise of virtues? I must be poor and want before I can exercise the virtue of gratitude; miserable and in torment (70) before I can exercise the virtue of patience. How deep do we dig and for how coarse gold! And what other touchstone have we of our gold but comparison, whether we be as happy as others, or as (75) ourselves at other times? O poor step toward being well, when these spots do only tell us that we are worse than we were sure of before!

1. The speaker of the passage is

   A. an Old Testament prophet
   B. a sick person
   C. a physician
   D. a man who has died and is recalling his last days
   E. a geographer

2. The comparisons in the first 16 lines of the passage are to illustrate the fact that

   A. the western oceans are larger than the eastern
   B. life contains both happiness and sorrow
   C. good fortune and bad fortune cannot be measured
   D. the sorrow in life outweighs the happiness
   E. neither misery nor joy is lasting in men's lives

3. As it is used in line 21, "dogmatical" means

   A. arrogantly asserted
   B. authoritatively affirmed

   C. asserted without any reference to evidence
   D. suggested, formulated
   E. ungrammatically stated

4. The argument in lines 25–32 is that because the disease has now been identified

   I. it may be so serious that the doctors can be of no use
   II. it can be more easily treated
   III. the physicians recognizing its contagion may refuse to treat the disease

   A. I only
   B. II only
   C. I and II only
   D. I and III only
   E. I, II, and III

5. In line 36, the word "intestine" is used to

   A. modify "voluntary confessions"
   B. refer to a part of the body
   C. mean murderous or fatal
   D. mean forceful or violent
   E. mean domestic or internal

6. The metaphor in lines 33–36

    A. argues that an unseen enemy is more dangerous than an open one

    B. compares a disease and physicians to an invader and a town under siege

    C. argues that the enemy has been discovered too late to be defeated

    D. argues that the temporary defeat of an enemy is no consolation

    E. compares the enemy to an army with the advantage

7. We can infer that the latest symptoms of the speaker's disease have appeared

    A. without raising his physicians' increased concern

    B. without having been noticed by the physicians

    C. without increasing the concern of the speaker

    D. because they have been induced by medicines

    E. in the natural course of his illness

8. In line 53, "that" refers to

    A. "repentance" (line 50)

    B. "faint" (line 51)

    C. "to know the worst" (lines 51–52)

    D. "remediless" (line 53)

    E. "that that" (line 54)

9. In lines 62–65, the comparison of happiness to coinage in which the "allay is more than the metal" is parallel to the comparison of

    A. the sea and land as equal (lines 1–2)

    B. drinking misery and tasting happiness (lines 16–17)

    C. the taste of man (lines 24–25)

    D. the voluntary confessions and confessions under torture (lines 36–39)

    E. the woman in childbirth (lines 55–60)

10. The "coarse gold" of line 72 is

    A. riches

    B. virtue

    C. patience

    D. misery

    E. happiness

11. The style of the paragraph is most notably characterized by its use of

    A. extended metaphors

    B. carefully reasoned syllogism

    C. reasoning from the specific to the general

    D. ironic understatements

    E. citation of intellectual authorities

12. The tone of the passage may be best described as

    A. ambiguous

    B. skeptical

    C. pessimistic

    D. servile

    E. anxious

GO ON TO THE NEXT PAGE

Practice Test 3

187

Questions 13–27. *Read the following poem carefully before you begin to answer the questions.*

Another Letter to her Husband,
Absent upon Public Employment

As loving hind that (hartless) wants her deer,
Scuds through the woods and fern with hark'ning ear,
Perplext, in every bush and nook doth pry,
Her dearest deer, might answer ear or eye;
(5) So doth my anxious soul, which now doth miss
A dearer dear (far dearer heart) than this,
Still wait with doubts, and hopes, and failing eye,
His voice to hear or person to descry.
Or as the pensive dove doth all alone
(10) (On withered bough) most uncouthly bemoan
The absence of her love and loving mate,
Whose loss hath made her so unfortunate,
Ev'n thus do I, with many a deep sad groan,
Bewail my turtle true, who now is gone,
(15) His presence and his safe return still woos,
With thousand doleful sighs and mournful coos.
Or as the loving mullet, that true fish,
Her fellow lost, not joy nor life do wish,
But launches on that shore, there for to die,
(20) Where she her captive husband doth espy.
Mine being gone, I lead a joyless life,
I have a loving peer, yet seem no wife;
But worst of all, to him can't steer my course,
I here, he there, alas, both kept by force.
(25) Return my dear, my joy, my only love,
Unto thy hind, thy mullet, and thy dove,
Who neither joys in pasture, house, nor streams,
The substance gone, O me, these are but dreams.
Together at one tree, oh let us browse,
(30) And like two turtles roost within one house
And like the mullets in one river glide,
Let's still remain but one, till death divide.
Thy loving love and dearest dear,
At home, abroad, and everywhere.

13. Which of the following best identifies
the genre of this poem?

  A. verse meditation

  B. verse epistle

C. elegy

D. love lyric

E. verse essay

14. In line 6, the parenthetical phrase "far dearer heart" is

   I. more logically printed without the parentheses

  II. in apposition to "dearer dear"

 III. an apostrophe to the absent husband

  A. I only

  B. I and II only

  C. I and III only

  D. II and III only

  E. I, II, and III

15. On what figure of speech do lines 1–8 chiefly rely?

  A. simile

  B. metaphor

  C. metonymy

  D. synecdoche

  E. allegory

16. In line 19, "launches" is best defined as

  A. boats

  B. sets afloat

  C. puts to sea

  D. sets in operation

  E. throws herself

17. The images of the deer, the dove, and the mullet (lines 1–20) are alluded to later in the poem in all of the following words or phrases EXCEPT

  A. "pasture" (line 27)

  B. "house" (line 27)

  C. "browse" (line 29)

  D. "glide" (line 31)

  E. "abroad" (line 34)

18. Of the following definitions of "substance," which is the primary meaning in line 28?

  A. wealth, resources

  B. that which exists independently

  C. essence, reality

  D. material, physical matter

  E. passport, true meaning

19. In line 28, the phrase "these are but dreams" can be best paraphrased as

  A. my dreams are of your return

  B. I dream of you so long as you are gone

  C. these dreams are mine

  D. these dreams have no reality

  E. on the other hand, dreams are more real

20. Of the following, which is the best synonym for "house" in line 30?

  A. dovecote

  B. manor

  C. hiding place

  D. dwelling place

  E. shelter

GO ON TO THE NEXT PAGE

21. Grammatically, the sentence in the last two lines of the poem (lines 33–34) differs from the rest of the poem because it has no

    A. subject

    B. verb

    C. prepositions

    D. pronouns

    E. adjectives

22. The last two lines of the poem are used to

    A. recapitulate the argument of the poem

    B. reassert the optimism of the speaker

    C. serve as a signature to a letter

    D. express what the speaker most wishes for

    E. reassert the universality of the mutual love of husband and wife

23. All of the following words refer to the dove figure of speech EXCEPT

    A. "mate" (line 11)

    B. "turtle" (line 14)

    C. "coos" (line 16)

    D. "peer" (line 22)

    E. "house" (line 27)

24. On which of the following structural devices does the poem chiefly depend?

    A. a series of parallel analogies

    B. a series of contrasts

    C. an alternation of the specific and the general

    D. a logically developed argument

    E. a series of literal assertions about the same subject

25. With which of the following words does the poem exploit a double meaning?

    A. "hind" (line 1)

    B. "deer" (line 1)

    C. "bough" (line 10)

    D. "turtle" (line 14)

    E. "coos" (line 16)

26. Which of the following best describes the logical structural divisions of the poem?

    A. lines 1–4; lines 5–8; lines 9–12; lines 13–16; lines 17–20; lines 21–24; lines 25–26; lines 27–28; lines 29–31; lines 32–34

    B. lines 1–10; lines 11–16; lines 17–28; lines 29–31; lines 32–34

    C. lines 1–8; lines 9–16; lines 17–20; lines 21–24; lines 25–28; lines 29–32; lines 33–34

    D. lines 1–16; lines 17–22; lines 23–34

    E. lines 1–16; lines 17–24; lines 25–30; lines 31–34

27. To a modern reader, which of the following is NOT an off-rhyme?

    A. "eye" / "descry" (lines 7–8)

    B. "mate" / "unfortunate" (lines 11–12)

    C. "groan" / "gone" (lines 13–14)

    D. "browse" / "house" (lines 29–30)

    E. "deer" / "everywhere" (lines 33–34)

Questions 28–40. Read the following passage carefully before you begin to answer the questions.

from Joan of Arc

What is to be thought of *her?* What is to be thought of the poor shepherd girl from the hills and forests of Lorraine, that — like the Hebrew shepherd boy
(5) from the hills and forests of Judea — rose suddenly out of the quiet, out of the safety, out of the religious inspiration, rooted in deep pastoral solitudes, to a station in the van of armies, and to the
(10) more perilous station at the right hand of kings? The Hebrew boy inaugurated his patriotic mission by an *act,* by a victorious *act,* such as no man could deny. But so did the girl of Lorraine, if we read her
(15) story as it was read by those who saw her nearest. Adverse armies bore witness to the boy as no pretender; but so they did to the gentle girl. Judged by the voices of all who saw them *from a sta-*
(20) *tion of good-will,* both were found true and loyal to any promises involved in their first acts. Enemies it was that made the difference between their subsequent fortunes. The boy rose to a splendor and
(25) a noonday prosperity, both personal and public, that rang through the records of his people, and became a byword among his posterity for a thousand years, until the sceptre was departing from Judah.
(30) The poor, forsaken girl, on the contrary, drank not herself from that cup of rest which she had secured for France. She never sang together with the songs that rose in her native Domrémy as echoes to
(35) the departing steps of invaders. She mingled not in the festal dances at Vaucouleurs which celebrated in rapture the redemption of France. No! for her voice was then silent; no! for her feet
(40) were dust. Pure, innocent, noble-hearted girl! whom, from earliest youth, ever I believed in as full of truth and self-sacrifice, this was amongst the strongest pledges for *thy* truth, that never once —
(45) no, not for a moment of weakness — didst thou revel in the vision of coronets and honor from man. Coronets for thee! Oh no! Honors, if they come when all is over, are for those that share thy blood.
(50) Daughter of Domrémy, when the gratitude of thy king shall awaken, thou wilt be sleeping the sleep of the dead. Call her, King of France, but she will not hear thee. Cite her by the apparitors to
(55) come and receive a role of honor, but she will be found *en contumace.* When the thunders of universal France, as even yet may happen, shall proclaim the grandeur of the poor shepherd girl that
(60) gave up all for her country, thy ear, young shepherd girl, will have been deaf for five centuries. To suffer and to do, that was thy portion in life; that was thy destiny; and not for a moment was it
(65) hidden from thyself. Life, thou saidst, is short; and the sleep which is the grave is long; let me use that life, so transitory, for the glory of those heavenly dreams destined to comfort the sleep which is so
(70) long! This pure creature — pure from every suspicion of even a visionary self-interest, even as she was pure in senses more obvious — never once did this holy child, as regarded herself, relax
(75) from her belief in the darkness that was travelling to meet her. She might not prefigure the very manner of her death; she saw not in vision, perhaps, the aerial altitude of the fiery scaffold, the specta-
(80) tors without end on every road, pouring into Rouen as to a coronation, the

GO ON TO THE NEXT PAGE

surging smoke, the volleying flames, the hostile faces all around, the pitying eye that lurked but here and there, until na-
(85) ture and imperishable truth broke loose

from artificial restraints; — these might not be apparent through the mists of the hurrying future. But the voice that called her to death, *that* she heard forever.

28. The Hebrew shepherd boy, lines 1–29, is

   A. Jesus

   B. Solomon

   C. Moses

   D. David

   E. Isaac

29. For which of the following reasons were the Hebrew shepherd boy and the French shepherd girl alike?

   I.   They were religiously inspired.

   II. Their motives were patriotic.

   III. They initially won victories.

   IV. The armies they opposed testified to their greatness.

   A. II and IV only

   B. I, II, and III only

   C. I, III, and IV only

   D. II, III, and IV only

   E. I, II, III, and IV

30. The first 38 lines of the passage are organized by a use of

   A. comparison and contrast

   B. arguing the general from the specific

   C. repeated rhetorical questions

   D. recurrent appeals to authority

   E. syllogistic logic

31. The series of three sentences from line 30 to line 38 ("The poor . . . of France") have which of the following in common?

   I.   They describe Joan's inability to participate in the victory she had won.

   II. They are all expressed through negatives.

   III. They describe figurative rather than literal events.

   A. II only

   B. III only

   C. I and II only

   D. II and III only

   E. I, II, and III

32. The passage attributes Joan's tragedy to

   A. her innocence

   B. her enemies

   C. envy of her success

   D. adverse armies

   E. the King of France

33. Phrases like "if we read her story as it was read by those who saw her nearest" (lines 14–16) or "the voices of all who saw them from a station of good-will" (lines 19–20) suggest that

   A. there can be no doubt about Joan's greatness

   B. there have been hostile interpretations of Joan's story

   C. the author has consulted all the relevant historical sources

   D. we can trust only the testimony of eyewitnesses

   E. the truth should be sought in both written and eyewitness reports

34. In line 47, the word "coronets" is most precisely defined as

   A. trumpets

   B. praises

   C. flowers

   D. medals

   E. crowns

35. From details of this passage, we can infer that Joan dies

   A. by fire

   B. by hanging

   C. in battle

   D. by gunfire

   E. at the hands of the king

36. In lines 76–89, the account of Joan's death is presented as

   A. her prophetic vision of the future

   B. the report of an eyewitness

   C. what Joan may not have foreseen

   D. an instance of state suppression of religion

   E. an illustration in a medieval manuscript

37. Although the passage contains only one paragraph, it could most easily be broken into two paragraphs after

   A. "Judah" (line 29)

   B. "dust" (line 40)

   C. "no!" (line 48)

   D. "thee" (line 54)

   E. "her" (line 76)

38. The passage employs all of the following EXCEPT

   A. apostrophe

   B. exclamation

   C. direct quotation

   D. extended definition

   E. parallel syntax

GO ON TO THE NEXT PAGE

39. At one time or more, the passage uses direct address to which of the following?

   I.   a general reader

  II.   Joan of Arc

 III.   the King of France

 IV.   the enemies of Joan of Arc

  A. I only

  B. II and IV only

  C. I, II, and III only

  D. II, III, and IV only

  E. I, II, III, and IV

40. The speaker's attitude toward Joan of Arc is one of

  A. awed veneration

  B. rational approval

  C. guarded criticism

  D. bemused uncertainty

  E. vexed incredulity

Questions 41–55. Read the following poem carefully before you begin to answer the questions.

S. I. W.

I will to the King,
And offer him consolation in his trouble,
For that man there has set his teeth to die,
And being one that hates obedience,
Discipline, and orderliness of life,
I cannot mourn him.

> — W. B. Yeats

I. THE PROLOGUE

Patting good-bye, doubtless they told the lad
He'd always show the Hun a brave man's face;
Father would sooner him dead than in disgrace, —
Was proud to see him going, aye, and glad.
(5)   Perhaps his mother whimpered how she'd fret
Until he got a nice safe wound to nurse.
Sisters would wish girls too could shoot, charge, curse;
Brothers — would send his favourite cigarette.
Each week, month after month, they wrote the same,
(10) Thinking him sheltered in some Y.M. Hut,
Because he said so, writing on his butt
Where once an hour a bullet missed its aim
And misses teased the hunger of his brain.
His eyes grew old with wincing, and his hand
(15) Reckless with ague. Courage leaked, as sand
From the best sand-bags after years of rain.

But never leave, wound, fever, trench-foot, shock,
Untrapped the wretch. And death seemed still withheld
For torture of lying machinally shelled,
(20)   At the pleasure of this world's Powers who'd run amok.

He'd seen men shoot their hands, on night patrol.
Their people never knew. Yet they were vile.
"Death sooner than dishonour, that's the style!"
So Father said.

II. THE ACTION
(25)   One dawn, our wire patrol
Carried him. This time, Death had not missed.
We could do nothing but wipe his bleeding cough.
Could it be accident? — Rifles go off . . .
Not sniped? No. (Later they found the English ball.)

III. THE POEM
(30)   It was the reasoned crisis of his soul
Against more days of inescapable thrall,
Against infrangibly wired and blind trench wall
Curtained with fire, roofed in with creeping fire,
Slow grazing fire, that would not burn him whole
(35)   But kept him for death's promises and scoff,
And life's half-promising, and both their riling.

IV. THE EPILOGUE
With him they buried the muzzle his teeth had kissed,
And truthfully wrote the Mother, "Tim died smiling."

41. The title of the poem is an army abbreviation for self-inflicted wound used by the British as, say, K.P. or G.I. are used by the American army; that such an abbreviation exists suggest that

I.   it is common for soldiers to wound or kill themselves

II. the army is reluctant to face the fact that soldiers may kill themselves

III. the army does not wish the civilian population to know about suicides at the front

A. I only
B. II only
C. III only
D. II and III only
E. I, II, and III

42. The poem takes place during

A. the Civil War
B. World War I
C. World War II
D. the Vietnam War
E. any fictitious British war

GO ON TO THE NEXT PAGE

43. The chief speaker of the poem is

- **A.** an omniscient unnamed narrator
- **B.** the dead soldier's parents
- **C.** another soldier
- **D.** Tim
- **E.** the dead soldier's commanding officer

44. The diction of the phrase "nice safe wound" in line 6 represents that of the

- **A.** commanding officer
- **B.** dead soldier
- **C.** narrator of the poem
- **D.** soldier's father
- **E.** soldier's mother

45. In line 17, "leave, wound, fever, trench-foot, shock" are

- I. reasons for leaving the trenches
- II. the common dangers of life in the trenches
- III. potential causes of death in the trenches

- **A.** I only
- **B.** II only
- **C.** I and II only
- **D.** II and III only
- **E.** I, II, and III

46. Line 20 metrically is different from the rest of the prologue because

- **A.** its rhythm is trochaic
- **B.** it has more syllables

- **C.** it has no alliteration
- **D.** it has no rhyming line
- **E.** it uses feminine rhyme

47. In line 29, "ball" is a

- **A.** sphere
- **B.** root
- **C.** dance
- **D.** bullet
- **E.** uniform

48. The effect of part III is to

- I. obliquely call into question the soldier's decision to kill himself
- II. dramatize the inescapable horrors of trench warfare
- III. justify the soldier's choice of suicide

- **A.** I only
- **B.** II only
- **C.** I and II only
- **D.** I and III only
- **E.** II and III only

49. The "muzzle" of line 37 is

- **A.** the butt or handle of a gun
- **B.** the front of the barrel of a gun
- **C.** a medal
- **D.** a blindfold
- **E.** a mouthpiece

50. The poet uses the word "truthfully" in the last line of the poem because

    A. it will console the family of the dead soldier

    B. "smiling" refers to the happiness of the soldier whose war is over

    C. he realizes that "Tim died smiling" is not the truth

    D. "Tim died smiling" is the literal truth

    E. the poem has been too pessimistic to this point

51. The poem directly presents the words or thoughts of which of the following?

    I. Tim

    II. the narrator

    III. members of the patrol

    A. II only

    B. I and II only

    C. I and III only

    D. II and III only

    E. I, II, and III

52. With which of the following does the poem implicitly or explicitly find fault?

    I. the world's Powers

    II. Tim's family

    III. the wire patrol

    A. I only

    B. I and II only

    C. I and III only

    D. II and III only

    E. I, II, and III

53. All the following words or phrases are ironic EXCEPT

    A. "always" (line 2)

    B. "sooner him dead than in disgrace" (line 3)

    C. "nice safe wound" (line 6)

    D. "Courage leaked, as sand" (line 15)

    E. "Yet they were vile" (line 22)

54. The only feminine rhyme in the poem occurs in

    A. the second and third lines of the Yeats quotation

    B. line 20

    C. lines 26 and 27

    D. line 35

    E. lines 36 and 38

55. The crucial action of the poem takes place

    A. in The Prologue (I)

    B. between The Prologue (I) and The Action (II)

    C. in The Action (II)

    D. in The Poem (III)

    E. between The Poem (III) and The Epilogue (IV)

IF YOU FINISH BEFORE TIME IS CALLED, CHECK YOUR WORK ON THIS SECTION ONLY. DO NOT WORK ON ANY OTHER SECTION IN THE TEST.

Section II: Essay Questions

Time: 2 Hours

3 Questions

Question 1

(Suggested time — 40 minutes. This question accounts for one-third of the total essay section score.)

Directions: Read the following poem carefully. Then write an essay in which you discuss how the use of language in the poem determines the reader's response to the speaker and his situation.

The Farmer's Bride

Three Summers since I chose a maid,
Too young maybe — but more's to do
At harvest-time than bide and woo.
When us was wed she turned afraid
(5)   Of love and me and all things human;
Like the shut of a winter's day
Her smile went out, and 'twadn't a woman —
More like a little frightened fay.
One night, in the Fall, she runned away.

(10)   'Out 'mong the sheep, her be,' they said,
'Should properly have been abed;
But sure enough she wadn't there
Lying awake with her wide brown stare.
So over seven-acre field and up-along across the down
(15)   We chased her, flying like a hare
Before our lanterns. To Church-Town
All in a shiver and a scare
We caught her, fetched her home at last
And turned the key upon her, fast.

(20)   She does the work about the house
As well as most, but like a mouse:
Happy enough to chat and play
With birds and rabbits and such as they,
So long as men-folk keep away.

(25)   'Not near, not near!' her eyes beseech
When one of us comes within reach.
The women say that beasts in stall
Look round like children at her call.
I've hardly heard her speak at all.

GO ON TO THE NEXT PAGE

(30)   Shy as a leveret, swift as he,
      Straight and slight as a young larch tree,
      Sweet as the first wild violets, she
      To her wild self. But what to me?

      The short days shorten and the oaks are brown,
(35)   The blue smoke rises to the low grey sky,
      One leaf in the still air falls slowly down,
      A magpie's spotted feathers lie
      On the black earth spread white with rime,
      The berries redden up to Christmas-time.
(40)   What's Christmas-time without there be
      Some other in the house than we!

      She sleeps up in the attic there
      Alone, poor maid, 'Tis but a stair
      Betwixt us. Oh! My God! The down,
(45   The soft young down of her, the brown,
      The brown of her — her eyes, her hair, her hair!
                    — Charlotte Mew

Question 2

(Suggested time — 40 minutes. This question accounts for one-third of the total essay score.)

Directions: Read carefully the following passage from Thackeray's *Vanity Fair*. Write an essay that defines the targets of Thackeray's criticism and how the choice of details, the diction, and the syntax convey the satire.

Miss Crawley was, in consequence, an object of great respect when she came to Queen's Crawley, for she had a balance at her banker's which would have (5) made her beloved anywhere.

What a dignity it gives an old lady, that balance at the banker's! How tenderly we look at her faults, if she is a relative (and may every reader have a score (10) of such), what a kind, good-natured old creature we find her! How the junior partner of Hobbs & Dobbs leads her smiling to the carriage with the lozenge upon it, and the fat wheezy coachman! (15) How, when she comes to pay us a visit, we generally find an opportunity to let our friends know her station in the world! We say (and with perfect truth) I wish I had Miss MacWhirter's signature (20) to a cheque for five thousand pounds. She wouldn't miss it, says your wife. She is my aunt, say you, in an easy careless way, when your friend asks if Miss MacWhirter is any relative? Your (25) wife is perpetually sending her little testimonies of affection, your little girls work endless worsted baskets, cushions, and footstools for her. What a good fire there is in her room when she comes to (30) pay you a visit, although your wife laces her stays without one! The house during her stay assumes a festive, neat, warm, jovial, snug appearance not visible at other seasons. You yourself, dear sir, for- (35) get to go to sleep after dinner, and find yourself all of a sudden (though you

invariably lose) very fond of a rubber. What good dinners you have — game every day. Malmsey-Madeira, and no
(40) end of the fish from London. Even the servants in the kitchen share in the general prosperity; and, somehow, during the stay of Miss MacWhirter's fat coachman, the beer is grown much stronger,
(45) and the consumption of tea and sugar in the nursery (where her maid takes her meals) is not regarded in the least. Is it so, or is it not so? I appeal to the middle classes. Ah, gracious powers! I wish you
(50) would send me an old aunt — a maiden aunt — an aunt with a lozenge on her carriage, and a front of light coffee-coloured hair — how my children should work work-bags for her, and my Julia
(55) and I would make her comfortable! Sweet, sweet vision! Foolish, foolish dream!

Question 3

(Suggested time — 40 minutes. This question accounts for one-third of the total essay section score.)

Directions: Injustice, either social or personal, is a common theme in literature. Choose a novel or a play in which injustice is important. Write an essay in which you define clearly the nature of the injustice and discuss the techniques the author employs to elicit sympathy for its victim or victims. You may use one of the following works or another work of equivalent literary merit.

Othello	*An American Tragedy*
King Lear	*The Jungle*
A Doll's House	*Invisible Man*
All My Sons	*A Passage to India*
A Streetcar Named Desire	*Native Son*
Antigone	*The Grapes of Wrath*
Justice	*The Color Purple*
Billy Budd	*Animal Farm*
Tess of the D'Urbervilles	*1984*
Jude the Obscure	*Crime and Punishment*
Cry, the Beloved Country	*Catch-22*
Beloved	*Oliver Twist*

IF YOU FINISH BEFORE TIME IS CALLED, CHECK YOUR WORK ON THIS SECTION ONLY. DO NOT WORK ON ANY OTHER SECTION IN THE TEST.

Practice Test 3

Scoring Practice Test 3

Answer Key

Section I: Multiple-Choice Questions

First Prose Passage	First Poem
1. B	**13.** B
2. D	**14.** D
3. B	**15.** A
4. C	**16.** E
5. E	**17.** E
6. C	**18.** C
7. D	**19.** D
8. C	**20.** A
9. B	**21.** B
10. E	**22.** C
11. A	**23.** D
12. C	**24.** A
	25. B
	26. C
	27. A

Second Prose Passage

28. D
29. E
30. A
31. C
32. B
33. B
34. E
35. A
36. C
37. B
38. D
39. C
40. A

Second Poem

41. A
42. B
43. C
44. E
45. A
46. B
47. D
48. E
49. B
50. D
51. E
52. B
53. D
54. E
55. B

Practice Test 3 Scoring Worksheet

Use the following worksheet to arrive at a probable final AP grade on Practice Test 3. While it is sometimes difficult to be objective enough to score one's own essay, you can use the sample essay answers that follow to approximate an essay score for yourself. You may also give your essays (along with the sample essays) to a friend or relative to score if you feel confident that the individual has the knowledge necessary to make such a judgment and that he or she will feel comfortable in doing so.

Section I: Multiple-Choice Questions

$$\underset{\substack{\text{right} \\ \text{answers}}}{\underline{\hspace{2cm}}} - (^1/_4 \text{ or } .25 \times \underset{\substack{\text{wrong} \\ \text{answers}}}{\underline{\hspace{2cm}}}) = \underset{\substack{\text{multiple-choice} \\ \text{raw score}}}{\underline{\hspace{3cm}}}$$

$$\underset{\substack{\text{multiple-choice} \\ \text{raw score}}}{\underline{\hspace{3cm}}} \times 1.25 = \underset{\substack{\text{multiple-choice} \\ \text{converted score}}}{\underline{\hspace{3cm}}} (\text{of possible } 67.5)$$

Section II: Essay Questions

$$\underset{\substack{\text{question 1} \\ \text{raw score}}}{\underline{\hspace{2cm}}} + \underset{\substack{\text{question 2} \\ \text{raw score}}}{\underline{\hspace{2cm}}} + \underset{\substack{\text{question 3} \\ \text{raw score}}}{\underline{\hspace{2cm}}} = \underset{\text{essay}}{\underline{\hspace{2cm}}}$$

$$\underset{\substack{\text{essay} \\ \text{raw score}}}{\underline{\hspace{3cm}}} \times 3.055 = \underset{\substack{\text{essay} \\ \text{converted score}}}{\underline{\hspace{3cm}}} (\text{of possible } 82.5)$$

Final Score

$$\underset{\substack{\text{multiple-choice} \\ \text{converted score}}}{\underline{\hspace{3cm}}} + \underset{\substack{\text{essay} \\ \text{converted score}}}{\underline{\hspace{3cm}}} = \underset{\substack{\text{final} \\ \text{converted score}}}{\underline{\hspace{3cm}}} (\text{of possible } 150)$$

Probable Final AP Score

Final Converted	Probable AP Score
150–100	5
99–86	4
85–67	3
66–0	1 or 2

Answers and Explanations for Practice Test 3

Section I: Multiple-Choice Questions

First Prose Passage

Like the Bacon essay in the first practice exam, this "Meditation" by John Donne is challenging prose. It was written early in the seventeenth century.

1. **B.** As a rule, the first question of each set of multiple-choice questions is an easy one. Here the speaker does not identify himself until lines 25–28, where he speaks of his "malignant and pestilential disease" and uses the pronoun "me."

2. **D.** Each of the first three sentences begins with "We say"; they go on to speak of the sea in the two hemispheres, the stars under the northern and southern poles, and the sorrow and joy in human life. In line 11, Donne contradicts our suggesting that the seas, stars, or joys and sorrows are equally divided. There is far more misery than happiness. The passage does make the points of choices **A** and **B**, but they are not the thesis that the 16 lines are used to demonstrate.

3. **B.** It is often the case when a multiple-choice question asks you to define a reasonably familiar word that the common modern meaning is not the right answer. The AP exam is not likely to test vocabulary as the SAT does. You must look very carefully at the context of the word in the passage. We all know that the word "dogmatic" means "arrogantly asserted," and a student who answers this question without checking the passage would choose **A**. But it is used in this passage in a different sense, and the clue we are given is the linking of "dogmatical" with "positive." Here the meaning is "authoritatively affirmed." In theology, "dogma" is an authoritatively affirmed doctrine.

4. **C.** The lines say nothing about the physicians' fear of contagion. The depressing consequence of the identification is that the disease may be so far advanced that the doctors can do nothing to help (lines 31–33); the small consolation is that they now know better how to deal with the disease (lines 29–30).

5. **E.** This is another instance where you should not assume that you know a word until you check the context. As a noun for organ of the body, "intestine" is an easy word. Here it is used as an adjective modifying "conspiracies" and meaning "internal" or "domestic."

6. **C.** The metaphor is comparing the identified disease to the enemy who reveals himself ("declares himself") after he is strong enough to survive and to win ("achieve his ends"). To know of this enemy whom it is too late to defeat, the passage argues, is "faint comfort."

7. D. The passage gives us no information about the physician's response to the symptoms, and it is clear that the speaker's concern has increased; we can eliminate choices **A**, **B**, and **C**. We must sort out more figures of speech to answer the question. Donne likens the new symptoms to two kinds of confession, that which is freely given and that which is obtained by torture. The freely given confession is like the natural development of a disease in which new symptoms appear (lines 38–43). The appearance of new symptoms induced by administering medicines ("the strength of cordials") is like the confession obtained by torture and is of less comfort to the sufferer.

8. C. The sentence may be paraphrased as follows: It is a small consolation to know the worst when that worst is something that cannot be remedied; it is even less comforting than knowing the worst to know something very bad and not know that the worst has been reached.

9. B. The allay, or alloy, of a counterfeit coin is the base metal (for example, iron) as opposed to the genuine (for example, gold). According to the figure, the alloy (misery) is larger than the genuine (happiness). In lines 16–17, the figure of drinking misery (swallowing it) as opposed to just tasting happiness makes the same depressing point.

10. E. The gold that requires such an effort to find is a metaphor for happiness. Lines 71–75 expand the figure using the word "happy."

11. A. Take away the metaphors and there would be hardly anything left on the page. What makes this passage so difficult and so interesting is its figurative language. None of the other options is so notable as the use of metaphor, though **C** is at least a remote possibility, because the author uses his own disease to make a case for the preponderance of misery over happiness in human life.

12. C. By far the best choice here is "pessimistic." The next best are "anxious" and "skeptical," but they are not strong enough. Neither "ambiguous" nor "servile" is at all appropriate.

First Poem

This poem by American poet Anne Bradstreet was probably written in the second half of the seventeenth century.

13. B. Though the poem expresses the speaker's love for her husband, it is not a lyric, normally a songlike expression of feeling. It is a verse epistle, that is, a letter in verse addressed by the wife to her husband, who is away.

14. D. The phrase is grammatically parenthetical, and the line without parentheses would be very obscure. The more likely use of the phrase is in apposition to "dearer dear." The phrase says she misses a dearer dear and heart. It is also possible that the phrase is an interjected direct address (apostrophe) to her absent husband.

15. A. The extended figure compares the female deer seeking her mate (hart) to the wife who misses her husband. The figure is a simile, not a metaphor, because it uses "As" in line 1 and "So" in line 5.

16. **E.** The verb "launch" can be transitive or intransitive. There is no object here, so the best choice of definitions is "throws herself," describing the unlikely event of a mullet that beaches herself to join her mate. This use of the verb is still common, as in the sentence "He launched into an attack on the media."

17. **E.** In line 27, the "pasture," "house," and "streams" are, respectively, where the deer, dove, and mullet live. In line 29, the verb "browse" refers to the deer, while "glide" in line 31 refers to the fish. In line 34, "abroad" refers to Bradstreet, not the animals.

18. **C.** Be sure to consult the text in questions about the meaning of a word. Here the line says that without the substance, alas, everything is unreal or just a dream. In this context, "reality" or "essence" is the best choice.

19. **D.** The "but" here means "only" or "merely." The best of the five answers is **D**. The dreams are the shadow, the insubstantial, the unreal.

20. **A.** Because this is a "house" for doves ("turtles" are turtledoves, not the reptiles), the best choice is dovecote.

21. **B.** The last two lines of the poem have no verb. The subjects of the phrase are "love" and "dear." "At" is a preposition, "Thy" a pronoun, and "loving" and "dearest" adjectives.

22. **C.** The explanation for the missing verb in the last lines is that they are the complimentary close and signature of the letter — two lines of verse instead of "very truly yours, Anne Bradstreet."

23. **D.** The noun "peer" as it is used here has no reference to the turtledove figure. The four other words are all part of the bird imagery of the poem.

24. **A.** Lines 1–8 develop an analogy of the wife and the hind. Lines 9–16 develop a similar comparison of the wife and the turtledove. Lines 17–24 make a third comparison using the mullet. The animals used in these similes are reintroduced in the metaphors of lines 25–28 and 29–32. Choices **B**, **C**, **D**, and **E** are potentially useful structural devices, but none of them is important in this poem.

25. **B.** The poem plays on the words "dear" and "deer" as well as on the words "hart" and "heart." Both of these wordplays are very common in English love poetry of the Renaissance.

26. **C.** The fastest way to solve a question of this sort, which may be very time consuming, is to identify at once a structural unit that you are very sure about. It is clear that the first coherent part of this poem must be the eight lines of the first sentence that make up the deer-wife simile. Look now at the answers and eliminate any option that does not begin with lines 1–8 as the first unit. In this case, we can isolate **C** right away. Now check the rest of answer **C**. Lines 9–16 are fine, the next simile. Lines 17–20 and 21–24 could have made up one unit, but both are complete sentences, and the division is plausible. The rest of the answer also makes good sense. If there had been two answers with lines 1–8 first, you would have to continue to work through both until you found an error. Your savings in time would still have been great. An easy system to use is to determine with certainty what the first unit and what the last unit are. If you can do this, you will probably have eliminated the four wrong answers right away. In this poem, for example, the last unit must be the signature lines, 33 and 34. Only one of the five answers has 33–34 as its last section, reconfirming **C** as the correct choice.

27. **A.** An off-rhyme, or slant-rhyme is an approximate rhyme where the vowels do not in fact have the same sound. The vowel sound of "eye" and "descry" or "eye" and "cry" is the same, so it is not an off-rhyme. But in the other four pairs, the two vowel sounds differ; all of them are off-rhymes.

Second Prose Passage

The passage is from the nineteenth century, Thomas de Quincy on Joan of Arc.

28. **D.** Though the passage never identifies the Hebrew shepherd by name, the author assumes his readers know enough of the Old Testament to recognize David. We are told of his religious inspiration, his leading armies, his initial victorious action (the defeat of Goliath), and his success and fame in the kingdom of Judah. The exams do not attempt to test your knowledge of history or religion, but they are written with the understanding that AP students will be familiar with the major themes of Greek and Roman myth and of the Judaic and Christian religious traditions. The exams will never ask you about a minor Old Testament prophet or the Egyptian myths of Anubis, but one or two of the multiple-choice questions may require a familiarity with Zeus or Sampson or Mars.

29. **E.** The passage cites all four of these likenesses: both rose "out of . . . religious inspiration" (lines 6–7); their missions are "patriotic" (line 12); inaugurated by a victorious "act" (lines 12–13); both are praised by "adverse armies" (line 16).

30. **A.** The passage begins with a comparison of the great achievements of both David and Joan (lines 1–24). In lines 25–37, DeQuincy describes the triumphs of David and the contrasting fate of the martyred Joan. The passage does begin with two questions, but repeated rhetorical questions are not the organizing principle of the passage. None of the other devices is used here.

31. **C.** All three sentences describe Joan's inability to participate in the victory. All three sentences are cast as negatives: "drank not," "never sang," and "mingled not." The lines are both literal and figurative. The "cup of rest" is figurative, but the songs may be literal, and the dances surely are real.

32. **B.** In lines 22–24, the author blames enemies for the difference between David's success and Joan's tragedy. It may be argued that all five options are reasonable answers, but the question calls for the answer attributed by the passage.

33. **B.** Both of these phrases suggest that DeQuincy's awestruck view of Joan is not the only one possible. The implication of the phrase "those who saw her nearest" is that those whose view of Joan questions her heroism are those who were not nearest — not close enough to know the truth. Similarly, "all who saw . . . from a station of good will" implies that those men in the adverse armies who judged Joan harshly were not to be believed because they were men of ill-will. The defensiveness of the phrases attests to an alternate interpretation.

34. **E.** A coronet is a small crown worn by princes or others of high rank. Though an ornamental band of flowers or jewels is also called a coronet, the first meaning is used here to symbolize rank and to accord with the word "honors."

35. **A.** Joan was burned at Rouen in 1431. The passage alludes to the "fiery scaffold," the "surging smoke," and the "volleying flames."

36. **C.** Oddly, the whole scene is presented as a vision of the future which Joan may not have foreseen. The verbs controlling the body of the sentence are "she might not prefigure" and "she saw not in vision, perhaps." The sentence illustrates the rhetorical device by which an author can get something said by appearing not to say it. The political candidate who says, "I will not allude to the fact that my opponent spent two years in prison for mail fraud" understands the technique.

37. **B.** The logical division in the paragraph is after "no! for her feet were dust." At this point, the contrast between the prosperous David and the forsaken Joan has been completed. In the following sentence, the author switches from the use of the third person ("she") to address Joan directly, using the second person ("thou" and "thy"). The subject is no longer the similarity or difference of Joan and David but the nature of Joan's difference from her countrymen. Choice **A** is unlikely, because it falls in the middle of the comparison of Joan and David. Choice **C** interrupts a consideration of the worldly honors that Joan rejected. Choice **D** interrupts a series of parallel imperatives ("Call her . . . Cite her . . ."), and **E** interrupts two closely related sentences.

38. **D.** The passage does not employ extended definition, but the other devices are used several times. Apostrophe (words addressed to a person or thing) is directed to the reader, Joan, and the King of France. There are nearly as many exclamation points in this passage as there are periods. Joan's words are quoted in lines 65–70. The first of many examples of parallel syntax is the second sentence, which repeats the first six words of the first sentence exactly.

39. **C.** The passage alludes to enemies of Joan but does not address them directly. The opening lines address the reader, lines 40–52 address Joan, and lines 52–56 address the King of France.

40. **A.** Nothing in the headlong prose of this passage suggests anything like the controlled approval or guarded disapproval suggested by **B**, **C**, **D**, and **E**. The only possible choice here is **A**.

Second Poem

The poem is by Wilfred Owen, a World War I poet who was killed shortly before the war ended in 1918.

41. **A.** If the event happens often enough for the army to have a familiar abbreviation for it, it cannot be very rare. The very existence of the abbreviation is a grim reminder of how common the event is. The soldier in the poem thinks about other men who have wounded themselves to escape the trenches (line 21), but at first rejects the idea. Although the second and third statements in this question may be true, the abbreviation does not suggest either, for the meaning of the letters is not secret.

42. **B.** A number of the details of the poem make it clear that the war is World War I. These include the terms "the Hun" for the German enemy, "sand-bags," "trench-foot," shell "shock," "wire patrol," and "trench wall," and the reference to "this world's Powers."

43. C. The speaker, we learn in II, is a member of the patrol ("our wire patrol") that finds Tim's body. The details of The Prologue are what he infers but does not certainly know. He uses "doubtless" in line 1 and "Perhaps" in line 5 to reveal that this is his version of events. This soldier's insight reconstructs the mental anguish of III. The narrator is not named, but because he is not quite omniscient, **C** is a better choice than **A**.

44. E. No one directly connected with war would use the word "nice" to describe a wound. The not-so-subtle satire here is directed at the whimpering and fretful mother who would nurse a nice wound.

45. A. The wounds, fevers, and maladies like trench-foot or shell shock are dangers of life in the trenches, and wounds and fevers may be life threatening. Leave is neither dangerous or potentially fatal. Like the others, it is a way of escaping from the trenches.

46. B. The line is probably scanned as follows:

    u u   / | u   u / | /   / | u   / | u /
    At the pleasure of this world's Powers who'd run amok.

"Powers" is probably a monosyllable here, and the line is a pentameter, with two three-syllable feet. The basic meter of the stanza is iambic pentameter, but there are many substitutions and many lines with nine or eleven syllables. Line 20 is not trochaic (**A**). Many lines in The Prologue have no alliteration, but line 20 has two words with initial "p" sounds. Line 20 rhymes with line 17 ("shock" / "amok") (**D**). This is a masculine rhyme (**E**).

47. D. Lines 27 and 28 present fragments of the wire patrol soldiers' words. Was it an accident? Maybe he was killed by a sniper's bullet? The parentheses make the suicide clear. It was an English not a German bullet.

48. E. Part III presents the dead soldier's decision to take his own life as a "reasoned crisis." With nothing but a continuation of the agony to look forward to and no hope of death to end his suffering, he makes his choice. The effect of the stanza is to dramatize the horrors of war and to show the justice or reason of the soldier's choice. The poem does not question his decision.

49. B. The muzzle is the front of the barrel of the gun.

50. D. The point of the grim last line is its physical specificity. To place the muzzle of the gun against his teeth, the soldier would have to twist his lips into a last smile.

51. E. Tim's words or thoughts are directly presented in lines 22–24. The narrator speaks most of the poem. Lines 27–28 present the words of members of the patrol.

52. B. The narrator, who is a member of the wire patrol, is an understanding and sympathetic commentator of whom the author wholly approves. The poem does criticize the unthinking chauvinism of Tim's family and the world's Powers, who are responsible for the war.

53. D. The events of the poem reveal the irony in claiming eternal valor for the dead soldier. The father's preference of death before dishonor (for someone else) is realized in a way he could not have foreseen. The real wound here is neither "safe" nor "nice." Tim's condemnation of others who wound themselves is premature. The phrase "Courage leaked as sand" is figurative, but it is not ironic.

54. **E.** A feminine rhyme is a rhyme on the next-to-last syllable followed by an unstressed last syllable that is identical: "go" and "flow" is a masculine rhyme, "going" and "flowing," feminine. The only feminine rhyme in the poem is lines 36 and 38, "riling" and "smiling."

55. **B.** Tim's suicide takes place after The Prologue and before The Action.

Section II: Essay Questions

Question 1: Charlotte Mew

The question which asks how the "use of language" determines the reader's response to the speaker and his or her situation opens the door for an essay on aspects of the poem chosen by the student. Almost everyone will write on diction, and most will write on imagery as well. Other possible topics in this essay include the use of the first person, the use of dialect, and the use of repetition.

"The Farmer's Bride" is a narrative poem about two characters. The pathos of the young bride, shy, silent, and terrified by the approach of any male, needs no comment. The question calls for our response to the husband and speaker of the poem. By using some words and constructions of a rural dialect, the poet creates a simple farmer articulate enough to suggest the full anguish of his unhappy marriage.

The first three lines are, perhaps, the least sympathetic to the speaker. Granting the possibility that his bride was "too young, perhaps," he defends their marriage as necessary for a farmer too busy to woo at length or wait around at harvest time. The rest of the poem presents the farmer's pained coping with an intolerable situation; his recaptured wife sleeps alone in the attic. His desire for her has not abated, yet he refers to her as "poor maid."

Most of the comparisons of the poem are similes, likening the bride to animals or plants. She is compared to a hare, a mouse, a leveret, a larch, and the first wild violets. Most of these figures suggest her skittishness, her fragility, her inhuman quality, "like a frightened fay." The husband is intensely aware of her beauty ("Sweet as the first wild violets"), which he cannot come near ("But what to me?"). His desperate frustration is poignantly dramatized by the repetitions of the last two lines. The reader's sympathies are equally divided between both of these innocent victims, whose tragedy is played out against the slow-changing background of the cycle of the seasons.

Student Essay

The same character can be interpreted by the reader in drastically different terms, depending upon the clues left for the reader by the author. Many of the heroes of our literature are actually anti-heroes, rogues who are nevertheless possessed of a certain rakish charm. Such a character might likely be presented as a despicable reprobate by one

213

author, a charismatic and entirely sympathetic devil by another. Subtle clues left by the author must be the guides careful readers heed to discover the true nature of a character who may seem culpable to objective analysis.

Charlotte Mew presents such a character in the farmer, narrator, and protagonist of her poem "The Farmer's Bride." A man who repeatedly thinks of his wife as an animal and a possession, who locks her in her room after she runs away unhappy, and fails to treat her as an equal, the farmer nevertheless becomes a profoundly sympathetic character. While it is important to keep in mind the mores and marital customs of the day, Mew makes the farmer likable without resorting to reminding readers that things are relative, that men often treated their wives in such a way in days past, and therefore the farmer was not an aberration in his own times. Mew accomplishes this by taking readers inside the farmer's mind, revealing that he is a complex human being.

The poem's language provides great insight into the farmer's character and makes the reader feel sorry for the beleaguered husband. The farmer's folksy tone and broken English elicit immediate reader sympathy for the rube. The rustic has no understanding of his wife as a human being, treating her as something of a curiosity. Mew writes, "Like the shut of a winter's day / Her smile went out, and 'twadn't a woman — / More like a little frightened fay. / One night, in the Fall, she runned away." She is like a fairy; she does not leave him, but rather runs away like an animal or supernatural sprite. The reader comes to realize that the farmer has no idea of his own possible inadequacies. He cannot conceive of any reason she might leave him personally, aside from that she "turned afraid" of "all things human." The farmer can only explain her disappearance as an enigma.

During the chase, she is again described by the farmer as something not human. She is found among the sheep (and he will later note that she seems most at home among the barn animals, when men are not around). When caught, the stray creature is "All in a shiver and a scare," like an animal in the headlights. She does her housework "like a mouse." While readers still identify with the narrator of the poem. Mew makes them aware of the wife's situation as well, feeling sorry for the vulnerable woman completely misunderstood by her well-meaning husband.

Mew's diction later implies that while the farmer may treat his captured wife unkindly, caging her like an animal, he is not himself unkind. She does not condemn, nor will the reader, because the poet's words make it clear that the farmer knows no better. While this may not be sufficient for absolution, it at least makes the reader look with soft eyes on the man's plight. Mew writes, "We caught her, fetched her home at last / And turned the key upon her, fast." The farmer has no cognizance that anything he is doing may be morally questionable. He "fetches" her rather than "grabbing" her or "snatching" her; "fetches" is a wholly innocuous word, and the farmer sees his actions as totally innocuous.

He is utterly perplexed as to the source of the barrier between him and his wife, who has "turned afraid." Still, the reader cannot help but feel sorry for a man who is so unhappy, so unable to communicate with someone he genuinely loves. The farmer pines away at poem's close: "'Tis but a stair / Betwixt us. Oh! my God! The down, / The soft young down of her, the brown, / the brown of her — her eyes, her hair, her hair!"

Pathos and pity rule the day. The reader ends up pitying the wife, trapped, incomplete, and the husband, lonely and longing, questioning. Mew's diction has been effective, and the reader is bound to respond to "The Farmer's Wife" with true feeling for both characters and leave it, perhaps, with a great understanding of the conflict between the sexes and the condition of humanity.

Response to the Student Essay

This student essay on Charlotte Mew's poem is instructive for its strengths and its limitations. It answers the question well, defining clearly the reader's response to the farmer and discussing how the diction and imagery function in the poem. The paper would certainly be scored in the upper half of the scale, probably at seven of a possible nine points. Papers with high scores would focus more rigorously on the language of the poem and deal more fully with some of the subjects like tone, point of view, or dialect, which this essay merely mentions. The writing here is uneven. The essay would be better without the first paragraph. It is not necessary to begin your papers with uplifting generalizations about literature or life. Be careful about your tone. An essay that condescends to the "mores and marital customs" of an earlier period as less enlightened than our own should not refer to a west of England dialect as "broken" or to a farmer as a "rube."

Question 2: William Makepeace Thackeray

The following essay on the passage from *Vanity Fair* is typical of the student responses to this question.

Student Essay

In Thackeray's *Vanity Fair*, diction, syntax, and choice of detail are all used to convey a feeling of satire as Thackeray defines the targets of his criticism as the middle class relations of rich older ladies.

The first important detail that Thackeray gives the reader is a hint as to the nature of the passage as he notes, ". . . for she had a balance at her banker's which could have made her beloved anywhere." The author continues by describing "What a dignity it gives an old lady, that balance at the banker's! How tenderly we look at her faults, if she is a relative . . . what a kind, good-natured old creature we find her!" Immediately the reader sees what sort of relationship exists between old, rich women and their younger nieces and nephews who are burdened by the cost of owning homes and raising children. From this initial detail of the old lady's wealth, a satirical tone is apparent, and Thackeray is no doubt criticizing the greedy, younger relations who are hoping for an inheritance. This tone is also exemplified by the author's use of

"we" instead of "they." This use of the first person makes Thackeray appear to be supporting the avaricious relatives in their efforts, which makes his true disgust of their actions more forceful. The author's friendly tone and warm understanding only emphasize his true feelings, making the use of satire effective.

Again, both satire and disgust are brought forth in an artful manner as Thackeray describes how the children make ". . . endless worsted baskets, cushions, and footstools for her." These self-serving notions are confirmed as the speaker openly states his desire for his aunt's ". . . signature to a cheque for five thousand pounds." Thackeray also includes descriptions of how rich and expensive the meals are when this aunt visits, how the house "assumes a festive, neat, warm, jovial, snug appearance . . ." All these efforts are in an attempt to become unforgettable to this rich aunt as it comes time to draw up a will, and Thackeray compels readers to admit to this truth as he writes simply, "I appeal to

215

the middle classes." It is not until the end of the passage that he contradicts himself, revealing his sincere feelings, as he writes, "Sweet, sweet vision! Foolish, foolish dream!"

Thackeray's diction and choice of detail define the targets of his criticism, emphasizing his true feelings as he writes satirically about the nature of relationships between different family members.

Response to the Student Essay

This paper would be scored no higher than a six. The essay quotes from the question in its first sentence ("diction, syntax, and choice of detail") but never deals with the syntax. The final sentence speaks only of "diction and choice of detail." Most students will have no trouble dealing with these two topics. The better papers notice that the details describing the family's kowtowing to the rich relation include not just the husband, wife, and children; accommodations are made to impress even her fat coachman and her maid. That the family should court Miss MacWhirter by spending unusual amounts of money to insure her comfort is apt. Because money is the root of their values, what could be more natural?

Thackeray's satire is contained in a single long paragraph with a wide range of sentence forms. He begins with five exclamations introduced by "what" or "how," but no answer is needed to these questions. He moves then to dialogue, quoting the imagined words of the imagined audience, husband and wife. More exclamations introduced by "what" alternate with loose sentences. A direct question is put to the reader: "Is it so, or is it not?" Then, an appeal to the middle class. Then, a prayer to the "gracious powers." Then, three final exclamations. The paragraph has very long (up to forty-eight words) and very short (three words) sentences. Four times Thackeray interrupts himself with parentheses. The effect is to create a genial, intimate tone, a suggestion that this very carefully composed prose is spontaneous. Thackeray makes readers his accomplices and, by confessing his own venality, lures them, as it were, to confess their own.

Is the final "Foolish, foolish dream!" a rejection of the idea of courting a rich relation, a dropping of the mask to reveal the moralist? Or is it just a realistic comment on the extreme unlikelihood of the gracious powers' sending a rich aunt — something the speaker still longs for but which he is forced to admit is only a wish that can never come true?

Question 3: Open Question

The danger of an essay on a topic like this is that students will spend all of the essay defining the injustices by retelling the plot of the play or novel and neglect the second part of the question. This is a question where it is necessary to deal with the plot of the work you select, and so long as you keep in mind that what you say about the plot is to define the nature of a personal or social injustice, you should deal with the events of the work. But don't spend too much time on this easier task at the expense of the second requirement, discussing the techniques the author uses to make us sympathetic to the victims.

The two student essays that follow both handle the question well, and both make good points about the plays as a whole. Though the essay on Lear has some minor writing flaws and breaks off before its last paragraph is complete, it sees the connection between Lear's and the Duke of Gloucester's personal injustices and the larger issues of social injustice in the play. Both of these papers would receive high scores, sevens certainly and maybe eights.

Student Essay 1

The greatest tragedy is that of good intentions gone awry, the tragedy that leaves one to question what might have been. When sympathetic, basically decent people are driven by their characters toward a horrid outcome, when who is at fault for the tragic result becomes ambiguous — this is the greatest of tragedy. Sophocles' play *Antigone* tells such a story. Antigone is full of injustice, but Sophocles leaves no clear answers, and viewers (or readers) are left only with a sorrowful feeling toward both Antigone and Creon.

Central to the play is the enduring question of conflict between terrestrial and spiritual laws. Antigone wishes to bury her brother Polynices, but the king of Thebes dictates that only Eteocles, Polynices' brother and enemy in the attack on Thebes, be buried. Antigone falls victim to the apparent injustice of being unable to bury both of her brothers because of Creon's austere insistence that Polynices be left outside the city to rot. In the face of such moral injustice, Antigone feels a spiritual imperative to give Polynices a decent burial; she places the law of the gods as she understands it superior to Creon's dictate of Theban law.

Creon does not appear a complete villain, however. By burying her brother against Creon's orders, Antigone has defied the king and violated the law of the land, usurping his authority and thus, he feels, endangering the security of the entire kingdom. Creon's tragic flaw is his immutability, and he makes a victim of himself through his own stubbornness.

Sophocles lets his audience sympathize with both Antigone and Creon so that they might fully understand the intractable nature of the problem. In a world governed by law rather than anarchy, that law must be respected and upheld, despite differing personal opinions or reactions to it; if the law is wrong, then the law must be changed. Antigone clearly violates this tenet of orderly government. In contrast, Creon brings about perhaps the graver injustice of violating the precepts of the gods. Antigone feels the pain of Creon's spiritual injustice. Creon places the letter of the law and the form of procedure above essential truth and decency and this leads to Antigone's torment and his own downfall.

Sophocles guides readers to immediate sympathy with Antigone. She is a rebel, defying government and king, but Sophocles makes it eminently clear that Antigone is driven by moral impetus. She does what she does, making herself a victim of Creon's wrath, because she has no other choice but to obey her conscience. Creon, a wise and good-hearted ruler, is also sympathetic to audiences because of the same sense of inevitability about what he does. Each is driven by their own central qualities, their sense of duty, of right and wrong.

Through their dialogue and their lamentations (such as Antigone's initial discussion with Ismene about her intention to disobey the law), Sophocles serves to make the reader identify with the wrenching internal conflicts of the drama's participants, Indeed, more than anything else, Antigone is the story of conflicted souls in torment. This makes the injustices felt on both sides of the argument all the more acute.

Student Essay 2

Injustice, both social and personal, is a prevalent theme throughout literature. This is especially true of William Shakespeare's play *King Lear*. The private injustices that Lear and Duke Gloucester suffer lead to their understanding of the larger injustices in the world at large in which they hold privileged positions. The play presents a series of unjust actions beginning in the first scene when Lear resigns his kingship, an irresponsible action that is unjust to his subjects. The contest to decide which daughter gets the biggest share of the kingdom is unjust to all of his daughters and especially to Cordelia, who gets nothing because she tells the truth. Lear's banishing Kent is another injustice in this scene because, like Cordelia, Kent tells the truth.

Goneril and Reagan next act unjustly when they refuse to allow Lear to keep his knights. Lear rushes out into the storm, where he feels sympathy for Tom and his fool and realizes that as king he failed to care enough for the poor wretches of his kingdom. He says if the world's goods were divided more equally the heavens would be "more just." In the other plot, Gloucester unjustly condemns Edgar without even hearing his defense and in turn is unjustly betrayed by his bastard son and by Reagan and her husband. In his blind condition, Gloucester also sees the wider injustices of the world due to excess.

The actions of the play make us feel sorry for Lear and Gloucester. Just seeing these events, like Lear's going mad and suffering through the storm and Gloucester having his eyes gouged out, is horrifying. That both of them endure this suffering and use it to understand other people's suffering also makes us more sympathetic. Our sympathy is increased to a climax when Lear comes in carrying Cordelia's dead body.

Another reason we are sympathetic is that Lear speaks in such powerful poetry.

Answer Sheet for Practice Test 4

(Remove This Sheet and Use it to Mark Your Answers)

1 Ⓐ Ⓑ Ⓒ Ⓓ Ⓔ	21 Ⓐ Ⓑ Ⓒ Ⓓ Ⓔ	41 Ⓐ Ⓑ Ⓒ Ⓓ Ⓔ
2 Ⓐ Ⓑ Ⓒ Ⓓ Ⓔ	22 Ⓐ Ⓑ Ⓒ Ⓓ Ⓔ	42 Ⓐ Ⓑ Ⓒ Ⓓ Ⓔ
3 Ⓐ Ⓑ Ⓒ Ⓓ Ⓔ	23 Ⓐ Ⓑ Ⓒ Ⓓ Ⓔ	43 Ⓐ Ⓑ Ⓒ Ⓓ Ⓔ
4 Ⓐ Ⓑ Ⓒ Ⓓ Ⓔ	24 Ⓐ Ⓑ Ⓒ Ⓓ Ⓔ	44 Ⓐ Ⓑ Ⓒ Ⓓ Ⓔ
5 Ⓐ Ⓑ Ⓒ Ⓓ Ⓔ	25 Ⓐ Ⓑ Ⓒ Ⓓ Ⓔ	45 Ⓐ Ⓑ Ⓒ Ⓓ Ⓔ
6 Ⓐ Ⓑ Ⓒ Ⓓ Ⓔ	26 Ⓐ Ⓑ Ⓒ Ⓓ Ⓔ	46 Ⓐ Ⓑ Ⓒ Ⓓ Ⓔ
7 Ⓐ Ⓑ Ⓒ Ⓓ Ⓔ	27 Ⓐ Ⓑ Ⓒ Ⓓ Ⓔ	47 Ⓐ Ⓑ Ⓒ Ⓓ Ⓔ
8 Ⓐ Ⓑ Ⓒ Ⓓ Ⓔ	28 Ⓐ Ⓑ Ⓒ Ⓓ Ⓔ	48 Ⓐ Ⓑ Ⓒ Ⓓ Ⓔ
9 Ⓐ Ⓑ Ⓒ Ⓓ Ⓔ	29 Ⓐ Ⓑ Ⓒ Ⓓ Ⓔ	49 Ⓐ Ⓑ Ⓒ Ⓓ Ⓔ
10 Ⓐ Ⓑ Ⓒ Ⓓ Ⓔ	30 Ⓐ Ⓑ Ⓒ Ⓓ Ⓔ	50 Ⓐ Ⓑ Ⓒ Ⓓ Ⓔ
11 Ⓐ Ⓑ Ⓒ Ⓓ Ⓔ	31 Ⓐ Ⓑ Ⓒ Ⓓ Ⓔ	51 Ⓐ Ⓑ Ⓒ Ⓓ Ⓔ
12 Ⓐ Ⓑ Ⓒ Ⓓ Ⓔ	32 Ⓐ Ⓑ Ⓒ Ⓓ Ⓔ	52 Ⓐ Ⓑ Ⓒ Ⓓ Ⓔ
13 Ⓐ Ⓑ Ⓒ Ⓓ Ⓔ	33 Ⓐ Ⓑ Ⓒ Ⓓ Ⓔ	53 Ⓐ Ⓑ Ⓒ Ⓓ Ⓔ
14 Ⓐ Ⓑ Ⓒ Ⓓ Ⓔ	34 Ⓐ Ⓑ Ⓒ Ⓓ Ⓔ	54 Ⓐ Ⓑ Ⓒ Ⓓ Ⓔ
15 Ⓐ Ⓑ Ⓒ Ⓓ Ⓔ	35 Ⓐ Ⓑ Ⓒ Ⓓ Ⓔ	
16 Ⓐ Ⓑ Ⓒ Ⓓ Ⓔ	36 Ⓐ Ⓑ Ⓒ Ⓓ Ⓔ	
17 Ⓐ Ⓑ Ⓒ Ⓓ Ⓔ	37 Ⓐ Ⓑ Ⓒ Ⓓ Ⓔ	
18 Ⓐ Ⓑ Ⓒ Ⓓ Ⓔ	38 Ⓐ Ⓑ Ⓒ Ⓓ Ⓔ	
19 Ⓐ Ⓑ Ⓒ Ⓓ Ⓔ	39 Ⓐ Ⓑ Ⓒ Ⓓ Ⓔ	
20 Ⓐ Ⓑ Ⓒ Ⓓ Ⓔ	40 Ⓐ Ⓑ Ⓒ Ⓓ Ⓔ	

CUT HERE

Practice Test 4

Section I: Multiple-Choice Questions

Time: 60 Minutes

54 questions

Directions: This section contains selections from two passages of prose and two poems with questions on their content, style, and form. Read each selection carefully. Choose the best answer of the five choices.

Questions 1–12. Read the poem carefully before you begin to answer the questions.

> I had not minded walls;
> Were universe one rock
> And far I heard his silver call
> The other side the block,
>
> (5) I'd tunnel til my groove
> Pushed sudden through to his;
> Then my face take her recompense,
> The looking in his eyes.
>
> But 'tis a single hair,
> (10) A filament, a law,
> A cobweb wove in adamant,
> A battlement of straw,
>
> A limit like the veil
> Unto the lady's face,
> (15) But every mesh a citadel,
> With dragons in the crease.

1. In the second line of the poem, the word "Were" is

   A. an adjective, as in "were-wolf."

   B. a third person singular conditional verb with "if" understood.

   C. a third person plural verb in the past tense with "they" understood.

   D. a contraction of "we are."

   E. a second person singular past tense with "you" understood.

2. In line 3, the word "far" probably modifies

   A. "universe" (line 2).

   B. "rock" (line 2).

   C. "heard" (line 3).

   D. "call" (line 3).

   E. "side" (line 4).

GO ON TO THE NEXT PAGE

221

3. The lines "I'd tunnel till my groove / Pushed sudden through to his" are an example of

    A. hyperbole

    B. paradox

    C. simile

    D. apostrophe

    E. irony

4. In line 7, the word "recompense" is best understood to mean

    A. memory or recollection

    B. punishment or penalty

    C. survey or view

    D. joy or happiness

    E. reward or compensation

5. Which of the following is an example of <u>synesthetic imagery</u>, that is, the description of one sensory experience in terms of a different sense, such as Keats' phrase, "aromatic pain."

    A. "minded walls," line 1

    B. "universe . . . rock," line 2

    C. "silver call," line 3

    D. "my groove," line 5

    E. "looking in his eyes," line 8

6. Which of the following phrases requires some adjustment according to conventional grammatical rules?

    A. "I heard," line 3

    B. "his silver call," line 3

    C. "I'd tunnel," line 5

    D. "pushed sudden," line 6

    E. "looking in his eyes," line 8

7. All the following words are used to suggest the same quality EXCEPT

    A. "walls," line 1

    B. "rock," line 2

    C. "block," line 4

    D. "groove," line 5

    E. "adamant," line 11

8. Line 9 begins with "But" because

    A. lines 9–16 are contrasted with the universe of rock in lines 1–8.

    B. the speaker realizes the statement of lines 1–8 is insincere.

    C. lines 9–16 will precisely parallel lines 1–8.

    D. lines 1–8 are metaphorical, while lines 9–16 are literal.

    E. the speaker of lines 1–8 is different from the speaker of lines 9–16.

9. All the following words are used to suggest the Middle Ages EXCEPT

    A. "adamant," line 11

    B. "battlement," line 12

    C. "lady," line 14

    D. "citadel," line 15

    E. "dragons," line 16

10. All the following words are used to suggest the same quality EXCEPT

    A. "hair," line 9

    B. "filament," line 10

    C. "cobweb," line 11

    D. "straw," line 12

    E. "limit," line 13

11. On which of the following do lines 11–16 chiefly rely?

A. understatement

B. paradox

C. personification

D. internal rhyme

E. apostrophe

12. To fully understand the situation presented in the poem, a reader would have to know more about the specific reference of which of the following words?

A. "block," line 4

B. "groove," line 5

C. "recompense," line 7

D. "law," line 10

E. "veil," line 13

Questions 13–27. Read the following passage carefully before you begin to answer the questions.

Let not our veneration for Milton forbid us to look with some degree of merriment on great promises and small performance — on the man who hastens
(5) home because his countrymen are contending for their liberty, and when he reaches the scene of action, vapours away his patriotism in a private boarding school. This is the period of his life from
(10) which all his biographers seem inclined to shrink. They are unwilling that Milton should be degraded to a school-master; but, since it cannot be denied that he taught boys, one finds out that he taught
(15) for nothing, and another that his motive was only zeal for the propagation of learning and virtue; and all tell what they do not know to be true, only to excuse an act which no wise man will con-
(20) sider as in itself disgraceful. His father was alive; his allowance was not ample; and he supplied its deficiencies by an honest and useful employment.

It is told that in the art of education he
(25) performed wonders; and a formidable list is given of the authors, Greek and Latin, that were read in Aldersgate-street, by youth between ten and fifteen or sixteen years of age. Those who tell
(30) or receive these stories should consider that nobody can be taught faster than he

can learn. The speed of the horseman must be limited by the power of his horse. Every man that has ever under-
(35) taken to instruct others, can tell what slow advances he has been able to make, and how much patience it requires to recall vagrant inattention, to stimulate sluggishness, and to rectify absurd
(40) misapprehension.

He published about this time his <u>Areopagitica, a Speech of Mr. John Milton for the Liberty of unlicensed Printing</u>. The danger of such unbounded
(45) liberty, and the danger of bounding it, have produced a problem in the science of government which human understanding seems hitherto unable to solve. If nothing may be published but what
(50) civil authority shall have previously approved, power must always be the standard of truth; if every dreamer of innovations may propagate his projects, there can be no settlement; if every mur-
(55) murer at government may diffuse discontent, there can be no peace; and if every sceptic in theology may teach his follies, there can be no religion. The remedy against these ills is to punish the
(60) authors; for it is yet allowed that every

GO ON TO THE NEXT PAGE

society may punish, though not prevent, the publication of opinions which that society shall think pernicious; but this punishment, though it may crush the au-
(65) thor, promotes the book. It seems not

(70) more reasonable to leave the right of printing unrestrained because writers may be afterwards censured than it would be to sleep with doors unbolted because by our law we can hang a thief.

13. In line 14, the pronoun "one" refers to

    A. the author of this passage

    B. a biographer of Milton

    C. a reader of this passage

    D. a schoolmaster

    E. a reader of biographies of Milton

14. Which of the following points does the author make in the second paragraph of the passage?

    I.   Milton enjoyed a remarkable success as a teacher.

    II. The success of any teacher depends upon the ability of the students.

    III. Students are likely to be indolent, inattentive, and misinformed.

    A. I only

    B. I and II only

    C. I and III only

    D. II and III only

    E. I, II, and III

15. The image in lines 32–34 compares

    A. a teacher with a rider

    B. a horse with its rider

    C. a student with a rider

    D. human power with horse power

    E. a teacher with a horse

16. The author of the passage believes that Milton became a schoolmaster

    A. to encourage virtue and respect for learning in his students.

    B. to earn money.

    C. to share his learning with others.

    D. to promote the study of the works of Greek and Latin literature.

    E. to avoid military service.

17. According to the first and second paragraphs of the passage, early biographers of Milton

    I.   refused to see that he might be laughed at.

    II. deny that Milton had ever been a schoolmaster.

    III. lie about Milton's accomplishments as a schoolmaster.

    A. III only

    B. I and II only

    C. I and III only

    D. II and III only

    E. I, II, and III

18. In the first two paragraphs of the passage, the author presents other biographers of Milton as

   A. misinformed and verbose.

   B. florid and heavy-handed.

   C. incisive and authoritative.

   D. naive and objective.

   E. partisan and credulous.

19. We can infer from the third paragraph of the passage that Milton's *Areopagitica* is

   A. a defense of the classics of Greek and Latin literature.

   B. an argument for freedom of speech.

   C. a justification of his writings in poetry and prose.

   D. an argument against censorship.

   E. a seditious argument for the abolition of kingship.

20. In its context in lines 51–52, the phrase "power must always be the standard of truth" can be best understood to mean

   A. truth and power must always go together.

   B. nothing is more powerful than the truth.

   C. political authority dictates what the truth is.

   D. the real value of power is determined by its truthfulness.

   E. truth is determined by powerful moral standards.

21. In line 54, the word "settlement" may be best defined as

   A. colonizing a new land.

   B. establishment in life.

   C. gradual subsidence.

   D. adjustment of a claim.

   E. freedom from disturbances.

22. The phrase "if every skeptic in theology may teach his follies" (lines 56–58) makes it clear that the author believes that

   I. some theologians may be skeptical.

   II. theologians should be teachers.

   III. skeptical theologians are in error.

   A. II only

   B. I and II only

   C. I and III only

   D. II and III only

   E. I, II, and III

23. Which of the five sentences in the third paragraph best exemplifies the use of parallel construction?

   A. the first (lines 41–44, "He published . . .")

   B. the second (lines 44–47, "The danger . . .")

   C. the third (lines 49–59, "If nothing . . .")

   D. the fourth (lines 58–65, "The remedy . . .")

   E. the fifth (lines 65–70, "It seems . . .")

GO ON TO THE NEXT PAGE

24. The final sentence of the passage (lines 65–70) argues that

   A. the threat of punishment will prevent authors from publishing dangerous or seditious works.

   B. any publication should be permitted so long as the author can be punished.

   C. punishing controversial authors will increase the popularity of their works.

   D. there are some writings that should not be allowed to be published.

   E. the threat of punishment will not prevent the publication of dangerous writings.

25. The last sentence of the passage (lines 65–70) is an example of

   A. simile

   B. metaphor

   C. understatement

   D. overstatement

   E. paradox

26. We can infer from the passage that the author regards Milton with

   A. veneration and sympathy

   B. interest and skepticism

   C. detachment and indifference

   D. suspicion and contempt

   E. curiosity and bafflement

27. Which of the following best describes the style of the passage?

   A. metaphorical

   B. argumentative

   C. objective

   D. conversational

   E. introspective

Questions 28–41. Read the following poem carefully before you begin to answer the questions.

Fair is my love, and cruel as she's fair;
Her brow shades frowns, although her eyes are sunny,
Her smiles are lightning, though her pride despair,
And her disdains are gall, her favors honey.
(5) A modest maid, decked with a blush of honor,
Whose feet do tread green paths of youth and love;
The wonder of all eyes that look upon her,
Sacred on earth, designed a saint above.
Chastity and Beauty, which were deadly foes,
(10) Live reconciled friends within her brow:
And had she pity to conjoin with those,
Then who had heard the plaints I utter now?
Oh had she not been fair and thus unkind,
My muse had slept, and none had known my mind.

Note: designed, line 8= designated

28. The poem is an example of a

    A. blank verse lyric

    B. Shakespearean (or English) sonnet

    C. ballad

    D. Petrarchan (or Italian) sonnet

    E. verse epistle

29. In lines 1–4, all the following pairs are specifically contrasted EXCEPT

    A. fair — cruel

    B. brow — eyes

    C. frowns — smiles

    D. gall — honey

    E. disdains — favors

30. In line 4, the word "gall" is used to suggest

    A. insulting behavior

    B. illness

    C. effrontery

    D. bitterness

    E. exasperation

31. Lines 5–8 differ from lines 1–4 and lines 9–12 because they

    I. focus only on the virtues of the lady.

    II. make no mention of her beauty.

    III. rhyme the first and third and the second and fourth lines.

    A. II only

    B. I and II only

    C. I and III only

    D. II and III only

    E. I, II, and III

GO ON TO THE NEXT PAGE

32. The grammar in lines 5–8 is unusual because these lines

  A. express a conditional idea.

  B. employ a dangling participle.

  C. have no main verb.

  D. contain errors of agreement.

  E. employ inconsistent verb tenses.

33. The implication of line 9 ("Chastity and Beauty, which were deadly foes") is that

  I. love is a battle between good and evil.

  II. the beautiful and the chaste are besieged by dangerous enemies.

  III. it is difficult to be both beautiful and chaste.

  A. I only

  B. III only

  C. I and III only

  D. II and III only

  E. I, II, and III

34. All the following specifically refer to Chastity and Beauty EXCEPT

  A. "which," line 9

  B. "deadly foes," line 9

  C. "reconciled friends," line 10

  D. "pity to conjoin," line 11

  E. "those," line 11

35. The answer to the question asked in line 12 ("Then who had heard the plaints I utter now?") is

  A. the lady

  B. other men in love

  C. no one

  D. the speaker

  E. indeterminable, because the question cannot be answered

36. Which of the following best paraphrases "my muse had slept" in line 14?

  A. I have never been in love.

  B. I could not have written poetry.

  C. My love did not awaken.

  D. I could not think about her.

  E. She has paid no attention to my love.

37. The primary rhetorical purpose of the poem is probably to

  A. celebrate the chastity of the lady.

  B. convince the lady to return his love.

  C. praise the restorative powers of poetry.

  D. console the speaker for his disappointment in love.

  E. complain about the changefulness of the lady.

38. The poem presents the lady as all the
following EXCEPT

    A. beautiful

    B. inspiring

    C. chaste

    D. modest

    E. kind

39. Of the following words or phrases,
which one can be said to refer to this
poem?

    A. "disdains," line 4

    B. "green paths of youth and love,"
line 6

    C. "reconciled friends," line 10

    D. "plaints," line 12

    E. "muse," line 14

40. The poem employs all the following
EXCEPT

    A. rhetorical question

    B. personification

    C. antithesis

    D. contrary to fact construction

    E. understatement

41. Which of the following best describes
the major structural divisions of the
poem?

    A. lines 1–4, lines 5–8, lines 9–12,
lines 13–14.

    B. lines 1–12, lines 13–14.

    C. lines 1–5, lines 6–8, lines 9–14.

    D. lines 1–8, lines 9–10, lines 11–12,
lines 13–14.

    E. lines 1–13, line 14.

*Questions 42–54. Read the following passage carefully before you begin to answer the
questions.*

Her name was Aho, and she belonged
to the last culture to evolve in North
America. Her forbears came down from
the high country in western Montana
(5) nearly three centuries ago. They were a
mountain people, a mysterious tribe of
hunters whose language has never been
positively classified in any major group.
In the late seventeenth century, they be-
(10) gan a long migration to the south and
east. It was a journey toward the dawn,
and it led to a golden age. Along the way
the Kiowas were befriended by the
Crows, who gave them the culture and
(15) religion of the Plains. They acquired
horses, and their ancient nomadic spirit
was suddenly free of the ground. They

acquired Tai-me, the sacred Sun Dance
doll, from that moment the object and
(20) symbol of their worship, and so shared
in the divinity of the sun. Not least they
acquired the sense of destiny, therefore
courage and pride. When they entered
upon the southern Plains they had been
(25) transformed. No longer were they slaves
to the simple necessity of survival; they
were a lordly and dangerous society of
fighters and thieves, hunters and priests
of the sun. According to their origin
(30) myth, they entered the world through a
hollow log. From one point of view,
their migration was the fruit of an
old prophecy, for indeed they emerged
from a sunless world. Although my

GO ON TO THE NEXT PAGE

(35) grandmother lived out her long life in the shadow of Rainy Mountain, the immense landscape of the continental interior lay like memory in her blood. She could tell of the Crow, whom she had (40) never seen, and of the Black Hills, where she had never been. I wanted to see in reality what she had seen more perfectly in the mind's eye, and traveled fifteen hundred miles to begin my pilgrimage. (45) Yellowstone, it seemed to me, was the top of the world, a region of deep lakes and dark timber, canyons and waterfalls. But, beautiful as it is, one might have the sense of confinement there. The skyline (50) in all directions is close at hand, the high wall of the woods and deep cleavages of shade. There is a perfect freedom in the mountains, but it belongs to the eagle and the elk, the badger and the bear. The (55) Kiowas reckoned their stature by the distance they could see, and they were bent and blind in the wilderness. Descending eastward, the highland meadows are a stairway to the plain. In (60) July the inland slope of the Rockies is luxuriant with flax and buckwheat, stonecrop and larkspur. The earth unfolds and the limit of the land recedes.

Clusters of trees, and animals grazing (65) far in the distance, cause the vision to reach away and wonder to build upon the mind. The sun follows a longer course in the day, and the sky is immense beyond all comparison. The great (70) billowing clouds that sail upon it are shadows that move upon the grain like water, dividing light. Farther down, in the land of the Crows and Blackfeet, the plain is yellow. Sweet clover takes hold (75) of the hills and bends upon itself to cover and seal the soil. There the Kiowas paused on their way; they had come to the place where they must change their lives. The sun is at home on the plains. (80) Precisely there does it have the certain character of a god. When the Kiowas came to the land of the Crows, they could see the dark lees of the hills at dawn across the Bighorn River, the pro- (85) fusion of light on the grain shelves, the oldest deity ranging after the solstices. Not yet would they veer southward to the caldron of the land that lay below; they must wean their blood from the (90) northern winter and hold the mountains a while longer in their view. They bore Tai-me in procession to the east.

42. The primary purpose of the speaker of the passage is to

A. briefly sketch autobiographical information.

B. describe a series of mythical events.

C. summarize the Kiowa tribal history.

D. pay tribute to the memory of his grandmother.

E. comment upon a popular misunderstanding.

43. In line 11, the Kiowa migration is described as "a journey toward the dawn" because

I. it moves in an easterly direction.

II. it moves toward a land of greater sunlight.

III. it is a movement toward a more enlightened way of life.

A. III only

B. I and II only

C. I and III only

D. II and III only

E. I, II, and III

44. Before the migration described in the passage, the Kiowa

    A. used horses only for agricultural purposes.

    B. had a difficult struggle to survive.

    C. were unable to read or write.

    D. had no religious beliefs.

    E. lived chiefly by agriculture.

45. In which of the following does the diction demonstrate the author's refusal to idealize the Kiowas?

    A. "pride," line 23.

    B. "fighters," line 28.

    C. "thieves," line 28.

    D. "hunters," line 28.

    E. "priests," line 28.

46. In the analogy of lines 29–34, the speaker compares

    A. the Kiowa origin myth and the myth of Eden.

    B. a fruit and a prophecy.

    C. the great plains and the limitless sky.

    D. a hollow log and the mountain world.

    E. the sunless world and the world of afterdeath.

47. The speaker undertakes his "pilgrimage" from Yellowstone eastward in order to

    I. revisit the scenes of his grandmother's childhood.

    II. retrace the route of the Kiowa migration.

    III. see scenes his grandmother has described.

    A. II only

    B. I and II only

    C. I and III only

    D. II and III only

    E. I, II, and III

48. The author's description of the Kiowa as "bent and blind in the wilderness" in line 57 is

    I. a phrase that dramatizes the freedom of the plains.

    II. an example of hyperbole.

    III. an example of literal description.

    A. I only

    B. I and II only

    C. I and III only

    D. II and III only

    E. I, II, and III

GO ON TO THE NEXT PAGE

49. The passage expresses the difference in the Kiowa's history by the use of all the following contrasts EXCEPT

   A. language and silence

   B. light and darkness

   C. northwest and southeast

   D. plain and mountain

   E. space and confinement

50. In lines 67–68, "the sun follows a longer course in the sky" because

   A. the summer sun moves more slowly across the sky.

   B. the sky is more visible in the plains than in the mountains.

   C. the days in the south are longer than those in the north.

   D. the distances from east to west are greater than those from north to south.

   E. the sun is reenacting the migration of the Kiowa.

51. Lines 69–72 ("The great billowing clouds that sail upon it are shadows that move upon the grain like water, dividing light") contain examples of all the following EXCEPT

   A. a metaphor comparing clouds and ships.

   B. a metaphor comparing clouds and shadows.

   C. a simile comparing either grain or motion to water.

   D. a metaphor comparing the sky and the sea.

   E. a metaphor comparing light and darkness.

52. In lines 85–86, the phrase "the oldest deity ranging after the solstices" describes

   A. the mythic battle of light and darkness.

   B. the cosmic journeys of the sun.

   C. the fertility spirits of the earth.

   D. the reflection of light on the fields of grain.

   E. the natural word of the plains animals.

53. The passage probably uses the figure "the caldron of the land that lay below"(line 88) to suggest its

   A. association with witchcraft.

   B. metallic color.

   C. enclosure by a circle of surrounding mountains.

   D. extreme distance from the mountains.

   E. greater warmth.

54. Of the following, which is a significant characteristic of the style of the passage?

   A. frequent use of metaphor

   B. frequent use of carefully developed similes

   C. frequent use of rhetorical questions

   D. frequent use of periodic sentences

   E. frequent use of parallel constructions

IF YOU FINISH BEFORE TIME IS CALLED, CHECK YOUR WORK ON THIS SECTION ONLY. DO NOT WORK ON ANY OTHER SECTION IN THE TEST.

Section II: Essay Questions

Time: 2 hours

3 Questions

Question 1

(Suggested time: 40 minutes. This question accounts for one-third of the total essay section score.)

Directions: The following passage is from Sir James Frazer's anthropological study *The Golden Bough*. Read the passage carefully and write an essay in which you discuss the literary techniques the author uses and their effect. Your essay should include some consideration of the diction, imagery, and syntax of the passage.

In antiquity this sylvan landscape was the scene of a strange and recurring tragedy. On the northern shore of the lake, right under the precipitous cliffs on (5) which the modern village of Nemi is perched, stood the sacred grove and sanctuary of Diana Nemorensis, or Diana of the Wood.

The lake and the grove were some-(10) times known as the lake and grove of Aricia. But the town of Aricia was situated about three miles off, at the foot of the Alban Mount, and separated by a steep descent from the lake, which lies (15) in a small crater-like hollow on the mountain side. In this sacred grove there grew a certain tree round which at any time of the day, and probably far into the night, a grim figure might be seen to (20) prowl. In his hand he carried a drawn sword, and he kept peering warily about him as if at every instant he expected to be set upon by an enemy. He was a priest and a murderer; and the man for (25) whom he looked was sooner or later to murder him and hold the priesthood in his stead. Such was the rule of the sanctuary. A candidate for the priesthood could only succeed to office by slaying (30) the priest, and having slain him, he retained office till he was himself slain by a stronger or craftier.

The post which he held by this precarious tenure carried with it the title of (35) king; but surely no crowned head ever lay uneasier, or was visited by more evil dreams, than his. For year in year out, in summer and winter, in fair weather and in foul, he had to keep his lonely watch, (40) and whenever he snatched a troubled slumber it was at the peril of his life. The least relaxation of his vigilance, the smallest abatement of his strength of limb or skill of fence, put him in jeop-(45)ardy; grey hairs might seal his death warrant. To gentle and pious pilgrims at the shrine the sight of him might well seem to darken the fair landscape, as

GO ON TO THE NEXT PAGE

(50) when a cloud suddenly blots the sun on a bright day. The dreamy blue of Italian skies, the dappled shade of summer woods, and the sparkle of waves in the sun, can have accorded but ill with that stern and sinister figure. Rather we pic-
(55) ture to ourselves the scene as it may have been witnessed by a belated way-farer on one of those wild autumn nights when the dead leaves are falling thick and the winds seem to sing the dirge of
(60) the dying year. It is a sombre picture, set to melancholy music — the background of forest showing black and jagged against a lowering and stormy sky, the sighing of the wind in the branches, the
(65) rustle of the withered leaves under foot, the lapping of the cold water on the shore, and in the foreground, pacing to and fro, now in twilight and now in gloom, a dark figure with a glitter of
(70) steel at the shoulder whenever the pale moon, riding clear of the cloud-rack, peers down at him through the matted boughs.

Question 2

(Suggested time: 40 minutes. This question accounts for one-third of the total essay section score.)

Directions: Read the following poems carefully. Then write an essay in which you consider the similarities and differences in style and meaning. You may wish to consider such topics as the use of detail, imagery, point-of-view, and symbolism.

Up-Hill

Does the road wind up-hill all the way?
Yes, to the very end.
Will the day's journey take the whole long day?
From morn to night, my friend.

(5) But is there for the night a resting place?
A roof for when the slow dark hours begin.
May not the darkness hide it from my face?
You cannot miss that inn.

Shall I meet other wayfarers at night?
(10) Those who have gone before.
Then must I knock, or call when just in sight?
They will not keep you standing at that door.

Shall I find comfort, travel-sore and weak?
Of labor you shall find the sum.
(15) Will there be beds for me and all who seek?
Yea, beds for all who come.

— Christina Rossetti

The Long Hill

I must have passed the crest a while ago
And now I am going down —
Strange to have crossed the crest and not to know,
But the brambles were always catching the hem of my gown.

(5)   All the morning I thought how proud I should be
To stand there straight as a queen,
Wrapped in the wind and sun with the world under me
But the air was dull, there was little I could have seen.

It was nearly level along the beaten track
(10)   And the brambles caught in my gown
But it's no use now to think of turning back.
The rest of the way will be only going down.

— Sara Teasdale

Question 3

(Suggested time: 40 minutes. This question accounts for one-third of the total essay section score.)

Directions: Often, a play or novel presents a character who cannot be trusted, but whose true nature is eventually revealed. Choose a novel or a play in which a devious character plays an important part and write an essay in which you discuss how and why this character is unmasked and the relevance of the character to the meaning of the work as a whole. You may choose a work from the list below or another novel or play of literary merit.

Othello
The Wild Duck
King Lear
All My Sons
Sense and Sensibility
Billy Budd
David Copperfield
Wide Sargasso Sea
Great Expectations
Lord of the Flies
Hedda Gabler
Much Ado About Nothing
The Little Foxes
Miss Julie

IF YOU FINISH BEFORE TIME IS CALLED, CHECK YOUR WORK ON THIS
SECTION ONLY. DO NOT WORK ON ANY OTHER SECTION IN THE TEST.

Answer Key

Section I: Multiple-Choice Questions

<table>
<tr><td>First Poem</td><td>First Prose Passage</td></tr>
<tr><td>1. B</td><td>13. B</td></tr>
<tr><td>2. C</td><td>14. D</td></tr>
<tr><td>3. A</td><td>15. A</td></tr>
<tr><td>4. E</td><td>16. B</td></tr>
<tr><td>5. C</td><td>17. C</td></tr>
<tr><td>6. D</td><td>18. E</td></tr>
<tr><td>7. D</td><td>19. D</td></tr>
<tr><td>8. A</td><td>20. C</td></tr>
<tr><td>9. A</td><td>21. E</td></tr>
<tr><td>10. E</td><td>22. C</td></tr>
<tr><td>11. B</td><td>23. C</td></tr>
<tr><td>12. D</td><td>24. D</td></tr>
<tr><td></td><td>25. A</td></tr>
<tr><td></td><td>26. B</td></tr>
<tr><td></td><td>27. B</td></tr>
</table>

Second Poem

28. B
29. C
30. D
31. B
32. C
33. B
34. D
35. C
36. B
37. B
38. E
39. D
40. E
41. A

Second Prose Passage

42. C
43. E
44. B
45. C
46. D
47. D
48. B
49. A
50. B
51. E
52. B
53. E
54. A

Practice Test 4 Scoring Worksheet

Use the following worksheet to arrive at a probable final AP grade on Practice Test 4. While it is sometimes difficult to be objective enough to score one's own essay, you can use the sample essay answers that follow to approximate an essay score for yourself. Better yet, give your essays (along with the sample scored essays) to a friend or relative who you think is competent to score the essays.

Section I: Multiple-Choice Questions

$$\underset{\substack{\text{right}\\\text{answers}}}{\underline{\hspace{2cm}}} - (^1\!/_4 \text{ or } .25 \times \underset{\substack{\text{wrong}\\\text{answers}}}{\underline{\hspace{2cm}}}) = \underset{\substack{\text{multiple-choice}\\\text{raw score}}}{\underline{\hspace{2cm}}}$$

$$\underset{\substack{\text{multiple-choice}\\\text{raw score}}}{\underline{\hspace{2cm}}} \times 1.25 = \underset{\substack{\text{multiple-choice}\\\text{converted score}}}{\underline{\hspace{2cm}}} (\text{of possible } 67.5)$$

Section II: Essay Questions

$$\underset{\substack{\text{question 1}\\\text{raw score}}}{\underline{\hspace{2cm}}} + \underset{\substack{\text{question 2}\\\text{raw score}}}{\underline{\hspace{2cm}}} + \underset{\substack{\text{question 3}\\\text{raw score}}}{\underline{\hspace{2cm}}} = \underset{\substack{\text{essay}\\\text{raw score}}}{\underline{\hspace{2cm}}}$$

$$\underset{\substack{\text{essay score}}}{\underline{\hspace{2cm}}} \times 3.055 = \underset{\substack{\text{essay}\\\text{converted score}}}{\underline{\hspace{2cm}}} (\text{of possible } 82.5)$$

Final Score

$$\underset{\substack{\text{multiple-choice}\\\text{converted score}}}{\underline{\hspace{2cm}}} + \underset{\substack{\text{essay}\\\text{converted score}}}{\underline{\hspace{2cm}}} = \underset{\substack{\text{final}\\\text{converted score}}}{\underline{\hspace{2cm}}} (\text{of possible } 150)$$

Probable Final AP Score

Final Converted Score	Probable AP Score
150–100	5
99–86	4
85–67	3
66–0	1 or 2

Section I: Multiple-Choice Questions

First Poem

The poem is by Emily Dickinson.

1. **B.** The verbs in the first two stanzas of the poem are conditional. The "I had not minded walls" of line 1 is an abbreviated way of saying "I would not have minded walls." Lines 2–6 are saying "if the universe were a single rock, and I heard him calling from its other side, I would tunnel through it."

2. **C.** It is more likely that "far" is an adverb rather than an adjective here. It means "from afar," or "from a distance" and modifies the verb "heard."

3. **A.** The lines are a hyperbole, an exaggeration or overstatement. The vow to tunnel through a rock as wide as the universe is like the more commonly used lovers' hyperboles, promises to climb the highest mountains or drink the ocean dry.

4. **E.** The word "recompense" means "reward" or "compensation." In another hyperbole, the speaker says that simply to look in his eyes is reward enough for tunneling through the universe.

5. **C.** The "call" is a sound, but it is described by a color, an adjective of sight, "silver."

6. **D.** We expect the adverb "suddenly" to modify the verb "pushed." The interchange of adverb and adjectives is a commonly used license in poetry written before the twentieth century, and especially common in the poems of Emily Dickinson.

7. **D.** Four of the five words suggest the hardness of the barrier. The "groove" is the means of bringing the two together.

8. **A.** The poem turns on the word "But" and the last two stanzas present the opposite of the walls or rock, the filament, cobweb, law which the speaker does "mind" and cannot break through.

9. **A.** The references to parts of a castle ("battlement" and "citadel") and to dragons are easy to identify. The harder choice is between "lady" and "adamant," both words in common use in modern English. But "adamant" (a very hard stone) has no medieval associations, while we do think of the knight and his "lady" as a common feature of the romances of the Middle Ages.

10. **E.** Four of these five words suggest the fragility or apparent weakness of the barrier, but the "limit" is the barrier itself.

11. **B.** The lines rely chiefly on paradox, the strong weakness of the "limit." The phrases "cobweb wove of adamant" or "battlement of straw" are paradoxical, as is the veil with dragons in the last stanza.

12. **D.** The word that challenges the reader most is "law." What law? Does the poem describe the love for a married man from whom the speaker must be separated by the marriage laws? Or is it a moral law? or a natural law? With only the poem to go by, we cannot know. The words "block," "groove," "recompense," and "veil" are all used figuratively, or as part of figures of speech, but "law" stands apart because it seems to be literal. The block or the lady's veil don't really exist, but the law does and it separates even more effectively than a wall or a dragon.

First Prose Passage

The passage is from Dr. Johnson's "Life of Milton."

13. **B.** The pronoun "They" at the beginning of this sentence refers to "biographers," and the "one" and "another" refer to "They," that is, the biographers of Milton who are unwilling to see Milton as merely a schoolmaster.

14. **D.** Though the other biographers claim remarkable success for Milton's teaching, the author here refuses to judge. He does, however, say that the teacher is only as good as his students and that the students are likely to be limited, implying that Milton's success was no greater than that of most teachers.

15. **A.** If the speed of the rider is no faster than the horse's, then the speed with which a master can teach can be no faster than the speed with which the student can learn. The teacher is the rider here, the student the horse.

16. **B.** The author frankly states that Milton taught to earn money. His "father was still alive" (that is, he had not yet inherited his father's estate) and his "allowance was not ample," so he needed the money.

17. **C.** The first sentence of the passage suggests a comic anti-climax in Milton's life that "veneration" may prevent our seeing, and the first two paragraphs mock those biographers whose veneration of Milton causes them to make of his school-mastering something it was not. But "it cannot be denied that he taught boys."

18. **E.** Eager to see Milton as superior in every way, the other biographers are well described as partisan and credulous, that is, unreasonably devoted and willing to believe too easily.

19. **D.** Though in a sense *Areopagitica* is an argument for freedom of speech, the more specific answer here is an argument against censorship. The tract is titled "for the Liberty of unlicensed Printing."

20. **C.** The whole sentence is saying that when civil authority can determine what can and cannot be published, then the power of this authority will determine what is "true," that is, "truth" as authority sees it. This is the side of the argument with which Milton would agree.

21. **E.** Though you can find all five of these definitions of "settlement" in a dictionary, the meaning here is "freedom from disturbances."

22. **C.** If there can be a "skeptic in theology," there must be a skeptical theologian (I). If what the skeptic teaches are "follies," the skeptical theologians must be in error (III). The phrase does not assert or suggest that theologians should be teachers.

23. **C.** The third sentence has four clauses that begin with "if." The use of parallel structure is even clearer in lines 52–58, where each of three clauses begins with "if every" and is followed by a second clause that begins with "there can be no. . . ."

24. **D.** The sentence is saying it makes no more sense to allow anything to be published than it does to sleep with unlocked doors. Better to prevent a crime, than allow it and then punish the guilty party. The passage makes the point about punishment increasing an author's popularity, but not in the last sentence.

25. **A.** The figure here is a simile. We tend to think similes will always use a "like" or an "as" to make identification easy, but here the word that makes this an expressed comparison is "than."

26. **B.** You will occasionally find questions like this one where none of the five answers will seem very good. In cases like this, you should work by the process of elimination. Which one is the best of the lot? Here, "veneration and sympathy" **A** is clearly wrong, in **D**, "contempt" is probably too strong a word, while "indifference" in **C** and "bafflement" in **E** are inappropriate. That leaves only **B**.

27. **B.** This is another question where the right answer may not strike you as the best word to describe the style here, but at least it is not inaccurate. One could be tempted by "objective," but though the author may be more objective than the biographers cited in the first two paragraphs, you can make a better case for "argumentative" as characteristic of all three paragraphs in the passage.

Second Poem

The poem, typical of the love sonnets of the late sixteenth century, was written by Samuel Daniel.

28. **B.** The poem is a Shakespearean or English sonnet: fourteen lines long, in iambic pentameter, and rhymed in three quatrains and a couplet (ABAB, CDCD, EFEF, GG). An Italian sonnet uses only two rhymes in the first eight lines (ABBAABBA).

29. **C.** Though we may think of frowns and smiles as opposites, the poem opposes the shade of her frown with the sunniness of her eyes and her cheering ("lightning") smile with her dispiriting pride.

30. **D.** Here "gall" is used to suggest bitterness, the opposite of the sweetness of honey.

31. **B.** Lines 1–4 and 9–12 present both the beauty and the cruelty (that is, that she turns the lover down) of the lady, but lines 5–8 describe only good points, her modesty, honor, youth, and piety. All three quatrains rhyme the first and third and the second and fourth lines.

32. C. The lines have no main verb. We should probably understand the subject and verb to be "My love is" or "She is."

33. B. The poem does not say that Beauty is evil. It presents Chastity and Beauty as enemies only of each other. The implication is that it is not difficult to be beautiful and unchaste, or to be chaste and not beautiful, but as the Ovidian (and male) notion has it, "she is chaste whom no one has asked."

34. D. Of the four, only "pity to conjoin" does not refer to the Chastity and Beauty.

35. C. The question is answered in line 14. One consolation of the lady's refusal is that the poet is inspired to write this poem. If she had not been "unkind" to him, he would have had no reason to complain in verse.

36. B. The "muse" is the goddess who inspires the artist. If the muse had slept, the poet could not have written this poem.

37. B. Although the poem does most of these things, its primary rhetorical purpose is probably to convince the lady to return his love. Most of the thousands of poems written in this tradition assume that the lady is part of the audience of the poem; by hearing about how much the lover is suffering, about how much he loves her, and about how wonderful he thinks she is, the lady may regret her "cruelty" and accept the poet's love.

38. E. In line 13, the poem specifically calls the lady "unkind."

39. D. The "plaints I utter now" are this poem, by which the poem lets us and the lady know "his mind."

40. E. One could accuse the poem of overstatement, not of understatement. Line 12 is a rhetorical question; line 9 uses personification; lines 1–4 use antithesis several times; line 11 is a contrary to fact construction (if she had pity, but she doesn't).

41. A. The most common structure of the Shakespearean sonnet follows the divisions of the rhyme scheme, that is, three sections of four lines each, followed by a couplet (two lines). Look carefully at the punctuation of a poem. It is the surest guide to structure.

Second Prose Passage

The passage is from the Introduction to N. Scott Momaday's *The Way to Rainy Mountain*.

42. C. The passage describes the history of the Kiowas, a series of real, not mythical events.

43. E. All three answers are correct. The migration is to the east and south, from the enclosure of the mountain to the open spaces of the plains. Lines 25–29 make clear that the journey is also to a far richer life.

44. B. Lines 25–26 describes the Kiowas after their migration as "no longer slaves to the simple necessity of survival."

45. C. The author describes the Kiowas as "lordly and dangerous" but includes the word "thieves" in his description of their new ways of life.

46. D. The passage refers to the migration as the fruit of an old prophecy, and an emergence from a sunless world. The migration is from the sunless world of the mountain forest (the dark inside the hollow log) to the open, sunlit world of the plains.

47. D. The speaker wishes to retrace the route of the Kiowas and to see the lands his grandmother has spoken of. They are not the scenes of her childhood, but scenes she has seen only "in the mind's eye."

48. B. The phrase is a hyperbole and a metaphor, not a literal description. It is used to emphasize how the "stature" of the tribe dramatically increases in a land where they can see for miles. In the mountains, they had been, as it were, "bent and blind."

49. A. The passage contrasts the confining, dark, northern mountain life before the migration with the open, sunlit, southeast plains life. There is no mention of silence in the passage.

50. B. The main point here is that the longer journey of the sun is visible from the plains. Because the land described here is "in July," the days would be longer, though the speed of the sun will not have changed.

51. E. The use of "sail upon it" (the sky) is a metaphor likening the clouds and ships (**A**) and the sky and the sea (**D**). The phrase "shadows that move upon the grain like water" uses a simile ("like water") though it is not fully clear if the figure means that the shadows move like water or that the grain is like water (**C**). The "clouds . . . are shadows" (**B**) is a metaphor.

52. B. The "deity" is the sun; "ranging after the solstices" describes the sun's apparent journey to northern and southern limits throughout the year.

53. E. The caldron is probably intended to suggest warmth. Before the image is used, the author refers to the "northern winter" of the mountains. Because the Kiowa are descending the eastern slope of the Rockies, there is no circular enclosure of mountains.

54. A. Of the five choices here, metaphor is the most often used in the passage. The four others are used sparingly or not at all.

Section II: Essay Questions

Question One

Student Essay One

In the passage by Sir James Frazer from The *Golden Bough* the author tells about an ancient religious custom in Greece (?). In this custom any man who wanted to become a priest had to kill whoever was currently the priest. If he did, he could be priest and also king ("the post which he held by this precarious tenure carried with it the title of king"). But then someone else who wanted to become a priest would want to kill him, which is why the author used the word "precarious." This could be described as a very ironic situation, as when the author says "He was a priest and a murderer." The author of this passage used many different kinds of images, such as cloud, blue skies, wave, dead leaves, and so on. Most of them are from nature. The effect of these images is to make the author's description of the ancient custom very interesting. He just doesn't tell about it, he paints a picture of what happens so the reader's imagination is set free. The writer also uses good diction in the passage so that it is almost like a poem. His syntax also adds to the vividness as in the following line — "The least relaxation of his vigilance, the smallest abatement of his strength of limb or skill of fence, put him in jeopardy." The reader can almost see the man as he waits for his enemies. Personification and alliteration ("pious pilgrims") are also two other important things used by the author to paint a picture. It is a sign of how good Sir James Frazer is that even though he is educating his readers about an ancient custom he is not doing so like a dry, boring teacher but is telling an exciting story that even children would enjoy. In conclusion, this passage has a strong effect on the reader because of the author's techniques such as imagery, diction, and syntax.

Student Essay Two

The passage begins matter-of-factly, like a guide book describing a scene in nature. But the passage changes with the introduction of the "grim figure" carrying a sword and "peering warily about." From this point on, the passage uses diction, imagery, and syntax to paint a really eerie picture. The effect is to give the passage a feeling of awe and horror, more like a scene from a mystery novel or horror movie than an anthropology book. The writer chooses his words to increase the feelings of mystery — "sinister," "wild," "dirge," "sombre," "melancholy," "dark," "gloom." He loads on the adjectives in pairs like "black and jagged" and "lowering and stormy." The images are also sinister. He uses similies (the stalking priest darkens the landscape like a cloud) and metaphors (winds sigh and sing a dirge, and the moon "peers" down). The image of the last six lines of the passage describing the autumn night with the priest stalking in the darkness is really scary. The syntax is also part of the story. The author utilizes parallel constructions often. The sentence beginning "For year in, year out, in summer and winter, in fair weather or in foul" has a number of parallel phrases. So does the next sentence which uses "the least relaxation" and "the smallest abatement." In the last sentence of the passage has a series of four parallels beginning with "the . . . of" and two with "now in." Diction, images, and syntax are combined to make a powerful picture of a weird event.

Comments on the Student Essays

The first essay is a good example of a kind of weak essay that often turns up. The student does not know how to discuss the techniques that the question calls for. There are references to "imagery, diction and syntax," but the rest of the essay makes clear that he or she has no real understanding of any of the three. It does list several "images" from nature, but the examples are incoherent because the effect of "blue skies" is entirely different from the effect of "dead leaves." All the images are lumped together with the deadly adjective "interesting." The insipid remarks on diction ("good") and syntax ("adds vividness") give no hint that the writer understands what either word means. The example of personification ("pilgrims") is not a personification.

Though the second essay is as short as the first, it answers the question very well. It understands the effect of the diction and the syntax in the passage and it defines clearly just what the effect is ("a feeling of awe and horror," "mystery"). The words and phrases it selects to support its comments on diction are carefully chosen. The writer understands two different meanings of "image," and gives excellent examples of both. The remarks on syntax are equally accurate and insightful. Despite its brevity, this is a first-rate answer.

Question 2

Comments on Question 2

The obvious connection of the two poems is they both use the hill as a metaphor for life. In Rossetti's poem, life is a climb with death at the summit, while Teasdale compares life to the ascent and descent of a hill. A good discussion of the differences will probably comment on the the fact that Rossetti casts her poem as a dialogue with one speaker asking questions in the odd-numbered lines, and a second answering in the even-numbered. Teasdale's poem, on the other hand, is a monologue with the speaker examining her disappointing life which is now on the way down. Rossetti's poem is about the rest that comes with death, while Teasdale's presents a life whose promise has never been fulfilled.

Most of the student essays on these poems were middle or upper half papers, suggesting that the poems are easier than those that usually appear on the exam. The following, though not without some weakness in the writing, is a good example of a shorter paper that would be scored near the top of the scale.

Student Essay

The big difference between these two poems is the tone. The first, "Uphill," although it is about death, is upbeat, emphasizing that death is restful, comforting, and universal. The end of the journey of life is a welcoming inn where everyone who has died will find rest from the labors of life. The poem reminds me of the Scotch ballad "Edward, Edward" where two people are speaking. There the mother asks question after question, and the son Edward answers each one. Like "Uphill," the whole poem is made up of questions and answers. Here the poet has the first person (someone who is still alive) ask the questions, and a second person (maybe a clergyman) gives the answers.

The diction of the poem becomes more and more comfortable. It begins with the harsher words like "uphill" and "the whole, long day," to describe the journey, but it gets calmer with words like "resting place," "inn," "comfort," and "beds for all." The second poem is more pessimistic. There is only one speaker, and she is frustrated and irritable. Though her journey should be easier because it is now not downhill (not "uphill all the way"), she is dissatisfied with her life which has turned out the way she expected it would.

The diction here shows the frustration of the woman. Instead of "comfort," and "beds," there are "brambles," and "dull," and "it's no use." The woman here has expected her life would be like the fabulous view from a mountaintop, but all she got was "the air was dull," and nothing to see, so now she has given up on life.

As for being like each other, both poems are about hills, and both have the same rhymes. There are four lines in each verse and the rhyme is line one and three, and lines two and four: "way-day, end-friend" and "ago-know, down-gown." The big difference is that the first is hopeful but the second is a downer.

Question 3

Student Essay One

In *King Lear* by Shakespeare Gonerill and Reagan are characters who cannot be trusted. At the beginning of the play they tell their father King Lear how much they love him so that they will get bigger shares of the country. His other daughter Cordelia also deceives him because she won't say she loves him though she really does. As the story moves on Gonerill and Reagan perform many devious and untrustworthy actions such as pushing their father out of their castle into a storm and poking out another old man's eyes. In the end Gonerill and Reagan's deviousness is out in the open and Cordelia comes back to take care of her father. Gonerill poisons Reagan but when this is found out she kills herself. Cordelia is also killed, but she has been good not evil at the end of the story.

Student Essay Two

Shakespeare's play <u>King Lear</u> depicts a struggle between characters who embody goodness and virtue and those who are evil and trecharous. The battle between good and evil ultimately results in the demise of Shakespeare's protagonist King Lear and his kingdom. The plight of the character Edmund who embodies evilness and deception illustrates the initial success of trechary but the ultimate victory of goodness. Edmund's eventual unmasking reveals his overzealous greed and manipulation and his demise is a victory for the natural order and his brother Edgar who exemplifies the need to possess self-knowledge and an accurate vision of the world.

At the beginning of the play, Edmund states he will not allow his illegitimate birth prevent him from inheriting his father's land, and he devises a plan to deceive both his father and his brother. As Edmund's power ascends, so does his desire for greater power. He manipulates other people like Regan and Goneril for his own selfish purposes. His last evil act is to order the death of Lear and Cordelia.

Edmund's eventual downfall occurs when Edgar acquires a letter that Edmund wrote plotting the killing of Goneril's husband Lord Albany. He is accused of treason but is allowed to defend himself in a duel against an unknown competitor. His opponent is his brother Edgar who is seeking revenge for the suffering Edmund by his deceit inflicted on both him and his father, Gloucester. Edmund is fatally wounded, but before his death confesses the entirety of his trechary and deception.

Edmund's rise and initial success come as a result of other characters' lack of self-knowledge and clear vision. Gloucester is easily fooled by Edmund because, like King Lear, he lacks self-knowledge and understanding of the people around him. Although Edmund initially topples the natural order of the kingdom, the ultimate unmasking of his evilness and Edgar's success underscore the idea of the need for accurate vision and the ultimate victory of a natural order. Edgar's victory over Edmund reveals that the only way to live successfully is to possess compassion, love and forgiveness.

Comments on the Student Essays

The first essay is in big trouble from the start. The question calls for "<u>a</u> character," not two. It doesn't help that the student misspells both names, and misrepresents Cordelia's actions in the first act. Unlike her sisters, she does not deceive her father; she simply refuses to play his game. The next two paragraphs are no better. A kindly reader may give this vacuous paper a 2, but it would probably be scored a 1. A reminder: If the questions say write on "a character," write on one, not two or three. If the question says write on a novel or a play, write on only one novel or only one play. The second essay, despite a few problems in diction and spelling, would get a high score. Edmund is probably the best character to choose, and this paper explains his deviousness and how and why he is unmasked very well. It also deals well with Edmund's relevance to meanings of the work as a whole, citing several key themes: Edmund's death as a "victory for the natural order," the "need for accurate vision," and importance of "compassion, love, and forgiveness."

Answer Sheet for Practice Test 5

1 Ⓐ Ⓑ Ⓒ Ⓓ Ⓔ	21 Ⓐ Ⓑ Ⓒ Ⓓ Ⓔ	41 Ⓐ Ⓑ Ⓒ Ⓓ Ⓔ
2 Ⓐ Ⓑ Ⓒ Ⓓ Ⓔ	22 Ⓐ Ⓑ Ⓒ Ⓓ Ⓔ	42 Ⓐ Ⓑ Ⓒ Ⓓ Ⓔ
3 Ⓐ Ⓑ Ⓒ Ⓓ Ⓔ	23 Ⓐ Ⓑ Ⓒ Ⓓ Ⓔ	43 Ⓐ Ⓑ Ⓒ Ⓓ Ⓔ
4 Ⓐ Ⓑ Ⓒ Ⓓ Ⓔ	24 Ⓐ Ⓑ Ⓒ Ⓓ Ⓔ	44 Ⓐ Ⓑ Ⓒ Ⓓ Ⓔ
5 Ⓐ Ⓑ Ⓒ Ⓓ Ⓔ	25 Ⓐ Ⓑ Ⓒ Ⓓ Ⓔ	45 Ⓐ Ⓑ Ⓒ Ⓓ Ⓔ
6 Ⓐ Ⓑ Ⓒ Ⓓ Ⓔ	26 Ⓐ Ⓑ Ⓒ Ⓓ Ⓔ	46 Ⓐ Ⓑ Ⓒ Ⓓ Ⓔ
7 Ⓐ Ⓑ Ⓒ Ⓓ Ⓔ	27 Ⓐ Ⓑ Ⓒ Ⓓ Ⓔ	47 Ⓐ Ⓑ Ⓒ Ⓓ Ⓔ
8 Ⓐ Ⓑ Ⓒ Ⓓ Ⓔ	28 Ⓐ Ⓑ Ⓒ Ⓓ Ⓔ	48 Ⓐ Ⓑ Ⓒ Ⓓ Ⓔ
9 Ⓐ Ⓑ Ⓒ Ⓓ Ⓔ	29 Ⓐ Ⓑ Ⓒ Ⓓ Ⓔ	49 Ⓐ Ⓑ Ⓒ Ⓓ Ⓔ
10 Ⓐ Ⓑ Ⓒ Ⓓ Ⓔ	30 Ⓐ Ⓑ Ⓒ Ⓓ Ⓔ	50 Ⓐ Ⓑ Ⓒ Ⓓ Ⓔ
11 Ⓐ Ⓑ Ⓒ Ⓓ Ⓔ	31 Ⓐ Ⓑ Ⓒ Ⓓ Ⓔ	51 Ⓐ Ⓑ Ⓒ Ⓓ Ⓔ
12 Ⓐ Ⓑ Ⓒ Ⓓ Ⓔ	32 Ⓐ Ⓑ Ⓒ Ⓓ Ⓔ	52 Ⓐ Ⓑ Ⓒ Ⓓ Ⓔ
13 Ⓐ Ⓑ Ⓒ Ⓓ Ⓔ	33 Ⓐ Ⓑ Ⓒ Ⓓ Ⓔ	
14 Ⓐ Ⓑ Ⓒ Ⓓ Ⓔ	34 Ⓐ Ⓑ Ⓒ Ⓓ Ⓔ	
15 Ⓐ Ⓑ Ⓒ Ⓓ Ⓔ	35 Ⓐ Ⓑ Ⓒ Ⓓ Ⓔ	
16 Ⓐ Ⓑ Ⓒ Ⓓ Ⓔ	36 Ⓐ Ⓑ Ⓒ Ⓓ Ⓔ	
17 Ⓐ Ⓑ Ⓒ Ⓓ Ⓔ	37 Ⓐ Ⓑ Ⓒ Ⓓ Ⓔ	
18 Ⓐ Ⓑ Ⓒ Ⓓ Ⓔ	38 Ⓐ Ⓑ Ⓒ Ⓓ Ⓔ	
19 Ⓐ Ⓑ Ⓒ Ⓓ Ⓔ	39 Ⓐ Ⓑ Ⓒ Ⓓ Ⓔ	
20 Ⓐ Ⓑ Ⓒ Ⓓ Ⓔ	40 Ⓐ Ⓑ Ⓒ Ⓓ Ⓔ	

CUT HERE

Practice Test 5

Section I: Multiple-Choice Questions

Time: 60 Minutes

52 Questions

Directions: This section contains selections from two passages of prose and two poems, with questions on their content, style, and form. Read each selection carefully. Choose the best answer of the five choices.

Questions 1–15. Read the passage carefully before you begin to answer the questions.

So that since the ever-praiseworthy poesy is full of virtue-breeding delightfulness, and void of no gift that ought to be in the noble name of learning; since
(5) the blames laid against it are either false or feeble; since the cause why it is not esteemed in England is the fault of poet-apes, not poets; since, lastly, our tongue is most fit to honor poesy, and to be hon-
(10) ored by poesy; I conjure you all that have had the evil luck to read this ink-wasting toy of mine, even in the name of the Nine Muses, no more to scorn the sacred mysteries of poesy, no more to
(15) laugh at the name of "poets," as though they were next inheritors to fools, no more to jest at the reverent title of a "rhymer"; but to believe, with Aristotle, that they were the ancient treasurers of
(20) the Grecians' divinity; to believe, with Bembus, that they were the first bringer-in of all civility; to believe, with Scaliger, that no philosopher's precepts can sooner make you an honest man
(25) than the reading of Virgil; to believe, with Clauserus, the translator of Cornutus, that it pleased the heavenly Deity, by Hesiod and Homer, under the veil of fables, to give us all knowledge,
(30) logic, rhetoric, philosophy, natural and moral, and Quid non?; to believe, with me, that there are many mysteries contained in poetry, which of purpose were written darkly, lest by profane wits it
(35) should be abused; to believe with Landin, that they are so beloved of the gods that whatsoever they write proceeds of a divine fury; lastly to believe themselves, when they tell you they will
(40) make you immortal by their verses.

Thus doing, your name shall flourish in the printers' shops; thus doing, you shall be of kin to many a poetical preface; thus doing you shall be most fair,
(45) most rich, most wise, most all; you shall dwell upon superlatives. Thus doing, your soul shall be placed with Dante's Beatrix, or Virgil's Anchises. But if (fie of such a but) you be born so near the
(50) dull-making cataract of Nilus that you cannot hear the planet-like music of poetry, if you have so earth-creeping a mind that it cannot lift itself up to look to the sky of poetry, or rather, by a

GO ON TO THE NEXT PAGE

(55) certain rustical disdain, will become such a mome as to be a Momus of poetry: then, though I will not wish unto you the asses ears of Midas, nor to be driven by a poet's verses (as Bubonax
(60) was) to hang himself, nor to be rhymed to death, as is said to be done in Ireland; yet thus much curse I must send you, in the behalf of all poets, that while you live, you live in love, and never get
(65) favor for lacking skill of a sonnet, and, when you die, your memory die from the earth for want of an epitaph.

Notes. lines 7–8, poet–apes = imitators of poets; lines 21, 23, 27, 36, Bembus, Scaliger, Clauserus, Landin = Renaissance men of letters; line 31, Quid non? = why not?, line 50, cataract = the people living near the falls of the Nile were said to be made deaf by the noise; line 56, mome = stupid person; line 56, Momus = a harsh critic.

1. The details of lines 1–10 suggest that this passage follows arguments about

   I. the low opinion of poetry in England.

   II. the moral effect of poetry.

   III. the suitability of English as a vehicle for poetry.

   A. II only

   B. I and II only

   C. I and III only

   D. II and III only

   E. I, II, and III

2. In line 12, the word "toy" can be best defined as

   A. trifle

   B. small animal

   C. pastime

   D. child's plaything

   E. flirtation

3. The argument of Scaliger that "no philosopher's precepts can sooner make you an honest man than the reading of Virgil" (lines 23–25) most closely resembles the view that poetry is

   A. "ever-praiseworthy," line 1.

   B. "full of virtue-breeding delightfulness," lines 2–3.

   C. "void of no gift that ought to be in the noble name of learning," lines 3–4.

   D. "the fault of poet–apes," lines 7–8.

   E. "sacred mysteries," lines 13–14.

4. In line 31, the speaker says "Quid non?" ("why not?") because he

   A. wishes to give authority to his argument by using Latin.

   B. wishes to alert the reader that the comment that follows is more important than those earlier in this series.

   C. is modestly hesitant about including himself with the other defenders of poetry.

   D. does not really believe that poetry contains "many mysteries."

   E. has introduced the other elements in this series with a similar parenthetical phrase.

5. In line 34, "darkly" can be best defined as

   A. with evil intentions

   B. gloomily

   C. illegibly

   D. obscurely

   E. with no knowledge

6. The subject and main verb of the sentence that makes up the first paragraph of the passage are

   A. "poesy is," line 2

   B. " I conjure," line 10

   C. "you," line 10 . . . "to scorn," line 13

   D. "you," line 10 . . . "believe," line 18.

   E. "they will make" lines 39–40

7. Which of the following is evidence of the speaker's modesty and lightness of tone?

   I. "all that have had the evil luck to read," lines 10–11

   II. "this ink-wasting toy of mine," lines 11–12

   III. "Quid non?" line 31

   A. II only

   B. I and II only

   C. I and III only

   D. II and III only

   E. I, II, and III

8. Which of the following accurately describes the first paragraph?

   I. It contains only one sentence.

   II. It makes extensive use of rhetorical questions.

   III. It makes extensive use of parallel clauses.

   A. I only

   B. I and II only

   C. I and III only

   D. II and III only

   E. I, II, and III

9. The speaker refers to Beatrix and Anchises (line 48) in order to

   A. ally himself with Dante and Virgil.

   B. provide examples of those immortalized in poetry.

   C. remind the reader of the historical sweep of poetry.

   D. provide examples of the "most fair, most rich, most wise," (lines 44–45).

   E. assert the priority of religious poetry.

10. The figures that describe poetry in lines 50–59 are used to suggest that it is

   A. heavenly

   B. musical

   C. prophetic

   D. ancient

   E. intellectual

GO ON TO THE NEXT PAGE

Practice Test 5

11. An "epitaph" (line 67) is

    A. a repeated term or phrase used to describe a person

    B. a monument in memory of a person buried somewhere else

    C. a characterizing word

    D. a composition in the form of a letter

    E. an inscription on a grave

12. Which of the following best represents the basic structure of the last sentence of the passage (lines 48–67)?

    A. But (line 48) . . . then (line 57) . . . while (line 63).

    B. But (line 48) . . . yet (line 62).

    C. if (line 48) . . . then though (line 57) . . . yet (line 62).

    D. if (line 48) . . . so (line 49) . . . then (line 57) . . . nor (line 58).

    E. if (line 48) . . . then (line 57) . . . while (line 63).

13. Which of the following rhetorical devices does the second paragraph of the passage employ?

    I. It first promises rewards, then threatens punishments.

    II. It uses allusions to classical literature to cajole and to intimidate.

    III. It says something by saying what it will not say.

A. II only

B. I and II only

C. I and III only

D. II and III only

E. I, II, and III

14. The content of the two paragraphs of this passage suggest that they are

    A. the opening paragraphs of an argument

    B. the preface to a publication by another author

    C. a digression in an essay on an unrelated subject

    D. the conclusion of an argument

    E. part of a letter written to a close friend

15. As a defender of poetry, the author of this passage resembles all the following EXCEPT

    A. Aristotle

    B. Hesiod

    C. Bembus

    D. Scaliger

    E. Landin

Questions 16–27. *Read the poem carefully before you begin to answer the questions.*

Ardelia's Answer to Ephelia Who Had
Invited Her to Come to Her in Town

Me, dear Ephelia, me in vain you court
With all your pow'rful influence to resort
To that great town, where friendship can but have
The few spare hours which meaner pleasures leave.
(5)   No! Let some shade, or your large palace be
Our place of meeting, love and liberty,
To thoughts and words, and all endearments free.
But to those walls excuse my slow repair,
Who have no business, no diversion there;
(10)   No dazzling beauty to attract the gaze
Of wond'ring crowds to my applauded face:
Nor to my little wit the ill-nature join'd
To pass a general censure on mankind;
To call the young, and unaffected, fools;
(15)   Dull all the grave, that live by moral rules;
To say the soldier brags who, asked, declares
The nice escapes and dangers of his wars,
The poet's vain that knows his unmatched worth,
And dares maintain what the best Muse brings forth.
(20)   Yet this the humour of the age is grown,
And only conversation of the town:
In satire vers'd and sharp detraction be,
And you're accomplished for all company.

Line 3, town = London

Line 5, shade = a retired place

16. Which of the following best describes the genre of this passage?

   A. lyric poem

   B. epistle

   C. dramatic monologue

   D. ballad

   E. mock-epic

17. In lines 3–4 ("where friendship can but have / The few spare hours which meaner pleasures leave") the author is saying that

   A. friendship is more important than the distractions of the city.

   B. the city is cruel to friends and friendships.

   C. there are no pleasures that mean more than those of friendship.

   D. there is no time for pleasure in the activity of the city.

   E. the pleasures of spare hours are more meaningful in the city.

GO ON TO THE NEXT PAGE

18. Ardelia is reluctant to meet Ephelia in town because

   A. she wishes to avoid a meeting with Ephelia anywhere.

   B. she is concerned about making a bad impression in the city.

   C. Ephelia's palace is more luxurious than her house in London.

   D. city activities will interfere with the expression of friendship.

   E. she knows that Ephelia prefers the city to the country.

19. The phrase "dazzling beauty to attract the gaze / Of wond'ring crowds to my applauded face" exemplifies all the following EXCEPT

   A. overstatement

   B. irony

   C. metaphor

   D. satiric comment

   E. paradox

20. In lines 9, 12–13 (" Who have . . . Nor to my little wit, the ill-nature join'd / To pass a general censure on mankind"), the speaker claims to have

   I. limited native intelligence.

   II. satiric skills.

   III. a dim opinion of mankind in general.

   A. I only

   B. I and II only

   C. I and III only

   D. II and III only

   E. I, II, and III

21. As they are used in line 15, the words "dull" and "grave" are respectively

   A. a transitive verb and noun which is the object of that verb.

   B. a transitive verb and an adjective modifying "all."

   C. an adjective and a noun which is the object of "call."

   D. two nouns, the second in apposition to the first.

   E. two adjectives modifying "rules."

22. In lines 16–17, the speaker does not condemn the soldier as a braggart because

   A. she understands his impulse to exaggerate his exploits.

   B. she overrates the importance of physical courage.

   C. he is unused to the conventions of polite society.

   D. he has been asked to speak.

   E. he values honesty more than he values modesty.

23. In line 20, the word "humour" can be best defined as

   A. the ability to appreciate the comic

   B. drollery

   C. indulgence

   D. disposition

   E. whim

24. The irony of lines 22–23 in this passage is that they

    A. urge learning upon an audience that is selfish and lazy

    B. recommend satire in a poem that criticizes the satiric

    C. are democratic, but the town-dwellers are aristocratic

    D. recommend intellectual skills to an audience that values the physical more than the mental

    E. are comic while the passage as a whole is serious

25. The poem implies that compared to the city, the country will offer

    A. more healthful air

    B. kinder people

    C. more beautiful scenery

    D. more cultural attractions

    E. more sophisticated company

26. The speaker of the poem would be most likely to value all the following highly EXCEPT

    A. satiric wit

    B. naivete

    C. moral strictness

    D. self-confidence

    E. forthrightness

27. The only variation in the rhyme pattern of the poem occurs in

    A. lines 1–4

    B. lines 5–7

    C. lines 8–9

    D. lines 14–15

    E. lines 20–2

Questions 28–40. Read the passage carefully before you begin to answer the questions.

To be leaders of society in the town of Dulham was as satisfactory to Miss Dobin and Miss Lucinda Dobin as if Dulham were London itself. Of late (5) years, though they would not allow themselves to suspect such treason, the most ill–bred of the younger people in the village made fun of them behind their backs, and laughed at their trea-(10) sured summer mantillas, their mincing steps, and the shape of their parasols.

They were always conscious of the fact that they were the daughters of a once eminent Dulham minister; but be-(15) side this unanswerable claim to the respect of the parish, they were aware that their mother's social position was one of superior altitude. Madam Dobin's grandmother was a Greenapple of Boston. (20) Madam Dobin had now been dead a great many years. She seemed an elderly woman to her daughters some time before she left them; later they thought she had really died comparatively young, (25) since their own years had come to equal the record of hers. To be sure, it was the fashion to appear older in her day, — they could remember the sober effect of really youthful persons in cap and (30) frisette; but whether they owed it to the changed times or to their own qualities,

GO ON TO THE NEXT PAGE

they felt no older themselves than they ever had. Beside upholding the ministerial dignity of their father, they were
(35) obliged to give a lenient sanction to the ways of the world for their mother's sake; and they combined the two duties with reverence and impartiality.

Several of her distinguished relatives
(40) attended Mrs. Dobin's funeral, which was long considered the most dignified and elegant pageant of that sort which ever had taken place in Dulham. It seemed to mark the close of a famous
(45) epoch in Dulham history, and it was increasingly difficult forever afterward to keep the tone of society up to the old standard. Somehow, the distinguished relatives had one by one disappeared,
(50) though they all had excellent reasons for the discontinuance of their visits. A few had left this world altogether, and the family circle of the Greenapples was greatly reduced in circumference.
(55) Sometimes, in summer, a stray

connection drifted Dulham-ward, and was displayed (not to say paraded) by the gratified hostesses. It was a disappointment if the guest could not be per-
(60) suaded to remain over Sunday and appear at church. When household antiquities became fashionable, the ladies remarked a surprising interest in their corner cupboard and best chairs, and
(65) some distant relatives revived their almost forgotten custom of paying a summer visit to Dulham. They were not long in finding out with what desperate affection Miss Dobin and Miss Lucinda clung
(70) to their mother's wedding china and other inheritances, and were allowed to depart without a single tea-cup. One graceless descendant of the Greenapples prowled from garret to cellar, and ad-
(75) mired the household belongings diligently, but she was not asked to accept even the dislocated cherry-wood footstool that she had discovered in the far corner of the parsonage pew.

28. In the first paragraph, the author of the passage regards the people who make fun of the Dobin sisters with

A. studied indifference
B. guarded disapproval
C. amused understanding
D. snobbish condescension
E. stern condemnation

29. In lines 46–48, the phrase "to keep the tone of society up to the old standard" reflects the point of view of

A. an objective narrator
B. any Dulham townsperson
C. the Dobin sisters
D. the author of the passage
E. the younger people of Dulham

30. In lines 50–51, the reference to the "excellent reasons for the discontinuance of their visits" by the sisters' "distinguished relatives" is

A. a reflection of the point of view of the author of the passage

B. a comic understatement of the fact that they are dead

C. an explanation for their renewed visiting later in the passage

D. a rationalization that the sisters are eager to believe

E. a poignant symbolization of the inexorable passage of time

31. The effect of the parenthetical phrase "not to say paraded" in line 57 is

I. to suggest the display was, in fact, parading.

II. to shield the Dobin Sisters from the charge of showing off.

III. to suggest the military bearing of the Dobins and their relatives.

A. I only

B. II only

C. I and II only

D. I and III only

E. I, II, and III

32. All the following are examples of metaphor or simile EXCEPT

A. "was as satisfactory to Miss Dobin and Miss Lucinda Dobin as if Dulham were London itself," lines 2–4.

B. "they would not allow themselves to suspect such treason," lines 5–6.

C. "the most dignified and elegant pageant of that sort," lines 41–42.

D. "close of a famous epoch in Dulham history," lines 44–45.

E. "the family circle...was greatly reduced in circumference" lines 53–54.

33. All the following are examples of humorously overstated diction EXCEPT

A. "treason," line 6.

B. "mincing steps," lines 10–11.

C. "unanswerable claim," line 15.

D. "distinguished relatives," line 39.

E. "forever afterward," line 46

34. In which of the following phrases does the diction reflect the point of view of the author of the passage rather than that of the Dobin sisters?

A. "leaders of society," line 1

B. "superior altitude," line 18

C. "most dignified and elegant," lines 41–42

D. "up to the old standard," lines 47–48

E. "not long in finding out," lines 67–68

GO ON TO THE NEXT PAGE

35. What the passage refers to as "household antiquities" in lines 61–62 would now be called

    A. garage-sale items

    B. old furniture

    C. antiques

    D. interior decorations

    E. family portraiture

36. In line 63, the word "remarked" may be best defined as

    A. discussed

    B. objected to

    C. discovered

    D. referred to

    E. noticed

37. In lines 64–67, the relatives renew their visits to the Dobin sisters because

    A. they feel guilty for having ignored them in the past

    B. they hope to inherit their estate

    C. they hope to cadge some old family possessions

    D. they feel strong family loyalty and pride in their lineage

    E. they hope to make an appearance in Dulham society

38. In line 77, the word "dislocated" means

    A. disjointed

    B. misappropriated

    C. broken-down

    D. misplaced

    E. disconcerted

39. The passage makes fun all of the following EXCEPT

    A. regarding old age as an ever-receding horizon

    B. pretensions to social superiority

    C. greed of collectors

    D. women who remain unmarried

    E. genealogical pride

40. The tone of the passage may be best described as

    A. cynical and scornful

    B. tender and poignant

    C. lyrical and nostalgic

    D. whimsical and effusive

    E. wry and amusing

Questions 41–52. Read the poem carefully before you begin to answer the questions.

Spring and Fall: To a Young Child

Margaret, are you grieving
Over goldengrove unleaving?
Leaves, like the things of man, you
With your fresh thoughts care for, can you?
(5)   Ah! as the heart grows older
It will come to such sights colder
By and by, nor spare a sigh
Though worlds of wanwood leafmeal lie;
And yet you *will* weep and know why.
(10)   Now no matter, child, the name:
Sorrow's springs are the same.
Nor mouth had, no nor mind, expressed
What heart heard of, ghost guessed:
It is the blight man was born for,
(15)   It is Margaret you mourn for.

Notes: line 8, wanwood = the wood colored by the pale autumn leaves;
line 8, leafmeal = with leaves fallen and decaying (compare "piecemeal");
line 13, ghost = spirit, soul.

41. Of the following, which best describes the situation of this poem?

    A. an adult is speaking to Margaret, a weeping child

    B. a child is speaking to Margaret, another child

    C. an adult at a funeral is speaking to another adult

    D. an adult at a funeral is speaking to a child, Margaret

    E. at the funeral of a child, Margaret, an adult is speaking to a child

42. In line 2, the phrase "goldengrove unleaving" can be paraphrased as

    A. reading about a sad autumnal scene

    B. being unable to find a way out of the golden woods

    C. a wood's losing its leaves in autumn

    D. remembering an autumn wood of long ago

    E. pressing fallen leaves in a book

GO ON TO THE NEXT PAGE

43. In line 3, the word "leaves" is

    A. the main verb of the sentence

    B. the subject of the the sentence

    C. the object of the verb "care"

    D. the object of the preposition "for"

    E. the direct object of the verb "can"

44. In line 7, the phrase "by and by, nor spare a sigh" can be paraphrased

    A. and will not even sigh, later on

    B. and a timely sigh will be insufficient

    C. and in time sigh deeply

    D. and will eventually sigh briefly

    E. though others may sigh then

45. The "blight" of line 14 refers to

    A. a natural disease of plants

    B. man's indifference to others

    C. the destructive impulses of man

    D. the ecological irresponsibility of man

    E. the mortality of man

46. The poem presents Margaret as simultaneously

    I. a child and an adult.

    II. one who grieves and is grieved for.

    III. living and dying.

    A. I only

    B. II only

    C. I and II only

    D. II and III only

    E. I, II, and III

47. The poet's attitude to the characters in the poem is best described as a combination of

    A. detachment and approval

    B. admiration and respect

    C. curiosity and dislike

    D. understanding and sympathy

    E. superiority and condescension

48. The poem presents the natural world as

    A. nurturing and benevolent

    B. hostile and unpredictable

    C. deceptive and inscrutable

    D. mechanistic and indifferent

    E. mutable and instructive

49. Which of the following is an example of *synecdoche,* a kind of metaphor in which a part stands for the whole as in "hand" for farm worker or "a herd of fifty head?"

    A. "fresh thoughts," line 4

    B. "heart," line 5

    C. "sigh," line 7

    D. "springs," line 11

    E. "blight," line 14

50. The full title of the poem can be interpreted as

    I.   two seasons of the year.

    II. Margaret and the speaker.

    III. to leap and to trip.

    A. I only

    B. I and II only

    C. I and III only

    D. II and III only

    E. I, II, and III

51. Of the following, which employs parallelism in grammar, meaning, and sound effect?

    I.   "Sorrow's springs are the same," line 11.

    II. "Nor mouth had, no nor mind expressed," line 12.

    III. "What heart heard of, ghost guessed," line 13.

    A. II only

    B. I and II only

    C. I and III only

    D. II and III only

    E. I, II, and III

52. The poem employs all the following metrical devices EXCEPT

    A. feminine rhyme

    B. alliteration

    C. internal rhyme

    D. onomatopoeia

    E. triplet

GO ON TO THE NEXT PAGE

Section II: Essay Questions

Time: 2 hours

3 Questions

Question 1

(Suggested time: 40 minutes. This question accounts for one-third of the total essay section score.)

Directions: Read carefully the following passage and write an essay on the purpose of the passage and some of the means the author uses to achieve it.

The more ignorant men are, the more convinced are they that their little parish and their little chapel is an apex to which civilization has painfully struggled up the
(5) pyramid of time from a desert of savagery. Savagery, they think, became barbarism; barbarism became ancient civilization; ancient civilization became Pauline Christianity; Pauline Christianity
(10) became Roman Catholicism; Roman Catholicism became the Dark Ages; and the Dark Ages were finally enlightened by the Protestant instinct of the English race. The whole process is summed up as
(15) Progress with a capital P. And any elderly gentleman of Progressive temperament will testify that the improvement since he was a boy is enormous.

The notion that there has been any
(20) such Progress since Ceasar's time is too absurd for discussion. All the savagery, barbarism, dark ages and the rest of it of which we have any record as existing in the past, exists at the present moment. A
(25) British carpenter or stonemason may point out that he gets twice as much money for his labor as this father did in the same trade, and that his suburban house with its bath, its cottage piano, its
(30) drawing room suite, and its album of photographs, would have shamed the plainness of his grandmother's. But the descendents of feudal barons, living in squalid lodgings on a salary of fifteen
(35) shillings a week instead of in castles on princely revenues, do not congratulate the world on the change. Such changes, in fact, are not the point. It has been known, as far back as our records
(40) go, that man running wild in the woods is different from man kennelled in a city slum; that a dog seems to understand a shepherd better than a hewer of wood and drawer of water can understand an
(45) astronomer; and that breeding, gentle nurture, and luxurious food and shelter will produce a kind of man with whom the common laborer is socially incompatible. The same is true of horses and
(50) dogs. Now there is clearly room for great changes in the world by increasing the percentage of individuals who are carefully bred and gently nurtured, even to finally making the most of every man
(55) and woman born. But that possibility existed in the days of the Hittites as much as it does today. It does not give the slightest real support to the common assumption that the civilized contemporaries of the Hittites were unlike their
(60) civilized descendents today.

This would appear the tritest commonplace if it were not that the ordinary citizen's ignorance of the past combines

(65) with this idealization of the present to mislead and flatter him. Our latest book on the new railway across Asia describes the dullness of the Siberian farmer and the vulgar purse-pride of the Siberian

(70) man of business without the least consciousness that the string of contemptuous instances given might have been saved by writing simply "Farmers and provincial plutocrats in Siberia are ex-

(75) actly what they are in England." The latest professor descanting on the civilization of the Western Empire in the fifth century feels bound to assume, in the teeth of his own researches, that the

(80) Christian was one sort of animal and the Pagan another. It might as well be assumed by implication, that a murder committed with a poisoned arrow is different from a murder committed with

(85) a Mauser rifle. All such notions are illusions. Go back to the first syllable of recorded time, and there you will find your Christian and your Pagan, your yokel and your poet, helot and hero,

(90) Don Quixote and Sancho, Tamino and Papageno, Newton and bushman unable to count to eleven, all alive and contemporaneous, and all convinced that they are the heirs of all the ages and the priv-

(95) ileged recipients of THE truth (all others damnable heresies), just as you have them today, flourishing in countries each of which is the bravest that ever sprang at Heaven's command from out

(100) the azure main.

Notes: Hittites (lines 56, 60) — a powerful people of Asia Minor of the period from 1200–1900 B.C.

Question 2

(Suggested time: 40 minutes. This question accounts for one-third of the total essay score.)

Directions: Read the following poem carefully. Then write an essay in which you discuss the devices the poet uses to reveal his attitudes toward men and war.

Channel Firing

That night your great guns, unawares,
Shook all our coffins as we lay,
And broke the chancel window-squares,
We thought it as the Judgment-day

(5) And sat upright. While drearisome
Arose the howl of wakened hounds:
The mouse let fall the altar-crumb,
The worms drew back into the mounds,

The glebe cow drooled. Till God called, "No;
(10) It's gunnery practice out at sea
Just as before you went below;
The world is as it used to be:

"All nations striving strong to make
Red war redder. Mad as hatters
(15) They do no more for Christes sake
Than you who are helpless in such matters.

GO ON TO THE NEXT PAGE

"That this is not the judgment-hour
For some of them's a blessed thing,
For if it were they'd have to scour
(20)   Hell's floor for so much threatening.

"Ha, ha. It will be warmer when
I blow the trumpet (if indeed
I ever do; for you are men,
And rest eternal sorely need)."

(25)   So we lay down again. "I wonder,
Will the world ever saner be,"
Said one, "than when He sent us under
In our indifferent century!"

And many a skeleton shook his head.
(30)   "Instead of preaching forty year,"
My neighbor Parson Thirdly said,
"I wish I had stuck to pipes and beer."

Again the guns disturbed the hour,
Roaring their readiness to avenge,
(35)   As far inland as Stourton Tower,
And Camelot, and starlit Stonehenge.

Notes: Line 9. glebe — the glebe is the land owned by a parish church.
A glebe cow would graze on glebe land near the church.

Line 35. Stourton tower — is a tower erected in the eighteenth century
to commemorate a military victory by King Alfred.

Question 3

(Suggested time: 40 minutes. This question accounts for one-third of the total essay section score.)

Directions: Often in fiction or drama, an inanimate object, a stage property, will play an important part in the development of the work. The property will often have a significant role in the plot, and it may also be used to reveal character (a miser gloating over a pile of gold coins), to convey a symbolic meaning (the skull of Yorick) or to perform some other purpose of the novelist or the playwright. Choose a novel or a play in which an object serves several purposes and write an essay in which you discuss how the author makes use of the property. Do NOT merely summarize the plot.

You may choose a work by one of the following authors or write on a work by another writer of equal literary merit.

Samuel Beckett

Lillian Hellman

Henrik Ibsen

Eugene O'Neill

William Shakespeare

Oscar Wilde

Tennessee Williams

Arthur Miller

William Golding

Thomas Hardy

Toni Morrison

Charles Dickens

F. Scott Fitzgerald

Joseph Conrad

Nathaniel Hawthorne

Graham Greene

IF YOU FINISH BEFORE TIME IS CALLED, CHECK YOUR WORK ON THIS
SECTION ONLY. DO NOT WORK ON ANY OTHER SECTION IN THE TEST.

Answer Key

Section I: Multiple-Choice Questions

First Prose Passage

1. E
2. A
3. B
4. C
5. D
6. B
7. E
8. C
9. B
10. A
11. E
12. C
13. E
14. D
15. B

First Poem

16. B
17. A
18. D
19. E
20. C
21. C
22. D
23. D
24. B
25. B
26. A
27. B

Second Prose Passage

28. C
29. C
30. D
31. A
32. D
33. B
34. E
35. C
36. E
37. C
38. D
39. D
40. E

Second Poem

41. A
42. C
43. D
44. A
45. E
46. D
47. D
48. E
49. B
50. B
51. D
52. D

Practice Test 5 Scoring Worksheet

Use the following worksheet to arrive at a probable final AP grade on Practice Test 5. While it is sometimes difficult to be objective enough to score one's own essay, you can use the sample essay answers that follow to approximate an essay score for yourself. Better yet, give your essays (along with the sample scored essays) to a friend or relative who you think is competent to score the essays.

Section I: Multiple-Choice Questions

$$\underset{\substack{\text{right} \\ \text{answers}}}{\underline{\hspace{2cm}}} - (\text{$^1\!/_4$ or }.25 \times \underset{\substack{\text{wrong} \\ \text{answers}}}{\underline{\hspace{2cm}}}) = \underset{\substack{\text{multiple-choice} \\ \text{raw score}}}{\underline{\hspace{2cm}}}$$

$$\underset{\substack{\text{multiple-choice} \\ \text{raw score}}}{\underline{\hspace{2cm}}} \times 1.29 = \underset{\substack{\text{multiple-choice} \\ \text{converted score}}}{\underline{\hspace{2cm}}} \text{(of possible 67.}$$

Section II: Essay Questions

$$\underset{\substack{\text{question 1} \\ \text{raw score}}}{\underline{\hspace{1.5cm}}} + \underset{\substack{\text{question 2} \\ \text{raw score}}}{\underline{\hspace{1.5cm}}} + \underset{\substack{\text{question 3} \\ \text{raw score}}}{\underline{\hspace{1.5cm}}} = \underset{\text{essay}}{\underline{\hspace{1.5cm}}}$$

$$\underset{\text{essay raw score}}{\underline{\hspace{2.5cm}}} \times 3.055 = \underset{\substack{\text{essay converted} \\ \text{score}}}{\underline{\hspace{2.5cm}}}$$

Final Score

$$\underset{\substack{\text{multiple-choice} \\ \text{converted score}}}{\underline{\hspace{2.5cm}}} + \underset{\substack{\text{essay} \\ \text{converted score}}}{\underline{\hspace{2.5cm}}} = \underset{\substack{\text{final} \\ \text{converted score}}}{\underline{\hspace{2.5cm}}} \text{(of possible 150)}$$

Probable Final AP Score

Final Converted Score	Probable AP Score
150–100	5
99–86	4
85–67	3
66–0	1 or 2

Answers and Explanations for Practice Test 5

Section I: Multiple-Choice Questions

First Prose Passage

The passage is from Sir Philip Sidney's sixteenth-century *Apology for Poetry*.

1. **E.** The lines speak of the responsibility of poet-apes for poetry's not being "esteemed in England." They also refer to its "virtue-breeding," that is, its moral effect, and of the English language as "most fit to honor poesy, and to be honored by" it.

2. **A.** Though in some contexts, "toy" could have the meaning in all five of these answers, here it means "trifle." Sidney is saying (though he may not believe it) that his *Apology for Poetry* is an insignificant work.

3. **B.** Scaliger's point is that the reading of Virgil will have as much moral effect as the reading of an ethical philosopher; Sidney's phrase "virtue-breeding" points to the same moral effect of poetry.

4. **C.** At this point in this very long sentence, the series of writers the author has cited includes Aristotle, Bembus, and Scaliger, important intellectual authorities. Sidney wants to add an idea of his own to theirs, but instead of including it without comment, he hesitates, as if asking himself, "Should I put my own name in this company?" and answers, "Well, why not?" The hesitation lets the reader know that he has thought twice before including himself here. The four other answer choices here are not only inferior, but untrue.

5. **D.** Though all these meanings could define "darkly" in some contexts, here the meaning is "obscurely." Poetry is presented as a mystery, that is, a truth not readily comprehended by reason, written so the unenlightened will not understand. The term used in this period for symbolic writing (allegory) is "dark conceit."

6. **B.** The "since" clauses in lines 1–10 are dependent, and we do not reach the main clause of this sentence until we get to "I conjure you" in line 10. The series of infinitives ("to scorn," "to laugh," "to jest," "to believe") that make up the rest of the sentence are controlled by "I conjure you."

7. **E.** All three of these phrases suggest the self-deprecating tone that Sidney uses. He says a reader of his work is unlucky in his choice of reading matter, that his piece is a waste of ink (we would say "not worth the paper it is written on"), a trifle, and he hesitates to include himself with other men of letters who have defended poetry.

8. **C.** The sentence is punctuated with only one period, so it can be said to be only one sentence. An attempt to re-punctuate it into shorter sentences will not work. The sentence relies heavily on parallel clauses, for example, those introduced by "no more to," and seven more introduced by "to believe." There are no rhetorical questions in this paragraph.

9. **B.** Beatrix (Beatrice, the beloved of Dante) and Anchises (the father of Aeneas) are examples of those immortalized in poetry. Though Beatrice was "most fair" and Anchises was "most wise," neither can be said to be "most rich." Dante placed Beatrice in heaven, and Virgil placed Anchises among the heroes in Elysium.

10. **A.** The two figures used are the simile "planet-like" and the metaphor " sky of poetry," both suggesting that is heavenly.

11. **E.** An <u>epitaph</u> is an inscription on a tomb. A repeated term or phrase and a characterizing word is an <u>epithet</u>; a monument to a person buried elsewhere is a <u>cenotaph</u>, and a letter is an <u>epistle.</u>

12. **C.** This kind of question is much easier to deal with if you work out your own response without looking at the answers. To go through and eliminate each answer one by one is very time-consuming. The best choice here is "if...then though...yet." The sentence begins with two "if" clauses, followed by three parallel clauses ("then though I will not...nor...nor") and concludes with the "yet" clause which contains the subject and main verb ("I must send") and is followed by two parallel clauses introduced by "while" and "when."

13. **E.** The paragraph promises rewards to the friends of poetry in lines 41–48, and curses its enemies in lines 62–67. The allusions to Beatrix and Anchises support the rewards, while the references to Midas and Bubonax are veiled threats. By saying I will <u>not</u> threaten you with Midas's ears or with the fate of Bubonax, Sidney contrives to alert the reader to these possibilities, that is, in the act of saying what he will not say, he says something. We still see this ancient rhetorical device when a parent says "I will not remind you to clean up your bedroom," meaning "Clean up your bedroom," or a politician says "I want to run a mud-free campaign, and so I will not mention that my opponent has been indicted for mail fraud."

14. **D.** The opening phrase "So that" and the following summary of points about poetry suggest that the passage is the conclusion of a longer piece which has already discussed the two sides to these arguments. The sonorous and witty final sentence has all the earmarks of a last word. What could possibly follow?

15. **B.** All these men are mentioned as defenders of poetry except Hesiod, a Greek poet, not a critic.

First Poem

The poem is by Anne Finch, Countess of Winchelsea.

16. **B.** The passage is from an epistle or verse letter, a favorite form in late seventeenth and eighteenth century literature. The epistle is like the dramatic monologue, because it has just one speaker, but in the dramatic monologue, the audience, though silent, is present, and a specific setting is usually implied. Ardelia's letter is an answer to an earlier letter Ephelia has written inviting her to visit her in London.

17. **A.** The lines are saying that in the city "meaner" (that is, inferior) pleasures such as the social demands of London use up most of the time, leaving only a "few spare hours" to the more important expression of friendship.

18. **D.** Ardelia suggests a meeting where friendship will not be subject to the distractions of the city because she values friendship more than she values the "pleasures" of the town. The poem expresses the common literary theme which presents the country as more wholesome and more innocent than the corrupted city.

19. **E.** The lines use overstatement to deny a beauty so "dazzling" that crowds wonder at and applaud a face; irony (Ardelia does not imagine she has an "applauded face"); metaphor, the comparison of the gaping Londoners to an applauding theater audience; and satiric comment, the implication that Londoners require movie-star beauty to win their approval and dismiss those without it. The lines do not use a paradox, an apparent self-contradiction.

20. **A.** The speaker modestly claims to have only "little wit," which in this context refers to mental powers rather than to the modern meaning of satiric cleverness. She says she does not have the "ill-nature" that would encourage the fashionable London practice of satire, and she has no wish to censure mankind in general.

21. **C.** Starting at line 12, the poem is saying I do not have the ill-nature to condemn mankind in general, nor to call those who are young and without affectations foolish, nor to call all the serious people ("the grave") who respect the rules of morality dull. Thus, "dull" is an adjective that modifies "all the grave" and "grave" is a noun, meaning those who are serious.

22. **D.** The soldier is responding to a request, made clear by the word "asked," that is, having been asked.

23. **D.** In this context, "humour" has no reference to comedy, but means temper, disposition, or temperament.

24. **B.** The lines recommend skill in satire to qualify for acceptance in the city. They reflect the point of view of the city dweller, but not that of the speaker who disapproves of the city's love of detraction.

25. **B.** The poem argues that the requisites for acceptance in city society is ill-nature, satiric skill, and a willingness to mock the morally serious. The poem is not concerned with the salubriousness or beauty of the country, but implies it is free from the city's vicious tongues.

26. A. The poem refuses to dispraise the young and unaffected (line 14), those who live by moral rules (line 15), the self-confident poet (lines 18–19), or the straightforward soldier (lines 16–17). It does condemn the city's embrace of satire as its only "conversation."

27. B. Twenty of the passage's twenty-three lines are couplets, that is two lines with the same rhyme, though some are off-rhymes such as "gaze" and "face" in lines 10–11. Lines 5–7 are a triplet, that is, three, rather than two rhymed lines ("be," "liberty," "free").

Second Prose Passage

The passage is from Sarah Orne Jewett's 1886 story, "The Dulham Ladies."

28. C. The challenge in this question, and in many of the questions on this passage, is to discriminate between the author's view and that of the Dobin sisters. The Dobin sisters take themselves very seriously; the author does not share this attitude. In this paragraph, the first sentence reveals the self-satisfaction of the Dobin sisters. The use of "treason" and "most ill-bred" reflect the sisters' ideas, but an amused understanding is the best choice to describe the author's response.

29. C. It is the Misses Dobin who would be concerned with the "tone of society" in Dulham, and they would see with alarm a falling away from "the old standard" which made them "the leaders of society."

30. D. The diction of "excellent reasons" is that of the Dobin sisters. They wish to believe there are good reasons for the end of the visits, and not to consider the possibility of any limitations in the attractions of Dulham.

31. A. The effect of "not to say paraded" is almost the same as saying "paraded." It puts the idea into the reader's mind, though indirectly. It shields the author who pretends to not want to use the word, but not the Misses Dobin.

32. D. The first choice here is a simile using "as if," and comparing London and Dulham. The metaphors are harder to see. Ask yourself if the words here are literal or figurative. Both "epoch" and "history," though they may seem to make Dulham seem more important than it is, make good literal sense, but "treason," "pageant," and "circle" are metaphorical.

33. B. The use of "mincing steps" is descriptive, but it is not, like the other choices, overstated or comic.

34. E. The inflation of the diction in the first four choices reflects the sisters' point of view, but it is the author's tone we hear in lines 67–68.

35. C. We would use the term "antiques." Because the furniture or china is so eagerly sought after by the Greenapple relatives, we can infer that the pieces were well above garage sale quality, and that the possibility of getting one of these items made a visit to Dulham worth enduring.

36. E. In this context, the word means "noticed."

37. C. The paragraph makes clear that the visits have been renewed only after antiques have become "fashionable," and that the motive behind the renewed interest in the Dobin sisters is the misguided hope of carrying off one or two of their old pieces.

38. D. In this context, the word means "mis-located" or "misplaced."

39. D. The passage laughs at the family pride and self-satisfaction of the Misses Dobin, but it does not mock them because they are spinsters.

40. E. The art of the passage is its adroit adoption of the language and point of view of the Dobin sisters in such a way as to reveal the distance between their very serious response and the author's amused response to life in Dulham.

Second Poem

The poem is by Gerard Manley Hopkins.

41. A. The poem presents a sympathetic adult who is speaking to the weeping child, Margaret.

42. C. The "goldengrove" is the wood with its yellow leaves in autumn. The poet coins the verbal "unleaving" which means losing its leaves. The child is weeping at the sight of the falling leaves.

43. D. The prose word order of this sentence would read "Can you care for leaves?" "Leaves" is the object of the preposition "for."

44. A. The phrase means later (by and by) you will not even sigh, (let alone weep as you do now). That is, as the child grows up, she will become indifferent to the falling of the leaves in autumn.

45. E. Because it is the "blight man was born for," the reference here cannot be to the disease of plants, the usual meaning of the word. Here the word refers to the mortality of man. The speaker interprets Margaret's weeping for the mortality of the leaves as her unconscious sorrow for her own mortality.

46. D. In line 1, Margaret is "grieving;" in line 15 she is "mourned for." She is also both living and dying, because the poem asserts the universal mortality of mankind. Lines 5 and 6 predict the child's future indifference to the fall of leaves, but she is not "simultaneously" a child and an adult.

47. D. The best choice here is understanding and sympathy. It is very hard to make any case for any of the four other answers.

48. E. The falling leaves attest to the mutability of the world of nature, and from the fall of leaf, the poem draws instruction about the fate of man.

49. B. The synecdoche is the use of "heart" for the young girl; the use of heart for a man or woman is one the most common uses of this figure.

50. B. The title clearly refers to the two seasons, spring and fall. Symbolically, the spring represents youth (Margaret) and fall, the older man (the speaker). The title also includes the dedication "to a young child."

51. D. Lines 12–13 are saying the child's heart or spirit (ghost) have intuitively understood what has never been explained (no mouth nor mind expressed). The two lines each use parallel grammar, repeated meanings (mouth-mind; heart-ghost), and sound effects (the "n's" and "m's," the "h's" and "g's."

52. D. There is no onomatopoeia. (the use of a word whose sound imitates its meaning, such as "screech" or "buzz") in the poem. Lines 1–2 use feminine rhyme ("grieving" and "unleaving"). There are a number of alliterations in the poem ("ghost guessed," for example). There is internal rhyme in line 7 ("by" and "sigh"). Lines 7–9 use a triplet, the rhyme of "sigh," "lie," and "why."

Section II: Essay Questions

Question 1

Student Essay One

In this passage the writer is attempting to compare people today with people in other periods of history such as savages, Pauline Christianity, the Dark Ages, etc. He is doing this in order to show that in spite of greater wealth and comfort for some people such as the "British carpenter and stone mason," other people such as "feudal barons" are in worse shape in the modern world than the past. He seems to be saying that in general the world hasn't improved that much no matter what we think.

The way he shows this point is mostly by comparison, for example: he says a man running wild in the woods is not that different than a man stuck in a city slum. Sometimes he is very sarcastic in getting his point across. He uses some vivid images to make his point, as in saying murder is the same if it is committed with a poison arrow or a modern gun. The words he chooses also help make his point clear to a reader. He refers to famous people of all times such as Don Quixote, Papageno, and Newton.

He seems to be a man who prefers the past to the present but not thinking the past is perfect either. He ends up his last paragraph with a long sentence that makes his main point even more that human beings are pretty much the same all over the world and even through the ages and we shouldn't think that the modern world is so much better than olden times.

Student Essay Two

This writer is out to shake up the complacency of the Englishmen who believe that history is "Progress with a capital P." In fact, he argues, there is little difference between the Hittites of 1200–1900 B.C. and men in the twentieth century. He goes on to say that there is no real difference between the English people of the present and Siberian, or Christians and Pagans. All times believe that they are the best, and they are all wrong. Men are just men — at all times and all places.

The author presents these surprising ideas with complete confidence, reducing the ideas that he is attacking as silly oversimplifications. He is not saying that things are not different, only that they are not better. One of the means he uses to make his points is citing specific details of the past and present: ie. the bath and piano of the modern carpenter. He makes fun of two recent books, one that praises the Christian at the expense of the Pagan by pointing out the murder is murder, no matter how it is committed, using the contrasting details of the "poison arrow" and the "Mauser rifle." He also uses reference to literature, quoting <u>Macbeth</u> ("the last syllable of recorded time") and referring to Don Quixote. The sentences are varied. The author uses the device of balancing one sentence against another to set one age against another. This balance of the same kind of sentence is to suggest that the two ages are also parallel.

There is not much imagery in the passage, though the first sentence uses a metaphor.

Comments on Student Essays

This is a difficult question. Unlike that of most of the prose that appears on the exam, the style here is plain. It is much harder to talk about the usual topics like diction and imagery in this passage than it is in a showy excerpt like the Frazer in Sample Exam 4. An accurate account of the content ("the purpose of the passage") is important and challenging because the author's argument is unexpected and depends upon his complete indifference to the material prosperity on which most of us base our ideas of progress. This passage is not about technological advances but about the unchanging nature of man.

The first essay, though badly written and naive, does understand the argument of the passage. Its handling of the author's means, however, is inadequate. It attempts to talk about such techniques as comparison, irony, and allusion, but the examples are undeveloped, misunderstood, or ill-chosen. The paper would likely be scored in the lower half at 4.

The second essay is much better. Well-written and well-supported, the paper defines the content of the passage fully and accurately. It talks well about the derisive tone of parts of the passage and its comments on the use of allusion are also excellent. This student essay demonstrates that a good response need not be lengthy or high-sounding. But, like this one, it depends on a careful reading of the passage and a rigorous focus on what the question calls for.

Question 2

Student Essay One

In this poem the poet is saying that war is evil and that mankind must work to make the world saner so that people will not keep killing their fellow men.

He uses images like "mad as hatters" to show the insanity of war.

The soldiers are depicted as almost dead. Their trenches are compared to coffins, and they are also called skeletons. These dead-like men are weak in that they would rather drink beer than preach peace. God speaks in the poem to warn these soldiers that judgement day will be coming and that everyone will have to answer for their sins. The sounds of the guns are compared to the sounds that there will be on judgement day.

Almost all of creation hates war, the poet is saying, even mice, worms, and glebe cows. Man, on the other hand, makes war bloodier and bloodier without any thought for their fellow creatures.

In the poem God is shown as indifferent to what happens to soldiers in war. He warns that it "will be warmer when I blow the trumpet," which is a reference to judgement day.

To get his attitude across the poem also uses personification, as when he says the guns are roaring to avenge. Guns don't avenge things: people do.

In the last two lines of the poem the poet mentions three places in England that have been and will continue to be torn by war — Stourton Tower, Camelot, and Stonehenge.

He mentions these places to show that war touches everyone and every place, that there is no escape from the loud guns and the bloody actions of soldiers.

The poet uses all these techniques to make a simple point that bloody, insane war must be stopped so that all God's creatures will be safe. If man doesn't do anything about war, he will suffer the consequences on judgement day.

Student Essay Two

Have you ever heard the saying the noise was so loud it could wake the dead? That is the basis of this poem.

This is an anti-war poem and it makes its anti-war protest by inventing a scene in which skeletons can sit up in their coffins in the cemetery and talk to other dead persons. The war in this poem takes place near the English Channel (the title is Channel Firing) so it is probably one of the World Wars, (the second because the guns are so powerful?) The point is not which war is bad, but all wars are. The poem says that man has always made war going back to the time of King Alfred and King Arthur (Camelot), and even before that (the time of Stonehenge).

In stanza 3 and 4, the anti-war ideas are spoken by God who says men are "mad as hatters." Stanza 3 says men do not change ("the world is as it used to be"). The wars just get bloodier and bloodier ("red wars redder").

The most important devices that the poem uses to get its point across are allowing God and the dead to speak — like in Thornton Wilder's Our Town. There are several speakers in this poem-play, including God and a preacher. The poem uses direct quotations as the dead people speak as they sit up in their coffins. The whole idea of such a thing happening is funny in both senses of the word.

The poem is odd in that there is a very small use of figures of simile and metaphor. "Mad as hatters" is the only simile, and "red wars redder" is the only metaphor I can find.

The diction is most important in the last stanza. Words like "disturbed" and "readiness to avenge" are gloomy, and the dark tone is increased by the three capitalized words in the last two lines that expand the poem from the modern times to the whole history of man making war.

Comments on Student Essays

Though it is a lower-half paper (a four, probably), the first essay compensates in part for its misreadings of the poem with good points about its anti-war meaning and the point of the allusions in the last stanza. It reverses the most common student error (taking a metaphor to be literal) by taking the real skeletons and their coffins as a metaphor for the soldiers and trenches of the First World War.

The second essay is very good on the meaning of the poem. Its remarks on the techniques are also sharp. It calls the poem "funny in both senses of the word," rightly putting its finger on the poem's use of the grotesque. Its discussion of the use of dialogue and of allusion are also convincing. A paper like this, on this difficult poem, would get a very high score.

Question 3

Student Essay One

Throughout literature authors have used inanimate objects in their works for many reasons, such as to develop a character, help the plot, or as a symbol of an idea. F. Scott Fitzgerald in <u>The Great Gatsby</u> used many such objects to help get his ideas across.

<u>The Great Gatsby</u> is a story about a man, Gatsby, who spends his whole life trying to win a woman (Daisy) who represents everything he wants, such as beauty, money, and class. Daisy loves Gatsby at first, but then she marries someone else (Tom). This leads to a terrible tragedy and finally Gatsby's death.

In this novel the main characters are rich and spend their lives entirely for pleasure, such as big parties, polo, fast cars, and drinking. They do not care about poorer people except to use them, as with the mechanic Wilson and his wife who is Tom's mistress. They are also very bigoted. For example, Tom thinks African-Americans are to blame for everything that is wrong with the world. These people also never think about morals or religion.

To show how bad things are in this rich world the author chooses an inanimate object to use a symbol. This object is a big billboard of the road from where the characters live to New York City. It is located in a place called The Valley of the Ashes and it shows a big pair of eyes looking down on everyone. (It is an ad for an eye-doctor named Doctor T.J. Ecklesburg.) The author refers to the eyes many times in the book. Towards the end they see a hit-and-run accident that kills Tom's mistress. After the accident Wilson thinks Gatsby was driving the car so he goes to Gatsby's mansion and shoots him and then commits suicide.

The eyes on the billboard are used by the author as a symbol that is looking down on everything that happens.

The end of the book is when Gatsby is murdered by Wilson and Tom and Daisy get away with what they did, so the eyes don't care any more what happens to these shallow people.

Student Essay Two

In <u>Othello</u> by William Shakespeare, the most important inanimate object or property is Desdemona's handkerchief. This handkerchief was given to Desdemona by Othello, and she drops it by mistake when she uses it to wipe his head. Emelia finds it and gives it to Iago because he has told her to steal it. Iago plants it in Cassio's house, and he (Cassio) finds it and gives it to a streetwalker who is his girl-friend. She gives it back to him while Othello is watching so Othello believe Iago's lies about Desdemona having a love affair with Cassio. As this shows, the handkerchief passes through the hands of all six of the important characters in the play. The plot would not work without it.

It affects the plot one last time after Othello has killed his wife. When Emelia tells Othello that Iago made her steal the handkerchief, Othello finally realizes that Desdemona was innocent and Iago has tricked him.

Othello has given Desdemona the handkerchief as a symbol of his love. He told her it had magic powers and if she lost it, she would lose his love. The handkerchief can be called an inanimate object which is a symbol of Othello's love which is lost when it falls into the hands of Iago.

The handkerchief is also used to show the character of Emelia. She doesn't really steal the handkerchief though Iago told her to. She finds it and Iago takes it away from her. She doesn't tell Desdemona what happened, but when Othello tells about the handkerchief at the end, Emelia realizes that Iago is evil. She exposes him, even though he is her husband, and at the cost of her own life.

Thus, the handkerchief is used to advance the plot, the symbols, and the character drawing of the play.

Comments on Student Essays

Like many weak papers, the first essay begins by simply repeating the question in the form of a statement. The next two paragraphs summarize the plot, awkwardly. Finally, in the fourth paragraph, we reach a symbolic inanimate object, the "big pair of eyes looking down on everyone." The explanation of its symbolism is no explanation at all.

On the other hand, the second essay is first-rate. It shows how Desdemona's handkerchief functions in the plot, tracing its passage from Desdemona to Emelia to Iago to Cassio to Bianca (notice that the writer who cannot remember Bianca's name sensibly identifies her clearly as "Cassio's girl friend"). The essay then gives a reasonable interpretation of the symbolic meaning of the handkerchief. Finally, it shows how Shakespeare uses the handkerchief to motivate Emilia's unmasking of Iago in the last act. All these topics might have been developed more fully, but what is here is to the point and just what the question asks for.

Answer Sheet for Practice Test 6

(Remove This Sheet and Use it to Mark Your Answers)

1 Ⓐ Ⓑ Ⓒ Ⓓ Ⓔ	21 Ⓐ Ⓑ Ⓒ Ⓓ Ⓔ	41 Ⓐ Ⓑ Ⓒ Ⓓ Ⓔ
2 Ⓐ Ⓑ Ⓒ Ⓓ Ⓔ	22 Ⓐ Ⓑ Ⓒ Ⓓ Ⓔ	42 Ⓐ Ⓑ Ⓒ Ⓓ Ⓔ
3 Ⓐ Ⓑ Ⓒ Ⓓ Ⓔ	23 Ⓐ Ⓑ Ⓒ Ⓓ Ⓔ	43 Ⓐ Ⓑ Ⓒ Ⓓ Ⓔ
4 Ⓐ Ⓑ Ⓒ Ⓓ Ⓔ	24 Ⓐ Ⓑ Ⓒ Ⓓ Ⓔ	44 Ⓐ Ⓑ Ⓒ Ⓓ Ⓔ
5 Ⓐ Ⓑ Ⓒ Ⓓ Ⓔ	25 Ⓐ Ⓑ Ⓒ Ⓓ Ⓔ	45 Ⓐ Ⓑ Ⓒ Ⓓ Ⓔ
6 Ⓐ Ⓑ Ⓒ Ⓓ Ⓔ	26 Ⓐ Ⓑ Ⓒ Ⓓ Ⓔ	46 Ⓐ Ⓑ Ⓒ Ⓓ Ⓔ
7 Ⓐ Ⓑ Ⓒ Ⓓ Ⓔ	27 Ⓐ Ⓑ Ⓒ Ⓓ Ⓔ	47 Ⓐ Ⓑ Ⓒ Ⓓ Ⓔ
8 Ⓐ Ⓑ Ⓒ Ⓓ Ⓔ	28 Ⓐ Ⓑ Ⓒ Ⓓ Ⓔ	48 Ⓐ Ⓑ Ⓒ Ⓓ Ⓔ
9 Ⓐ Ⓑ Ⓒ Ⓓ Ⓔ	29 Ⓐ Ⓑ Ⓒ Ⓓ Ⓔ	49 Ⓐ Ⓑ Ⓒ Ⓓ Ⓔ
10 Ⓐ Ⓑ Ⓒ Ⓓ Ⓔ	30 Ⓐ Ⓑ Ⓒ Ⓓ Ⓔ	50 Ⓐ Ⓑ Ⓒ Ⓓ Ⓔ
11 Ⓐ Ⓑ Ⓒ Ⓓ Ⓔ	31 Ⓐ Ⓑ Ⓒ Ⓓ Ⓔ	51 Ⓐ Ⓑ Ⓒ Ⓓ Ⓔ
12 Ⓐ Ⓑ Ⓒ Ⓓ Ⓔ	32 Ⓐ Ⓑ Ⓒ Ⓓ Ⓔ	
13 Ⓐ Ⓑ Ⓒ Ⓓ Ⓔ	33 Ⓐ Ⓑ Ⓒ Ⓓ Ⓔ	
14 Ⓐ Ⓑ Ⓒ Ⓓ Ⓔ	34 Ⓐ Ⓑ Ⓒ Ⓓ Ⓔ	
15 Ⓐ Ⓑ Ⓒ Ⓓ Ⓔ	35 Ⓐ Ⓑ Ⓒ Ⓓ Ⓔ	
16 Ⓐ Ⓑ Ⓒ Ⓓ Ⓔ	36 Ⓐ Ⓑ Ⓒ Ⓓ Ⓔ	
17 Ⓐ Ⓑ Ⓒ Ⓓ Ⓔ	37 Ⓐ Ⓑ Ⓒ Ⓓ Ⓔ	
18 Ⓐ Ⓑ Ⓒ Ⓓ Ⓔ	38 Ⓐ Ⓑ Ⓒ Ⓓ Ⓔ	
19 Ⓐ Ⓑ Ⓒ Ⓓ Ⓔ	39 Ⓐ Ⓑ Ⓒ Ⓓ Ⓔ	
20 Ⓐ Ⓑ Ⓒ Ⓓ Ⓔ	40 Ⓐ Ⓑ Ⓒ Ⓓ Ⓔ	

Section 1: Multiple-Choice Questions

Time: 60 Minutes

51 Questions

Directions: This section contains selections from two passages of prose and two poems, with questions on their content, style, and form. Read each selection carefully. Choose the best answer of the five choices.

Questions 1–13. Read the poem carefully before you begin to answer the questions.

The Legacy

When I died last (and, dear, I die
As often as from thee I go,
Though it be but an hour ago,
And lovers' hours be full eternity)
(5)   I can remember yet that I
Something did say and something did bestow
(Though I be dead) which sent me I should be
Mine own executor and legacy.

I heard me say, "Tell her anon
(10)   That myself (that's you, not I)
Did kill me, and when I felt me die,
I bid me send my heart when I was gone."
But I, alas, could find there none
When I had ripped me and searched where hearts did lie.
(15)   It killed me again that I who still was true
In life, in my last will should cozen you.

Yet I found something like a heart,
But colors it, and corners had;
It was not good, it was not bad,
(20)   It was entire to none, and few had part.
As good as could be made by art
It seemed; and therefore, for our losses sad,
I meant to send this heart instead of mine,
But oh, no man could hold it, for 'twas thine.

line 7, sent me = brought it about
line 15, still = always
line 18, colors...had = was deceptive, was painted to deceive
line 18, corners...had = was flawed, was imperfect
line 20, entire to = possessed exclusively by

GO ON TO THE NEXT PAGE

1. Which of the following most accurately describes the poem?

   A. The poem is a dialogue between the speaker and his beloved.

   B. The poem is the speaker's will left behind after his death.

   C. The poem presents the direct address of the speaker to his beloved.

   D. The poem presents a speaker directly addressing a general reader.

   E. The poem is a letter directed to the writer's beloved.

2. In line 4, the phrase "lovers' hours be full eternity" is saying that

   A. time flies when you are in love

   B. lovers are never on time

   C. lovers are so happy that they think they are in heaven

   D. the joys of love are everlasting

   E. to lovers, an hour apart seems like forever

3. The word "executor" in line 8 can be best understood to mean

   A. a chief officer or director

   B. an heir designated in a will to inherit money or property

   C. a funeral undertaker

   D. a person responsible for carrying out the terms of a will

   E. a hangman or executioner

4. In the first stanza, there are metaphors in all the following lines EXCEPT

   A. line 1

   B. line 3

   C. line 4

   D. line 7

   E. line 8

5. In stanza two, the phrase "myself (that's you, not I)" can be best explained by the fact that

   A. lovers were said to exchange hearts

   B. love has so confused the speaker that he cannot distinguish one person from another

   C. a man who is in love is not himself

   D. "that" refers to "her," not to "myself"

   E. the parenthesis is not to be understood as part of this sentence

6. In line 15, the speaker's second death ("it killed me again") is caused by

   A. his ripping open his chest in search of a heart

   B. his failure to keep his word to his beloved

   C. his separation from his loved one

   D. his fear of her being unfaithful to him

   E. his wish to make the loved one feel guilty

7. In line 16, the word "cozen" can be best defined as

   A. to intimidate

   B. to disinherit

   C. to be related to

   D. to cheat

   E. to care for

8. The idea in stanza one, line 8, of the speaker becoming "his own legacy" is explained in stanza 2 in

   A. line 9

   B. line 12

   C. line 13

   D. line 14

   E. line 16

9. In line 18, the phrase "corners had" is used to mean "was flawed" or "was imperfect" because

   I. the circle, not the square, was considered to be the perfect form.

   II. it is difficult to see around corners.

   III. four is thought to be a lucky number.

   A. I only

   B. II only

   C. III only

   D. I and II only

   E. I, II, and III

10. The idea of "it was entire to none" (line 20) is repeated in

   A. the second part of line 20 ("and few had part")

   B. line 21 ("as good as could be made by art")

   C. line 22 ("for our losses sad")

   D. line 23 ("this heart instead of mine")

   E. line 24 ("no man could hold it")

11. Unlike the first and second stanzas, the third stanza

   A. relies heavily on figurative language

   B. uses odd word order in order to make the lines rhyme

   C. is critical of the lover

   D. uses both the first and third person pronouns

   E. expresses the speaker's continued love for the lady

12. On which of the following characteristics of the lady does the poem focus?

   A. her beauty

   B. her sincerity

   C. her fickleness

   D. her vanity about her beauty

   E. her concern with appearances

GO ON TO THE NEXT PAGE

13. Which of the following best describes the purpose of the poem as a whole?

A. to express the speaker's love

B. to condemn the loved one's faithlessness

C. to come to terms with the imminence of separation

D. to stress the importance of mutuality in love

E. to lament the brevity of life and love

Questions 14–25. Read the passage carefully before you begin to answer the questions.

The dinner was a grand one, the servants were numerous, and everything bespoke the Mistress's inclination for show, and the Master's ability to support
(5) it. In spite of the improvements and additions which were making to the Norland estate, nothing gave any symptom of indigence; no poverty of any kind, except of conversation, appeared — but there,
(10) the deficiency was considerable. John Dashwood had not much to say for himself that was worth hearing, and his wife had still less. But there was no peculiar disgrace in this, for it was very much the
(15) case with the chief of their visitors, who almost all laboured under one or other of these disqualifications for being agreeable — want of sense, either natural or improved — want of elegance — want of
(20) spirits — or want of temper.

When the ladies withdrew to the drawing-room after dinner, this poverty was particularly evident, for the gentlemen <u>had</u> supplied the discourse with
(25) some variety —the variety of politics, inclosing land, and breaking horses — but then it was all over; and one subject only engaged the ladies till coffee came in, which was the comparative heights

(30) of Harry Dashwood, and Lady Middleton's second son William, who were nearly of the same age.

Had both the children been there, the affair might have been determined too
(35) easily by measuring them at once; but as Harry only was present, it was all conjectural assertion on both sides, and everybody had a right to be equally positive in their opinion, and to repeat it over and
(40) over again as often as they liked.

The parties stood thus;

The two mothers, though each really convinced that her own son was the tallest, politely decided in favor of the
(45) other.

The two grandmothers, with not less partiality, but more sincerity, were equally earnest in support of their own descendant.

(50) Lucy, who was hardly less anxious to please one parent than the other, thought the boys were both remarkably tall for their age, and could not conceive that there could be the smallest difference in
(55) the world between them; and Miss Steele, with yet greater address gave it, as fast as she could, in favour of each. Elinor, having once delivered her

(60) opinion on William's side, by which she offended Mrs. Ferrars and Fanny still more, did not see the necessity of enforcing it by any farther assertion; and

(65) Marianne, when called on for hers, offended them all, by declaring that she had no opinion to give, as she had never thought about it.

14. In line 15, the phrase "chief of" means

   A. the socially prominent of

   B. the leader of

   C. an important few of

   D. the richest of

   E. most of

15. Which of the following best describes the purpose of the first paragraph of the passage?

   A. moral instruction

   B. objective analysis

   C. ironic introduction

   D. satiric commentary

   E. reflective insight

16. In line 19, "want" can be best defined as

   A. desire

   B. abundance

   C. need

   D. lack

   E. poverty

17. In line 22, the phrase "this poverty" refers to

   A. the ladies' ill-temper.

   B. the ladies' inability to make intelligent conversation.

   C. the gentlemen's conversational ability.

   D. the deficiencies in the furnishings of the dining room.

   E. the delay in the service of the coffee.

18. In line 27, the pronoun "it" refers to which of the following?

   A. "poverty," line 22

   B. "discourse," line 24

   C. "variety," line 25

   D. "land," line 26

   E. "breaking," line 26

19. In lines 50–55, all the following are words or phrases that Lucy herself probably uses EXCEPT

   A. anxious to please

   B. remarkably tall

   C. conceive

   D. the smallest difference

   E. in the world

GO ON TO THE NEXT PAGE

20. From the comments on Miss Steele in lines 55–57 we can infer that, compared to her sister Lucy, she is

    A. equally insincere and more intelligent

    B. equally insincere and less intelligent

    C. more sincere and more intelligent

    D. less eager to please and more tactful

    E. less eager to please and less tactful

21. From their response to Elinor's opinion in line 59, we can infer that Mrs. Ferrars and Fanny are

    A. the grandmother and mother of Henry Dashwood

    B. the grandmother and mother of William Middleton

    C. the grandmother of Harry Dashwood and the mother of William Middleton

    D. the grandmother of William Middleton and the mother of Harry Dashwood

    E. the mother of Harry Dashwood and the mother of William Middleton

22. Of which of the following characters can we infer that the author of the passage most approves?

    A. Lucy

    B. Miss Steele

    C. Elinor

    D. John Dashwood

    E. Mrs. John Dashwood

23. On which of the following does the passage rely most?

    A. figurative language

    B. abstract generalization

    C. euphemism

    D. colloquial diction

    E. balanced compound sentences

24. Which of the following best describes the narrator of the passage?

    A. bitterly sardonic

    B. insightfully amused

    C. cooly objective

    D. quietly nostalgic

    E. overtly disillusioned

25. Which of the following describe the handling of point of view in the passage?

    I.   The narration is in the third person.

    II. The narrator is omniscient.

    III. The narrator consciously misleads the reader.

    A. III only

    B. I and II only

    C. I and III only

    D. II and III only

    E. I, II, and III

Questions 26–37. Read the passage carefully before you begin to answer the questions.

Magnolias in Snow

Snow alters and elaborates perspectives,
confuses South with North and would deceive
me into what egregious error
but for these trees that keep their summer green
(5)   and like a certain hue of speech mean South.

Magnolias stand for South, as every copy-
reader knows, and snow means North to me,
means home and friends I walked with under boughs
of hemlock when the cold of winter
(10)   was a carilloneur that played in china bells.

But still, snow-shine upon magnolia leaves
that wither into shapes of abstract sculpture
when brought inside for garnishment,
does compensate for things I must forego
(15)   if I would safely walk beneath these trees:

These dazzleclustered trees that stand in heaped
and startling ornaments of snow, a baroque
surprise. O South, how beautiful is change.

Note: This poem was written by an African-American poet in 1948.

26. The poem takes place in

    A. the library of a southern university

    B. winter in the American south

    C. an unspecified location

    D. winter in the American north

    E. March in New England

27. How does knowing that this poem was written in 1948 by a black writer help to explain its meaning?

    I.   It explains why a black man's confusing North and South before the Civil Rights Movement might be an "egregious error." (line 3)

    II. It explains why the speaker should be concerned with "walking safely." (line 15)

    III. It explains the appeal of the last line of the poem. (line 18)

    A. II only

    B. I and II only

    C. I and III only

    D. II and III only

    E. I, II, and III

GO ON TO THE NEXT PAGE

28. Lines 1 and 2 ("Snow alters and elaborates perspectives, / confuses South with North) can be understood to mean

    I.   the snow symbolizes the North as magnolias symbolize the South.

    II. by covering the land, the snow confuses the sense of direction.

    III. the unexpected southern snow is disconcerting to one who expects snow only in the North.

    A. II only

    B. I and II only

    C. I and III only

    D. II and III only

    E. I, II, and III

29. The phrase "hue of speech" in line 5 can be termed a synesthetic figure because

    I.   it is metaphorical.

    II. it interchanges sound and color.

    III. it is composed of words of only one syllable.

    A. I only

    B. I and II only

    C. I and III only

    D. II and III only

    E. I, II, and III

30. The simile in the first stanza compares

    A. magnolias and the Southern accent

    B. snow and a painter

    C. snow and a deceitful person

    D. South and North

    E. trees in summer and magnolias

31. The phrase "as every copyreader knows" (lines 6–7) is used to signify that

    A. southerners follow the reading tastes of the North

    B. newspapers determine our ideas of places

    C. the South is more imitative than the North

    D. the idea is a commonplace

    E. newsmen are well-read

32. The metaphor of lines 9–10 compares

    A. wintertime and white flowers

    B. the cold of winter and a bell-ringer

    C. the cold of winter and icicles

    D. snow-covered trees and a jazz musician

    E. the tinkle of ice and Asian music

33. In the third stanza, the speaker finds consolation for his loss in

    A. the safety of the natural world

    B. the idea of returning to the North

    C. the beauty of the natural world

    D. the hope of change in the future

    E. the excitement of taking risks

34. In line 14, the "things I must forego" refers to

    A. the speaker's northern friends

    B. the events of the speaker's future

    C. the differences between North and South

    D. the threats he faces in the South

    E. the dangers of northern cities

35. Which of the following would best clarify the syntax of lines 16–18?

   A. adding a hyphen to "dazzleclustered"

   B. revising "stand in heaped" to read "stand heaped in"

   C. changing "stand" to "standing"

   D. replacing the comma after "snow" with the verb "are"

   E. adding a comma after "baroque"

36. In line 17, "baroque" can be best defined as

   A. irregular and bizarre

   B. artistic and beautiful

   C. singular and unique

   D. musical and melodic

   E. foreign and curious

37. The poem uses the surprise of the snowfall to argue that

   A. all of America is in need of change

   B. nature is more unpredictable than man

   C. a different South would be better

   D. all natural events are beautiful

   E. greater love of nature can lead to greater love among men

Questions 38-51. Read the passage carefully before you begin to answer the questions.

A Visit to America

Across the United States of America, from New York to California and back, glazed, again, for many months of the year, there streams and sings for its
(5) heady supper a dazed and prejudiced procession of European lecturers, scholars, sociologists, economists, writers, authorities on this and that and even, in theory, on the United States of America.
(10) And, breathlessly between addresses and receptions, in planes, and trains and boiling hotel bedroom ovens, many of these attempt to keep journals and diaries. At first, confused and shocked by
(15) shameless profusion and almost shamed by generosity, unaccustomed to such importance as they are assumed, by their hosts, to possess, and up against the barrier of a common language, they write in
(20) their note-books like demons, generalizing away, on character and culture and the American political scene. But towards the middle of their middle-aged whisk through middle-western clubs and
(25) universities, the fury of their writing flags; their spirits are lowered by the spirit they are everywhere strongly greeted with and which in ever-increasing doses, they themselves lower; and
(30) they begin to mistrust themselves and their reputations — for they have found, too often, that an audience will receive a lantern lecture on, say, ceramics, with the same uninhibited enthusiasm that it
(35) accorded the very week before to a paper on the Modern Turkish novel. And, in their diaries, more and more do such entries appear as "No way of escape!" or "Buffalo!" or "I am beaten," until at last
(40) they cannot write a word. And twittering all over, old before their time, with eyes like rissoles in the sand, they are helped up the gang-way of the home-bound liner by kind bosom friends (of all kinds
(45) and bosoms) who bolster them on the back, pick them up again, thrust bottles,

GO ON TO THE NEXT PAGE

sonnets, cigars, addresses into their pock-
ets, have a farewell party in their cabin,
pick them up again, and snickering and
(50) yelping, are gone: to wait at the dockside
for another boat from Europe and another
batch of fresh green lecturers.

There they go, every spring, from
New York to Los Angeles: exhibition-
(55) ists, polemicists, histrionic publicists,
theological   rhetoricians,   historical
hoddy-doddies, balletomanes, ulterior
decorators, windbags and bigwigs and
humbugs, men in love with stamps, men
(60) in love with steaks, men after million-
aires' widows, men with elephantiasis of

the reputation (huge trunks and teeny
minds), authorities on gas, bishops, best-
sellers, editors looking for writers, writ-
(65) ers looking for publishers, publishers
looking for dollars, existentialists, serious physicists with nuclear missions,
men from the B.B.C. who speak as
though they had the Elgin Marbles in
(70) their mouths, potboiling philosophers,
professional Irishmen (very lepri-
corny), and I am afraid, fat poets with
slim volumes.

*Notes: rissoles, line 42 = a small, battered fried fish or meat
cake; Elgin Marbles; line 69 = the statuary from the
Parthenon in the British Museum*

38. The primary purpose of the passage is to

  A. describe an American phenomenon
  comically

  B. contrast the characters of
  Europeans and Americans

  C. depict a situation with an eye to
  correcting it

  D. comment on a mistaken popular
  assumption

  E. satirize the European intellectual

39. In line 15, the phrase "shameless
profusion" probably refers to America's

  A. immodest profession

  B. immoral behavior

  C. ignorant boasting

  D. material abundance

  E. unchallenged excellence

40. In lines 18–19, the phrase "the barrier of
a common language" is a reference to

  A. the failure of people to
  communicate successfully

  B. the American failure to understand
  European culture

  C. the differences between American
  and British English

  D. the differences between American
  and British accents

  E. the impenetrable jargon of the
  scientist and the social scientist

41. In the sentence "their spirits are
lowered by the spirit they are
everywhere strongly greeted with, and
which in ever-increasing doses they
themselves lower" (lines 26–29), the
words "spirits," "lowered," "spirit," and
"lower" can be best understood to mean

  A. feelings . . . depressed . . .
  ghost . . . threaten

  B. attitudes . . . let down . . .
  liquor . . . reduce

  C. feelings . . . decreased . . .
  feeling . . . stare gloomily

  D. attitudes . . . reduced . . .
  liveliness . . . sink

  E. frames of mind . . . depressed . . .
  enthusiasm . . . consume

42. In lines 29–36, the European lecturers begin to lose confidence in themselves because

  A. they fear the American audiences may not understand their topics

  B. the Americans are indiscriminately enthusiastic

  C. the Americans are chiefly interested in odd subjects like the Turkish novel

  D. the American audiences are severe and captious

  E. they know that their reputations are undeserved, and fear discovery

43. The first paragraph presents the typical visiting lecturer as progressing from

  A. modesty to adulation to self-importance

  B. enthusiasm to self-doubt to despair.

  C. fear to enjoyment to exhaustion

  D. expectation to disappointment to stupor

  E. snobbery to uncertainty to acceptance

44. The passage presents the American lecture audiences as all the following EXCEPT

  A. opportunistic

  B. cordial

  C. enthusiastic

  D. generous

  E. adulatory

45. In lines 54–57, the series "exhibitionists, polemicists, histrionic publicists, theological rhetoricians, historical hoddy-doddies, balletomanes" includes

  A. a deliberately puzzling paradox

  B. a circumlocution for "experts"

  C. an authorial aside

  D. a shift in the level of diction

  E. an understatement

46. In line 67, the author probably uses the phrase "nuclear missions" in order to

  A. demonstrate the wide range of lecture topics

  B. remind the reader of the potential seriousness of scientific studies

  C. mock the large number of European physicists lecturing in America

  D. satirize the American concern with science at the expense of the arts

  E. play on the similar phrase "nuclear fissions"

GO ON TO THE NEXT PAGE

47. In lines 68–70, the phrase describing the "men from the B.B.C. who speak as though they had the Elgin Marbles in their mouths" is

   I.   an allusion to a common description of a hoity-toity accent.

   II.   a play on two meanings of the word "marbles."

   III.   a reference to the linguistic versatility of the Europeans.

   A. I only

   B. II only

   C. I and II only

   D. II and III only

   E. I, II, and III

48. In lines 71–72, the parenthetic "very lepri-corny" is all of the following EXCEPT

   A. a pun

   B. an invented comic word

   C. a reference to a common Irish myth

   D. a satiric comment on commercial professional Irishness

   E. a euphemism to refer to the Irish

49. From the style and the closing words ("I am afraid, fat poets with slim volumes," lines 72–73) of the passage, we can infer that the speaker

   A. is apologetic about the contents of this prose.

   B. is aware of the disparity between what is expected of the lecturers and what they present.

   C. is a poet who is fat.

   D. is eager to cash in on American wealth.

   E. is disgusted by the greed of the lecturers.

50. All the following phrases suggest the speaker's reservations about the European lecturers EXCEPT

   A. "a dazed and prejudiced procession," (lines 5–6)

   B. "such importance as they are assumed, by their hosts, to possess," (lines 16–18)

   C. "Buffalo!" (line 39)

   D. "ulterior decorators" (lines 57–58)

   E. "windbags and bigwigs and humbugs," (lines 58–59)

51. The passage employs all the following devices usually associated with poetry rather than with prose EXCEPT

   A. internal rhyme

   B. alliteration

   C. simile

   D. iambic pentameter

   E. consonance

Section II: Essay Questions

Time: 2 hours

3 Questions

Question 1

(Suggested time: 40 minutes. This question accounts for one-third of the total essay section score.)

Directions: Read the following lyric poems carefully. Then write an essay in which you discuss the speakers' attitudes toward love and analyze the techniques the poets use to communicate their feelings.

      i
   When thou must home to shades of underground,
   And there arrived, a new admired guest,
   The beauteous spirits do engirt thee round,
   White Iope, blithe Helen, and the rest,
(5)   To hear the stories of thy finished love
   From that smooth tongue whose music hell can move,

   Then wilt thou speak of banqueting delights,
   Of masques and revels which sweet youth did make,
   Of tourneys and great challenges of knights,
(10)   And all these triumphs for thy beauty's sake;
   When thou hast told these honors done to thee,
   Then tell, O tell, how thou didst murder me.
                              — Thomas Campion

      ii
   Shall I wasting in despair
   Die because a woman's fair?
   Or make pale my cheeks with care,
   'Cause another's rosy are?
(5)   Be she fairer than the day,
   Or the flow'ry meads in May,
   If she be not so to me,
   What care I how fair she be?
   Shall my heart be grieved or pined
(10)   'Cause I see a woman kind?
   Or a well-disposed nature
   Joined with a lovely feature?
   Be she meeker, kinder than
   Turtledove or pelican,

GO ON TO THE NEXT PAGE

(15) If she be not so to me,
What care I how kind she be?...
Great, or good, or kind, or fair,
I will ne'er the more despair;
If she love me, this believe,
(20) I will die ere she shall grieve;
If she slight me when I woo,
I can scorn and let her go;
For if she be not for me,
What care I for whom she be?

— George Wither

Pelican is a traditional symbol of affection.

Question 2

(Suggested time: 40 minutes. This question counts one-third of the total essay score.)

Directions: Read the following passage carefully and write an essay in which you characterize the author's attitude toward literary critics and analyze the techniques he uses to convey it.

Criticism is a study by which men grow important and formidable at very small expense. The power of invention has been conferred by nature upon few, (5) and the labour of learning those sciences which may, by mere labour, be obtained, is too great to be willingly endured; but every man can exert such judgment as he has upon the works of others; and he (10) whom nature has made weak, and idleness keeps ignorant, may yet support his vanity by the name of critic.

I hope it will give some comfort to great numbers who are passing through (15) the world in obscurity, when I inform them how easily distinction may be obtained. All the other powers of literature are coy and haughty; they must be long courted, and at last are not always (20) gained; but Criticism is a goddess easy of access, and forward of advance, who will meet the slow, and encourage the timorous; the want of meaning she supplies with words, and the want of spirit (25) she recompenses with malignity.

This profession has one recommendation peculiar to itself, that it gives vent to malignity without real mischief. No genius was ever blasted by the breath of (30) critics. The poison which, if confined, would have burst the heart, fumes away in empty hisses, and malice is set at ease with very little danger to merit. The critic is the only man whose triumph is (35) without another's pain, and whose greatness does not rise upon another's ruin.

To a study at once so easy and so reputable, so malicious and so harmless, it cannot be necessary to invite my readers (40) by a long or laboured exhortation; it is sufficient, since all would be critics if they could, to show by one eminent example, that all can be critics if they will.

Question 3

(Suggested time: 40 minutes. This question accounts for one-third of the total essay section score.)

Directions: In plays and novels, the flight from guilt takes many forms. A chief character's attempt to find some kind of freedom from guilt, may become a conscious or an unconscius motivation in his or her life.

Choose an important character in a novel or play who attempts to to deal with guilt, and discuss how this motive affects the action and how it determines meaning in the work as a whole.

You may choose a work by one of the following authors or a work by another writer of equal merit.

William Shakespeare

Eugene O'Neill

Lillian Hellman

Tennessee Williams

August Strindberg

Aeschylus

Sophocles

Henrik Ibsen

Arthur Miller

Virginia Woolf

Herman Melville

Ralph Ellison

William Faulkner

Joseph Conrad

Charles Dickens

Toni Morrison

Charlotte Bronte

John Steinbeck

Feodor Dostoevski

Emily Bronte

Jane Austen

Franz Kafka

IF YOU FINISH BEFORE TIME IS CALLED, CHECK YOUR WORK ON THIS SECTION ONLY. DO NOT WORK ON ANY OTHER SECTION IN THE TEST.

Scoring Practice Test 6

Answer Key

Section I: Multiple-Choice Questions

First Poem

1. C
2. E
3. D
4. B
5. A
6. B
7. D
8. B
9. A
10. E
11. C
12. C
13. B

First Prose Passage

14. E
15. D
16. D
17. B
18. C
19. A
20. B
21. A
22. C
23. E
24. B
25. B

Second Poem

26. B
27. E
28. D
29. B
30. A
31. D
32. B
33. C
34. A
35. D
36. A
37. C

Second Prose Passage

38. A
39. D
40. C
41. E
42. B
43. B
44. A
45. D
46. E
47. C
48. E
49. C
50. C
51. D

Practice Test 6 Scoring Worksheet

Use the following worksheet to arrive at a probable final AP grade on Practice Test 6. While it is sometimes difficult to be objective enough to score one's own essay, you can use the sample essay answers that follow to approximate an essay score for yourself. Better yet, give your essays (along with the sample scored essays) to a friend or relative who you think is competent to score the essays.

Section I: Multiple-Choice Questions

$$\underset{\substack{\text{right}\\ \text{answers}}}{\underline{\hspace{1.5cm}}} - (1/4 \text{ or } .25 \times \underset{\substack{\text{wrong}\\ \text{answers}}}{\underline{\hspace{1.5cm}}}) = \underset{\substack{\text{multiple-choice}\\ \text{raw score}}}{\underline{\hspace{2cm}}}$$

$$\underset{\substack{\text{multiple-choice}\\ \text{raw score}}}{\underline{\hspace{2cm}}} \times 1.32 = \underset{\substack{\text{multiple-choice}\\ \text{converted score}}}{\underline{\hspace{2cm}}} (\text{of possible } 67.5)$$

Section II: Essay Questions

$$\underset{\substack{\text{question 1}\\ \text{raw score}}}{\underline{\hspace{1.5cm}}} + \underset{\substack{\text{question 2}\\ \text{raw score}}}{\underline{\hspace{1.5cm}}} + \underset{\substack{\text{question 3}\\ \text{raw score}}}{\underline{\hspace{1.5cm}}} = \underset{\text{essay}}{\underline{\hspace{1.5cm}}}$$

$$\underset{\text{essay question}}{\underline{\hspace{2cm}}} \times 3.055 = \underset{\substack{\text{essay converted}\\ \text{score}}}{\underline{\hspace{2cm}}}$$

Final Score

$$\underset{\substack{\text{multiple-choice}\\ \text{converted score}}}{\underline{\hspace{2cm}}} + \underset{\substack{\text{essay}\\ \text{converted score}}}{\underline{\hspace{2cm}}} = \underset{\substack{\text{final}\\ \text{converted score}}}{\underline{\hspace{2cm}}} (\text{of possible } 150)$$

Probable Final AP Score

Final Converted Score	Probable AP Score
150–100	5
99–86	4
85–67	3
66–0	1 or 2

Answers and Explanations for Practice Test 6

Section I: Multiple-Choice Questions

First Poem

"The Legacy" was written by John Donne.

1. **C.** Though it plays with the idea of the speaker's dying and leaving a will, the poem presents the direct address of a man (indicated by the use of "I") to a woman ("dear," "you," or "thee"). The first two stanzas make it clear that the speaker is in love with the woman.

2. **E.** In lines 1–4, the poem uses the conventional idea that separation from the loved one is death to the lover (a modern song would say "I can't live without you;" rejected by his first love, Romeo says "I live dead that live to tell it now.") The hours that seem like eternity to the lover are the hours apart from the beloved, another old chestnut of love poetry.

3. **D.** An executor is the person responsible for carrying out the terms of a will. If the speaker is dead because he is separated from his beloved, he would leave a will. The speaker elaborates on this notion, appointing himself executor to see to it that the legacy of his heart is delivered to the lady ("My heart is yours.") Several Donne poems develop the idea of the consequences of a lover's "death," "The Funeral," for example.

4. **B.** "Though it be but an hour ago" is a literal statement. There are metaphors in all of the other lines: separation as death; an hour as eternity; separation as death; the lover as executor and legacy.

5. **A.** Another commonly used notion in the love poetry of this period is the exchange of hearts between lovers. (Phrases like "My heart is yours" or "You have all my heart" still show up on valentines and in popular songs.) Option **C** is tempting, but it explains only the phrase "not I," while **A** also accounts for "that's you."

6. **B.** Here the lover (who dies as often as other men sneeze) dies a second time. Separation caused the first death in the first stanza. Here, because he fears he will be unable to fulfill the terms of his legacy which left his heart to her, he is so distraught that it kills him "again."

7. **D.** To "cozen" is to cheat, to deceive.

8. **B.** The speaker's becoming his legacy and executor is explained in line 12 of the second stanza: "I bid me send my heart when I was gone;" that is, I told myself to send my heart (the legacy) after my death ("when I was gone").

9. **A.** Because it is endless and everywhere the same, the circle is the symbol of perfection or eternity. This notion is behind Donne's most famous figure, the compasses at the end of "A Valediction: Forbidding Mourning."

10. **E.** "It was entire to none" means no one could possess it entirely; the closest in meaning to this is "no man could hold it."

11. **C.** This is a difficult poem because it relies so heavily on ancient conventions of love poetry, because the images are complicated, and because after two stanzas of love poetry, it suddenly becomes an attack on the lady as unfaithful. A reader of Donne will recall several other poems that appear to be love lyrics, but turn on the woman at the end: for example, "The Apparition," "The Blossom," and "The Funeral." Donne uses the same strategy in this poem. Options **A, B,** and **D** here are true of the poem as a whole, but they apply to the first and second stanzas, and not just the third.

12. **C.** When it fully reveals itself in the third stanza, the poem focuses upon the fickleness of the lady (lines 17–20, line 24).

13. **B.** Though the poem appears at first to be a love poem, the reader is left with condemnation of the faithless woman as its real subject.

First Prose Passage

The passage is from Jane Austen's novel *Sense and Sensibility*.

14. **E.** The phrase is best defined as "most of." The sentence goes on to use the phrase "almost all" which also refers to the visitors.

15. **D.** The paragraph is satiric rather than ironic, because it states straightforwardly the deficiencies of the Dashwoods ("John Dashwood had not much to say for himself that was worth hearing, and his wife had still less") and their visitors ("almost all of whom laboured under one or another of these disqualifications for being agreeable").

16. **D.** As it is used here, "want" means "lack."

17. **B.** In lines 8-9 of the first paragraph, the passage says "no poverty of any kind, except of conversation, appeared." In line 22, "this poverty" is that poverty of conversation, even worse when the men are no longer present.

18. **C.** The antecedent of "it" here is "variety" in line 25. So long as the men are present, there is at least some variety in the conversation, but when the women are left alone, that variety ("it") is ended, and the women can find only one topic, and that one is trivial.

19. **A.** The phrase "anxious to please" is the narrator's describing Lucy. The other four phrases are Lucy's gush intended to please both mothers and grandmothers.

20. **B.** Like her sister Lucy, Miss Steele is eager to say what she thinks will please and she shares Lucy's insincerity. But Miss Steele has not the sense to see that however eagerly she speaks, the boys cannot *both* be taller, so she cannot take both sides at the same time.

21. **A.** The passage has made it clear that each mother and grandmother believes her own descendant to be the taller. If Mrs. Ferrars and Fanny are miffed by Elinor's favoring the Middleton boy, we can infer that they are the grandmother and mother of young Harry Dashwood, and that Fanny is Mrs. Dashwood.

22. **C.** The passage never criticizes Elinor, who is shown to be honest and laconic. All four of the others are mocked: the Dashwoods in the first paragraph, Lucy and Miss Steele in the next-to-last.

23. **E.** None of the devices listed in options **A, B, C,** or **D** is much used in the passage, but many of the sentences employ parallel structures.

24. **B.** Options **D** and **E** are clearly inappropriate here. The passage is certainly satiric, but "bitterly sardonic" overstates the tone. Though **C** is possible, "insightful" and "amused" are both accurate descriptions of the narrator.

25. **B.** The narrator does not mislead the reader. The passage uses an omniscient narrator and the third person.

Second Poem

"Magnolias in Snow' was written by Robert Hayden.

26. **B.** The poem takes place in winter after a surprising snowfall in the American south.

27. **E.** The poem is very hard to follow if a reader is not aware of the time, place, and race of the speaker. If a poem like this were used on an exam, this information would be provided in a footnote, or in a question like this one. The poem takes place before the Civil Rights Movement when it might be dangerous for a black man to walk in public with white friends in the South. The northern black, like Hayden, must remind himself that actions that would be permissible in Detroit may be dangerous ("egregious error," "safely") in the South. This information also explains why, in the last line, the speaker wishes for a changed South.

28. **D.** The lines can mean that snow obscures the landscape and makes finding one's way difficult. They can also refer to how snow in the South may disconcert a Northerner who does not expect it.

29. **B.** A synesthetic figure is a metaphor or simile that describes one sensory experience in terms of another sense. Here speech (the sense of sound) is presented in terms of hue (the sense of sight). The phrase "hue of speech" is also a metaphor comparing an accent to a color. That the phrase is monosyllabic has nothing to do with its being a "synesthetic figure."

30. **A.** The simile in the first stanza compares magnolias ("these trees") and the Southern accent ("like a certain hue of speech"). A simile is an explicit comparison, usually using "like" or "as."

31. **D.** The point of the lines is that the use of magnolias as a symbol of the South is a well-worn idea. A copy-reader, a person whose job is to read and correct written work, would frequently come across this cliche.

32. **B.** The metaphor compares the "cold of winter" and a "carilloneur," that is, one who plays a carillon, a set of tuned bells. The poet may be thinking of the tinkle of icicles as bell like, and so the cold is like a carillon-player.

33. **C.** Lines 11–14 say that the beauty of the snow on the magnolias "does compensate for things I must forego."

34. **A.** The speaker in the South gives up his northern friends with whom he could walk safely through the scenes of a northern winter (under "boughs of hemlock" rather than magnolia).

35. **D.** None of the changes suggested in options **A, B, C,** and **E** would clarify the lines. The comma in line 17 replaces the understood verb "are."

36. **A.** Option **C** is the next-best, though redundant, definition, but "irregular and bizarre" is the best of the five choices.

37. **C.** The poem argues that as the "baroque surprise" of the magnolias in snow is beautiful, so the South itself could become better if it too were to change. The poem is understated and does not go further than to suggest a change without specifying what this change should be.

Second Prose Passage

The passage is by the Welsh poet Dylan Thomas.

38. **A.** The correct answer should consider the passage as a whole. Although the passage does contrast Europeans and Americans and does make fun of some of the lecturers, its primary purpose is to describe the flood of lecturers (including the author) which inundates America each year. The passage is describing the situation shortly after World War II, when, for the first time after many years, America and Europe were no longer cut off from each other.

39. **D.** The "shameless profusion" of which the Europeans are glad to take advantage, is the material abundance of America, the more striking to Europeans accustomed to the austerity of post-war Europe.

40. **C.** This a reference to the fact that although both the British and Americans speak English, the differences in vocabulary often interfere with understanding. Oscar Wilde, a lecturer in America in the 1890s, observed that the British and Americans had everything in common "except language."

41. **E.** The sentence is rich in word-play. It says that their spirits (frame of mind) are lowered (depressed) by the spirit (enthusiasm, but also alcoholic drink) they are everywhere strongly (robustly, but perhaps also with high alcoholic levels as in "strong spirits") greeted with and which in ever-increasing doses (amounts, in general but also referring to the measure of alcohol) they themselves lower (drink down; to lower a drink is to consume it).

42. **B.** When they realize that the American audiences receive anything from ceramics to the Turkish novel with equal enthusiasm, the European lecturers begin to fear their success is due more to the audience's lack of discrimination than to their own talent as speakers.

43. **B.** The lecturers pass from writing in their note-books "like demons" to the self-doubt that follows when they realize the audiences are always adulatory and to despairing entries like "I am beaten." A twittering lethargy is the last stage before they are shipped back to Europe.

44. **A.** The Americans are certainly cordial, enthusiastic, generous, and adulatory (flattering), but there is nothing in the passage to suggest that they are opportunistic.

45. **D.** In the middle of these long serious words, many ending in -ist, we find the odd, obscure and comic sounding "hoddy-doddies," an archaic British word for a short, dumpy person, a simpleton, or a cuckold.

46. **E.** Given the unserious tone of the passage and the author's fondness for word play, the most likely explanation of the phrase is an echo of "nuclear fissions" and "nuclear missions."

47. **C.** The B.B.C. accent, that is, the accent of most of the broadcasters on the British radio stations, was notoriously refined (the author, Dylan Thomas spoke with a Welsh accent). The phrase "to speak with marbles in the mouth," is often used to describe a consciously upper-class accent ("to speak with a hot potato in the mouth" is another version of the same idea).

48. **E.** The author is playing with the words "corny" (trite, unsophisticated) and "leprechaun," the often terminally cute figure of Irish folklore. The word is a pun, a neologism (an invented word), a reference to and satiric comment on Irishness, but not a euphemism (a word considered to be less offensive).

49. **C.** Given the ingenuity and playfulness of the language of the passage, and the otherwise unexplained apology of "I am afraid," a reader should be able to infer that the speaker is, in fact, a fat poet.

50. **C.** The word "Buffalo!" is used as a sample journal entry by one of the lecturers to reflect his increasing bewilderment, but it does not suggest any overt criticism as the other four phrases do.

51. **D.** The passage uses internal rhyme ("glazed . . . dazed," "planes . . . trains"), alliterations ("prejudiced procession"), simile ("like rissoles in the sand"), and consonance (the repetition of consonant patterns, "windbag...bigwig... humbug" which repeats the b-g pattern), but the passage is prose, and never employs a line made up of only five iambic feet as a poem might.

Section II: Essay Questions

Question 1

Student Essay 1

In the two poems by Thomas Campion and George Wither, love is discussed. Campion, through use of imagery, portrays love as a sly, dangerous thing, and women as beautiful but deceitful. Wither, through use of repetition of syntax and imagery, paints love as something to be pursued.

Thomas Campion portrays love as a beautiful deceitful woman just arrived in hell. He employs rich imagery to emphasize how beautiful and desired the woman is. Campion suggests that her beauty has been honored through "banqueting delights," "masques," and "revels which sweet youth did make." In addition, Campion says that tournaments have been held in her honor, as knights challenge each other for the chance to win her favor. However, despite all of these tributes to her beauty, the woman is anything but good and virtuous. Campion suggests this by referring to hell as her place of residence. In addition, the final line of the poem is the most important, for it concretely states that the woman is not what she appears to be. Campion accuses her of murder which explains why she is in hell. He thus expresses his complete distrust of love, for like this woman it may be beautiful on the outside but is evil inside.

George Wither also expresses the sentiment that love is fickle. However, instead of running away from love, Wither suggests that people should actively seek it out. He employs comparisons in his poem, for he continually compares women to various objects, for example "flowery meads in May" and "turtledove or pelican." Wither sarcastically questions whether he should care for a woman if he is not sure she is the right person for him, and displays blatant disrespect for females when he contends that he should not care what happens to the women he has been involved with. He repeats this sentiment at the end of each stanza, stressing that he does not need to pay attention to these women. This depicts females as mere objects to be toyed with, instead of living breathing human beings who merit the same respect Wither commands. Wither displays a blatant disrespect for women and for love. He will not give any female a chance if she is not immediately to his liking, and his behavior undoubtedly will prove problematic for him.

Both Thomas Campion and George Wither portray love as fickle. While Campion contends that it is the deviousness of females that ruin love, Wither shows it is the intolerance of males that discredits love.

Student Essay Two

The birds and the bees. These two poems represent two different feelings towards love: its beauty and its sting. The first poem, through use of allusion and metaphor, speaks of the beauty of love, but then there is an unfavorable outcome which is disastrous to the speaker. In the second poem, through use of detail and imagery, there is a slightly different attitude. The speaker declares that no time should be wasted nor should feelings be wasted if a woman is not right for him; he gives a feeling of indifference, or "who cares?" Both poems however, use a metaphor of death as the end of a relationship.

In the first poem, two illusions are made to mythological beings, Iope and Helen, who both can be associated with love. Campion compares his love to a "new admired guest." The love interest of the speaker tells of all the great events of their courtship, "banqueting delights," for example. He uses the metaphor of the "tourneys and great challenges of knights," how he fought for her in a sense, like a knight fighting for the hand of a fair maiden. The poet ponders, in the end, the sting — after all the "honors done" to her, how could she have "dumped" him? How could it have been an unrequited love? The lady love will sometime tell everyone about the "elegant aspects" of their relationship but he believes she would never tell truthfully how she hurt him.

In the second poem, the speaker is aware of the pleasantries of attraction and love, but unlike the speaker of the first poem, he declares that he will not "waste in despair" because he sees a pretty girl who does not like him. If he sees a beautiful girl with rosy cheeks and lovely features, he will not love her unless she loves in return. In the last stanza, he says, "If she love me, this believe, I will die ere she will grieve . . . ." It is to say he will do anything, even die, for her. Unlike the lover in the first poem, this death would not be a murder. The last line of the poem returns to an attitude "let things go and do not dwell on things that went wrong." While the speaker of the first poem will dwell on his unrequited love, the second speaker, if love goes wrong, shall continue to "live," dismiss the event and move on with life.

Comments on the Student Essays

The Campion poem depends on the conventional figure of speech that Donne makes use of in "The Legacy," that is, the lady holds life-and-death power over a lover and if she leaves or refuses him, the man will die. The murder of the last line is simply a commonplace metaphor and students who read it literally will miss the point of the poem. The hell here is the classical afterlife, not the Christian place of punishment. The poet makes a point of presenting this world as delightful: the lady ("a new admired guest") will be surrounded by the most beautiful women of myth who will yearn to hear the stories of her triumphant life. Notice how carefully the two sentences of poem are balanced. Both are "when . . . then" constructions, one of ten, one of two lines. Everything in the first eleven lines is calculated to flatter the lady, but in line twelve, the heartbroken poet ("tell, O tell!") warns that she will have to speak of her guilt as a metaphorical killer. The rhetorical purpose of the poem is to convince the lady to return his love, to give her a chance (and a reason) to accept his love and thus avoid having to admit to "murder."

The Campion poem is addressed to the lady, the audience he wishes to convince. The speaker of the Wither lyric, on the other hand, is talking to himself. The first two stanzas reject Campion's notion of dying for a beautiful or charming woman. If his feelings are not returned, the speaker will be untouched. But the final stanza reveals that the speaker can be quite as sentimental as any lover, if his love is returned. He will "die" to preserve her happiness. The last four lines reassert his sophisticated indifference to any unresponsive woman.

The first of the two essays crucially misreads the tone of the first eleven lines (mistaking the hell as a place of torment) and fails to see that the murder is a metaphor.

The second essay is much better. It recognizes that death is metaphorical and a common element in the two poems. Though its reading of Campion's lyric is incomplete, it does a good job on the meaning of the Wither poem, and it handles the change of tone in the last stanza especially well.

Question 2

This prose passage is shorter than those that normally appear on the exam. It is here to remind you that every so often the exam will include a poem or a prose question that tests your ability to recognize irony. All too often, good students miss the irony altogether and consequently get a very low score on the question. Many of the students writing on this passage read it without recognizing that the author (Dr. Johnson) was making fun of his own profession and wrote that the selection presented the critic as a superior being. They pointed (out of context) to such words as "important," "formidable," "distinction," and even "greatness" to support their case. I reprint here only an example of a good essay on this topic. Though to summarize a selection paragraph by paragraph is not usually a good strategy, it works well here because the passage is short and the question calls for an explanation of the author's attitude toward literary critics. The remarks on techniques (irony, syntax, diction, and imagery in this paper) are accurate and intelligent. Despite a few minor flaws in the writing, this is a paper that would earn a top score.

Student Essay

At first, this passage seems to favor critics and criticism, but a more careful reading shows that the author is sarcastic and he or she really despises critics and thinks that they are people who can't do harder things that take a lot of work. The first paragraph says they are weak, idle, ignorant and vain! The second paragraph goes on to say that other kinds of literary "distinction" are difficult, but criticism is easy to do if the critic only has words and malice. Paragraph three is harder to follow, but it seems to say that the "malignity," that is the nastiness, of the critics is good because is doesn't harm anybody. The last paragraph repeats the idea that anyone can be a critic, and that critics are "malicious" and "harmless."

The first technique the author uses to convey his contempt for critics is irony. He pretends to be praising criticism as an easy job that makes a critic "important," and "reputable." But the author really thinks critics are malicious people with no talent at all.

The sentence structure in the passage is not like modern writers. Most of the sentences are very long. For example, the second sentence in the second paragraph uses three semicolons and parallelism in "the want of meaning she supplies with words" and "the want of spirit she recompenses with malignity."

The author also uses diction and imagery to convey his meaning. In the second paragraph, criticism is personified as a goddess, and it is compared to a poison in paragraph three. This poison is like a gas that is allowed to escape without doing any harm. The author's real attitude toward critics is shown by his choice of words such as "weak," "idleness," "ignorant," and "malignant," all of which he applies to critics.

Thus the author's diction, imagery, sentence structure, and irony skillfully are combined to convey his hostile attitude toward literary critics.

Question 3

Student Essay One

Arthur Miller's play <u>Death of a Salesman</u> depicts a story of Willy Loman, a man whose dreams are so impossibly large that he has lost touch with reality. When he loses his job, he takes his own life in an effort to both show his family the truth of his success and rid himself of the guilt of wasting his life. The lack of success Willy has in ridding himself of his guilt through suicide shows his inability to accomplish his wishes.

Willy Loman's dreams seem simple, but he complicates them with conditions of attainment. He wants to be successful, and considers that to be making lots of money and being popular and well-liked by people. He also wants his sons, especially Biff, to be successful in life, and his vision for Biff had been football. He refuses help in order to attain his version of the American Dream, and believes that there must be ways to suddenly make lots of money and become a success.

In reality, he is making less money and losing the respect of his boss. His clients could care less who sells them the products they want. His house and refrigerator are falling apart just as he is about to finish paying for them. His son, Biff, who he had such high hopes for, jumps from one job to another unable to advance himself in any way because of his habit of stealing things. He continues to believe Biff and his other son Happy will make it big somehow, but instead of steady advancement in a company, he wants them to follow in his steps and sell goods to make a living. Willy believes in his own success as a salesman so much that he is unable to recognize his own failure when it stares him in the face. Not only does he lie to his wife Linda about how much money he makes, but he also falsely believes in his own popularity among the customers and the company he works for. He turns down offers of any kind of advancement, insisting that he make it by himself. Being unable to perpetuate the American Dream causes him to go deeper and deeper in his unreal fantasy world, where his brother Charlie, rich from the gold rush in Alaska, speaks to him.

Eventually Willy is forced to face the truth of the failure of his life as he sees it. When he loses his job, he realizes that his life has been useless. He commits suicide and hopes that the family will be able to live off the insurance money. Unfortunately, no one shows up to his funeral. This only exacerbates the message sent in the entirety of Willy's life: unable to achieve his dreams, he can never escape his guilt.

Student Essay Two

While the flight from guilt is typically associated with cowardice, it often spurs the action at the crux of a novel or play's denoument. Shakespeare's Hamlet is a prime example of the effect of guilt and conscience upon the development of a character and plot. Wracked by the death of his father, the King of Denmark, and his mother's union with Claudius, his uncle, Hamlet enters into an extended period of depression, catalyzed not only by his father's death, but by his inability to take action upon it. Guilt becomes intertwined with blood vengeance and a modern sensibility about the futility of action, but eventually conscience and guilt combine with duty and fuel Hamlet to action.

Hamlet's flight from guilt is defined through his soliloquies and confrontations with the specter of his father. While the Ghost urges him toward action, demanding "justice" and vengeance, Hamlet's soliloquies often betray his incertitude and desire to flee, even to contemplate suicide, to simply abandon the knowledge he has been given. He carries not only his own guilt about his failure to avenge his father's death, but also the guilt and shame he feels for his Mother, and the stain or rot on Denmark. Quick to forget his father, his mother rushes to Claudius' throne and bed, and in Hamlet's eye's, this reveals their true, wicked natures. However, they remain his family, and the hate he is forced to bear toward them combines with the anticipated guilt and horror over the belief that his actions will destroy his mother, and this amplifies his uncertainty.

The appearance of his father's Ghost adds a new fervor to Hamlet's beleaguered soliloquies. Instead of revealing a clear path, separating duty from desire, Hamlet is forced to confront the issues he had desperately been avoiding since the death of his father: his right to blood vengeance, and his willingness to perform it. "Conscience doth make cowards of us all," he says in the "To be or not to be" soliloquy, revealing his Christian-like sense of guilt and fear of suicide or violent retribution. Ironically, it is his guilt-ridden uncertainty that leads to strife and madness affecting the whole court — Ophelia's madness and Polonius' death. The inability to take direct action, the desire to hide from the guilt and anguish which plague him, paralyzes Hamlet with disgust. His inaction can be measured by the degree to which the Ghost was forced to tantalize him through guilt. The play within a play is set to exploit Claudius' sense of guilt — "to catch the conscience of the King." This drama rolls forward, eager to snare its victims, double-edged sword, in the end, causing Hamlet as much pain as his victims, dramatizing as never before the ambiguities of revenge. Hamlet never washes himself of the guilt that plagues him following his father's death, if only because the revenge he must enact is so closely related to those he loves. While avenging his father, he destroys his family, and death is the only respite that he can receive from the guilt that drives him throughout the play.

Comments on the Student Essays

These two essays are an instructive pair: The first almost wholly fails to deal with what the question asks, while the second focuses rigorously on the effect of Hamlet's feelings of guilt in Shakespeare's play. The first essay uses the word "guilt" twice in its first paragraph and as its last word, but it never discusses Willy Loman's guilt with any clarity. It begins by saying Willy's suicide is an attempt to escape his guilt (a plausible reading), but confuses this idea by saying the suicide is a failure. Does this mean Willy feels guilty after death? The rest of the essay recounts details of the play but never connects them to the question's "flight from guilt." The last sentence refers to "guilt," but the claim that the small turnout at Willy's funeral is proof that he can "never escape from guilt" makes no sense. The essay is equally weak on the other part of the question: how guilt determines the meaning the work as a whole. The Hamlet essay, on the other hand, deals specifically and convincingly with Hamlet's feelings of guilt. It explains Hamlet's feelings as a response both to his failure to avenge his father's murder and to the shame he feels for his mother and his country. Though its handling of the meaning of the play is thin, it does refer to the relevance of Hamlet's guilt to "the ambiguities of revenge," an important idea in the play. This essay would be scored in the upper half of the scale, while the paper on the Miller play would fall into the lower half.

Notes

Notes

Notes

Notes

Notes

Notes

Notes

CliffsNotes

LITERATURE NOTES

Absalom, Absalom!
The Aeneid
Agamemnon
Alice in Wonderland
All the King's Men
All the Pretty Horses
All Quiet on Western Front
All's Well & Merry Wives
American Poets of the 20th Century
American Tragedy
Animal Farm
Anna Karenina
Anthem
Antony and Cleopatra
Aristotle's Ethics
As I Lay Dying
The Assistant
As You Like It
Atlas Shrugged
Autobiography of Ben Franklin
Autobiography of Malcolm X
The Awakening
Babbit
Bartleby & Benito Cereno
The Bean Trees
The Bear
The Bell Jar
Beloved
Beowulf
The Bible
Billy Budd & Typee
Black Boy
Black Like Me
Bleak House
Bless Me, Ultima
The Bluest Eye & Sula
Brave New World
Brothers Karamazov
The Call of the Wild & White Fang
Candide
The Canterbury Tales
Catch-22
Catcher in the Rye
The Chosen
The Color Purple
Comedy of Errors...
Connecticut Yankee
The Contender
The Count of Monte Cristo
Crime and Punishment
The Crucible
Cry, the Beloved Country
Cyrano de Bergerac
Daisy Miller & Turn...Screw
David Copperfield
Death of a Salesman
The Deerslayer
Diary of Anne Frank
Divine Comedy-I. Inferno
Divine Comedy-II. Purgatorio
Divine Comedy-III. Paradiso
Doctor Faustus

Dr. Jekyll and Mr. Hyde
Don Juan
Don Quixote
Dracula
Eléctra & Medea
Emerson's Essays
Emily Dickinson Poems
Emma
Ethan Frome
The Faerie Queene
Fahrenheit 451
Far from the Madding Crowd
A Farewell to Arms
Farewell to Manzanar
Fathers and Sons
Faulkner's Short Stories
Faust Pt. I & Pt. II
The Federalist
Flowers for Algernon
For Whom the Bell Tolls
The Fountainhead
Frankenstein
The French Lieutenant's Woman
The Giver
Glass Menagerie & Streetcar
Go Down, Moses
The Good Earth
Grapes of Wrath
Great Expectations
The Great Gatsby
Greek Classics
Gulliver's Travels
Hamlet
The Handmaid's Tale
Hard Times
Heart of Darkness & Secret Sharer
Hemingway's Short Stories
Henry IV Part 1
Henry IV Part 2
Henry V
House Made of Dawn
The House of the Seven Gables
Huckleberry Finn
I Know Why the Caged Bird Sings
Ibsen's Plays I
Ibsen's Plays II
The Idiot
Idylls of the King
The Iliad
Incidents in the Life of a Slave Girl
Inherit the Wind
Invisible Man
Ivanhoe
Jane Eyre
Joseph Andrews
The Joy Luck Club
Jude the Obscure
Julius Caesar
The Jungle
Kafka's Short Stories
Keats & Shelley
The Killer Angels
King Lear
The Kitchen God's Wife
The Last of the Mohicans

Le Morte Darthur
Leaves of Grass
Les Miserables
A Lesson Before Dying
Light in August
The Light in the Forest
Lord Jim
Lord of the Flies
Lord of the Rings
Lost Horizon
Lysistrata & Other Comedies
Macbeth
Madame Bovary
Main Street
The Mayor of Casterbridge
Measure for Measure
The Merchant of Venice
Middlemarch
A Midsummer-Night's Dream
The Mill on the Floss
Moby-Dick
Moll Flanders
Mrs. Dalloway
Much Ado About Nothing
My Ántonia
Mythology
Narr. ...Frederick Douglass
Native Son
New Testament
Night
1984
Notes from Underground
The Odyssey
Oedipus Trilogy
Of Human Bondage
Of Mice and Men
The Old Man and the Sea
Old Testament
Oliver Twist
The Once and Future King
One Day in the Life of Ivan Denisovich
One Flew Over Cuckoo's Nest
100 Years of Solitude
O'Neill's Plays
Othello
Our Town
The Outsiders
The Ox-Bow Incident
Paradise Lost
A Passage to India
The Pearl
The Pickwick Papers
The Picture of Dorian Gray
Pilgrim's Progress
The Plague
Plato's Dialogues
Plato's The Republic
Poe's Short Stories
A Portrait of Artist...
The Portrait of a Lady
The Power and the Glory
Pride and Prejudice
The Prince
The Prince and the Pauper
A Raisin in the Sun

The Red Badge of Courage
The Red Pony
The Return of the Native
Richard II
Richard III
The Rise of Silas Lapham
Robinson Crusoe
Roman Classics
Romeo and Juliet
The Scarlet Letter
A Separate Peace
Shakespeare's Comedies
Shakespeare's Histories
Shakespeare's Minor Plays
Shakespeare's Sonnets
Shakespeare's Tragedies
Shaw's Pygmalion & Arms...
Silas Marner
Sir Gawain...Green Knight
Sister Carrie
Slaughterhouse-Five
Snow Falling on Cedars
Song of Solomon
Sons and Lovers
The Sound and the Fury
Steppenwolf & Siddhartha
The Stranger
The Sun Also Rises
T.S. Eliot's Poems & Plays
A Tale of Two Cities
The Taming of the Shrew
Tartuffe, Misanthrope...
The Tempest
Tender Is the Night
Tess of the D'Urbervilles
Their Eyes Were Watching God
Things Fall Apart
The Three Musketeers
To Kill a Mockingbird
Tom Jones
Tom Sawyer
Treasure Island & Kidnapped
The Trial
Tristram Shandy
Troilus and Cressida
Twelfth Night
Ulysses
Uncle Tom's Cabin
The Unvanquished
Utopia
Vanity Fair
Vonnegut's Works
Waiting for Godot
Walden
Walden Two
War and Peace
Who's Afraid of Virginia...
Winesburg, Ohio
The Winter's Tale
The Woman Warrior
Worldly Philosophers
Wuthering Heights
A Yellow Raft in Blue Water